Game Anim
Video Game Animation Explained

Jonathan Cooper

CRC Press
Taylor & Francis Group
Boca Raton London New York

CRC Press is an imprint of the
Taylor & Francis Group, an **informa** business

AN A K PETERS BOOK

CRC Press
Taylor & Francis Group
6000 Broken Sound Parkway NW, Suite 300
Boca Raton, FL 33487-2742

© 2019 by Taylor & Francis Group, LLC
CRC Press is an imprint of Taylor & Francis Group, an Informa business

No claim to original U.S. Government works

Printed on acid-free paper

International Standard Book Number-13: 978-1-1-3809-487-1 (Paperback)
978-1-1-3809-488-8 (Hardback)

Library of Congress Cataloging-in-Publication Data

Names: Cooper, Jonathan (Animator), author.
Title: Game anim: video game animation explained / Jonathan Cooper.
Other titles: Game animator
Description: Boca Raton, FL : CRC Press/Taylor & Francis Group, 2019. |
Includes bibliographical references and index.
Identifiers: LCCN 2018040843| ISBN 9781138094871 (pbk. : acid-free paper) |
ISBN 9781138094888 (hardback : acid-free paper)
Subjects: LCSH: Computer animation--Vocational guidance. | Video
games--Design--Vocational guidance.
Classification: LCC TR897.7 .C66 2019 | DDC 777/.7023--dc23
LC record available at https://lccn.loc.gov/2018040843

Visit the Taylor & Francis Web site at
http://www.taylorandfrancis.com

and the CRC Press Web site at
http://www.crcpress.com

For Clara & Jade,
whose adventures in real life
inspire me in the virtual.

Contents

Preface

It's an incredibly arrogant presumption to write a book on your chosen field, but in the intervening decades between my first falling in love with video game animation and now, the medium has become something of a desirable career path (and no one else was going to do it). I've seen animation grow from a one-person throwaway on small teams to one of the largest multifaceted disciplines on the biggest video game projects and an important prerequisite for any studio with even modest storytelling ambitions. And yet, due to the medium's relative youth, the real details of game development are not covered by online articles or video tutorials, which instead focus on the (still very important) act of animation creation itself.

As I finish up this manuscript back home on a trip to Scotland, I realize I was fortunate to have grown up not just with games but also with the means to create computer art—even more so because my hometown birthed some of the most celebrated video game series in the world. While game development always seemed like an attainable career to me, I understand that's not the case for everyone. Similarly, video game animation (and development as a whole) has for years been economically inaccessible to most due to the cost of animation packages and tools. But with the internet; social media; and, most recently, the democratization of development with free game engines, animation tools, and digital distribution allowing anybody with a computer to start developing and get games out to an audience, I feel the time is now right to get everyone up to speed on this exciting field.

Written over the course of several years (because I'm very much still actively shipping huge games), this book is the result of notes taken every time I hit a new development phase and listed everything I considered important, regardless of the project. With this book, I hope to impart much of nearly two decades of knowledge working on a variety of game types in both in-game and cinematic roles in animator, lead, and director positions to make the reader as rounded a game animator as possible. All of this is based on personal experience so is bound to cause some disagreement, as not every studio approaches game development the same way, but the following pages are what I have found to work across multiple studios regardless of team size and culture, and should allow the game animator to focus on what's important (which goes far beyond just making beautiful animations).

I really hope you find this book useful, and I can't wait to see what the aspiring animators of tomorrow will create. The medium of video game animation is so linked to technology that we are forever reinventing processes and techniques, always making characters and worlds even more believable to entertain players around the world.

Jonathan Cooper

Additional Legal Notices

The associated tutorial "Azri" character is property of Matthew Bachnick and is used under license, and cannot be used for commercial purposes.

The Last Guardian: ©2016 Sony Interactive Entertainment Inc.

For Assassin's Creed pictures: "© 2007-2017 Ubisoft Entertainment. All Rights Reserved. Assassin's Creed, Ubisoft, and the Ubisoft logo are trademarks of Ubisoft Entertainment in the US and/or other countries."

For Prince of Persia pictures : "© 2003 Ubisoft Entertainment. Based on Prince of Persia® created by Jordan Mechner. Prince of Persia is a trademark of Waterwheel Licensing LLC in the US and/or other countries used under license."

For Watch Dogs pictures: "© 2014 Ubisoft Entertainment. All Rights Reserved. Watch Dogs, Ubisoft and the Ubisoft logo are registered or unregistered trademarks of Ubisoft Entertainment in the U.S. and/or other countries.

Acknowledgments

There are too many talented folks I've worked with over the years who have contributed to my own growth as a game developer and animator to mention. Special thanks, however, must go to Mari Kuwayama for interview translations, Sophie Brennan for rigging the featured "Azri" character, and the following folks who helped with image approvals and other advice: Alison Mori, Joel Macmillan, Etienne Allonier, Jay Hosfelt, Dan Tudge, Peter Bartholow, Jamaal Bradley, Joe Hixson, Jake Clark, Chris Brincat, Jay Britton, Max Dyckhoff, Michael Barclay, Wasim Khan, Jeremy Yates and Richard Boylan. Thanks also to Dayna Galloway for use of an Abertay laptop when I needed it most, and to Sean Connelly for being an all-round great publisher.

Author

Jonathan Cooper is a video game animator from Scotland who has been bringing virtual characters to life since 2000. He has led teams on large projects such as the Assassin's Creed and Mass Effect series, with a focus on memorable stories and characters and cutting-edge video game animation. He has since been focusing on interactive cinematics in the latest chapters of the DICE and Annie award-winning series Uncharted and The Last of Us.

In 2008 he started the BioWare Montreal studio co-leading a team to deliver the majority of cinematic cutscenes for the 2011 British Academy of Film & Television Award (BAFTA) Best Game, Mass Effect 2.

In 2013 he directed the in-game team that won the Academy of Interactive Arts & Sciences (AIAS/DICE) award for Outstanding Achievement in Animation on Assassin's Creed III.

Jonathan has presented at the Game Developers Conference (GDC) in San Francisco and at other conferences across Canada and the United Kingdom, and holds a Bachelor of Design honors degree in animation.

You can follow him online at his website, www.gameanim.com, and on twitter at @GameAnim.

CHAPTER 1

The Video Game Animator

What It Means to Be a Video Game Animator

So you want to be a video game animator, but what exactly does that entail? And what, if any, are the differences between a video game animator and those in the more traditional linear mediums of film and television? While there are certainly a lot of overlap and shared skills required to bring a character to life in any medium, there are many unique technical limitations, and opportunities, in the interactive artform.

Artistry & Creativity

To begin with, having a keen eye for observation of movement in the world around you (and a desire to replicate and enhance it for your own creative ends) is the first step to becoming a great game animator. The willingness to not only recreate these motions but to envision how this movement might be controlled by yourself and others, allowing players to embody the characters you create, is a key factor in separating game animators from the noninteractive animators of linear mediums.

Understanding the fundamentals of weight, balance, mass, and momentum to ensure your characters are not only pleasing to the eye but meet with the player's understanding of the physics of the worlds they will inhabit are equally essential. A desire to push the envelope of visual and interaction fidelity within your explorable worlds, which can afford players new stories and experiences they could never have in the real world, with believable characters that are as real to them as any created in another medium, is a driving force in pushing this still-young medium forward.

The ultimate goal is immersion—where players forget they are in front of a screen (or wearing a virtual/augmented-reality headset), escaping their own physical limitations and instead being transported into our virtual world, assuming their character's identity such that it is "they themselves" (and no longer their avatar) who are in the game.

Technical Ability

Beautiful animations are only the first challenge. Getting them to work in the game and play with each other seamlessly in character movement systems is the real challenge. The best game animators get their hands dirty in the technical side of seeing their animations through every step of the way into the game. A good game animation team will balance animators with complementary levels of technical and artistic abilities, but strength in both areas is only a good thing.

Only in thoroughly understanding tools, processes, and existing animation systems will new creative opportunities open up to animators willing to experiment and discover new techniques and methods that might make animation creation more efficient or increase in quality.

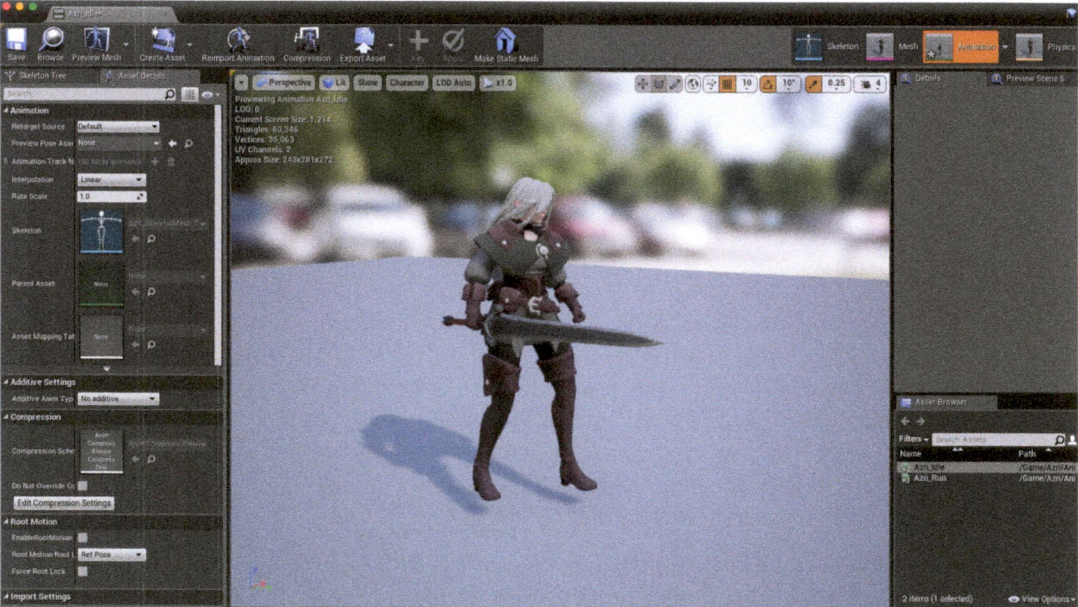

Animation inside a game engine.

Teamwork

Beyond simply making motions look clean and fluid, it is a game animator's responsibility to balance multiple (sometimes conflicting) desires to make a video game. A finished game is always more than the sum of its parts, and when all of a development team's disciplines pull in the same direction in unison is when we delight and surprise players the most.

Animators must work in concert with designers, programmers, artists, audio technicians, and more to bring their creations to life, so those harboring a desire to sit with headphones on and the door closed, focusing solely on their own area, will be quickly left behind in the race to create the best possible experiences.

A game animator can only truly succeed with a good awareness of the other disciplines in game development and the ability to speak their language, empathize with their needs, and know at least a little of all areas of game development.

Design Sense

Game animations do not exist in a bubble and are not simply created to look good, but must serve a purpose for the greater game. Animators handling player character animation, especially, must balance a game's "feel" with visual fidelity (though the two are not mutually exclusive).

Designers touting conventional wisdom will often fall back on the tenet of quicker animations equaling better and more reactive characters, but go too fast without the appropriate visual feedback and the characters will simply not exist believably in the world, destroying the illusion of life and hurting the "feel" in the opposite direction. Ultimately, it is a game animator's responsibility to create consistency in the game world, with everything displaying a relative weight and physics, and gravity being a constant throughout.

In game development, we might hope that "everyone is a designer," but the best game designers are the keepers of the game's goals with an idea of how to reach them. It is the game animators' role to know enough of design to ensure their creations do not hurt but serve the design goals while maintaining visual fidelity as much as possible.

Accepting the Nature of the Medium

It goes without saying that a great game animator must be passionate about his or her chosen field, but must understand that this chosen field is not just animation but game development as a whole.

Those wishing for the more easily-scheduled approach of traditional linear animation production will likely grow frustrated with the fluid nature of game development. You cannot plan how many iterations it will take a new mechanic to be fun, so it follows that you must always be open to schedules in a state of flux.

Avoid being precious about your work because it *will* change or be thrown away, but, similarly, don't be dissuaded, because you will always improve and refine your animation as the game progresses, no matter how many times you might rework it.

Life Experience

The best game animators love playing games and can find something to learn from every work, but they also go beyond simply referencing other games or movies. If we wish to truly improve our artistic works (and gaming as a whole), we must escape the echo chamber of comparing with and copying our peers and instead bring as much of our own varied life experience into our work as possible.

The blandest games are those that only reference their competition, and the most pedestrian animation choices are inspired only by other animation. Be passionate for games, but also be passionate for life and the world around you, and get away from the screen outside of work as much as possible.

Different Areas of Game Animation

While game animators in larger teams typically specialize, those at smaller studios may wear the many hats listed below. Regardless, even when specializing, it is incredibly valuable to understand other areas of game animation to open up opportunities for creativity across disciplines—often, the best results occur when lines are blurred such that an animator might excel in all moving aspects of a game.

Player Character Animation

The primary and easily most challenging aspect of game animation is the motion of characters under the player's control. This occurs in all but the most abstract of games and therefore is an important skill to focus on and for any game animator to have under his or her belt.

Character animation style and quality can vary greatly across different game types (and studios), depending upon their unique goals, but one thing is becoming more apparent as the medium progresses—bad character animation is unacceptable these days. Bringing up the baseline standard is one of the main goals of this book.

The Assassin is an excellent example of player character movement. (Copyright 2007–2017 Ubisoft Entertainment. All Rights Reserved. Assassin's Creed, Ubisoft, and the Ubisoft logo are trademarks of Ubisoft Entertainment in the US and/or other countries.)

Facial Animation

A relatively recent requirement, (due to advances in the quality of characters enabling us to bring cameras in close), is that even the most undiscerning player will be able to instinctively critique bad motion due to experience with other humans.

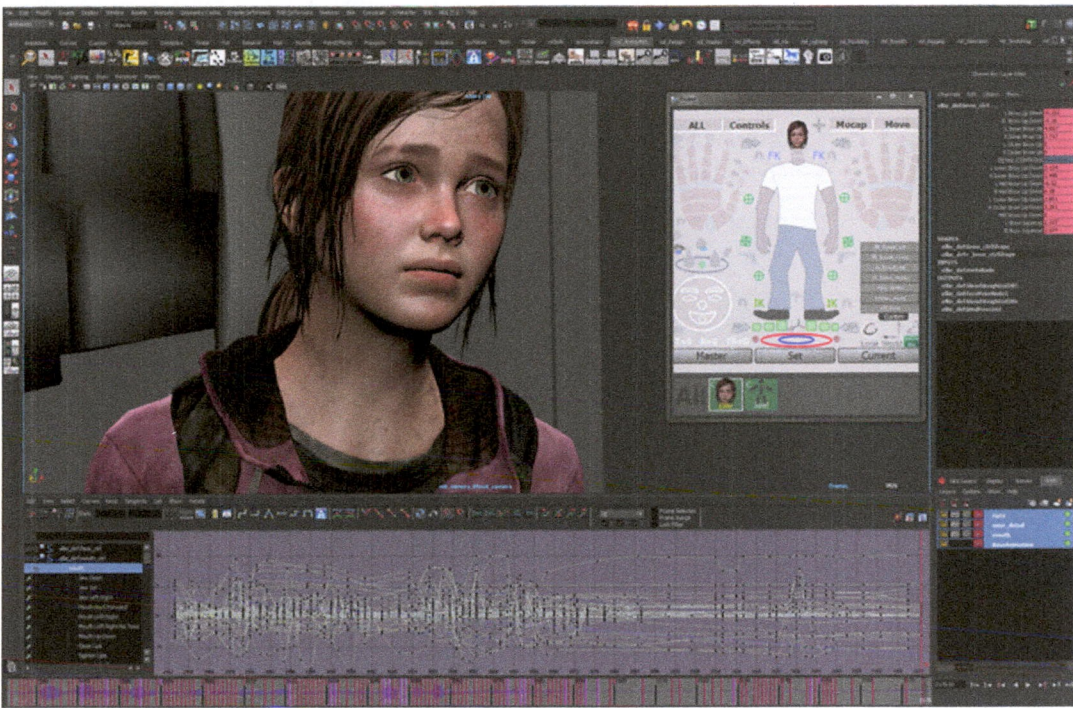

Great facial animation is a crucial element of story-based games like The Last of Us. (Courtesy of Sony Interactive Entertainment.)

How do we avoid these pitfalls when aiming to create believable characters that serve our storytelling aspirations? There are many decisions throughout a project's development that must work in concert to bring characters to life that are not just believable, but appealing.

Cinematics & Cutscenes

A mainstay of games with even the slightest degree of storytelling, cinematic cutscenes give developers the rare opportunity to author scenes of a game enough so that they play out exactly as they envision. A double-edged sword, when used sparingly and done well, they can bring us much closer to empathizing with characters, but used too much and they divorce us from not just our protagonists but the story and experience as a whole.

A well-rounded game animator should have a working knowledge of cinematography, staging, and acting to tell stories in as unobtrusive and economical a manner as possible.

Technical Animation

Nothing in games exists without some degree of technical wrangling to get it working, and game creation never ceases to surprise in all the ways it can break. A game animator should have at least a basic knowledge of the finer details of character creation, rigging, skinning, and implementation into the game—even more so if on a small team where the animator typically owns much of this responsibility alone.

A game animator's job only truly begins when the animation makes it into the game—at which point the systems behind various blends, transitions, and physical simulations can make or break the feel and fluidity of the character as a whole.

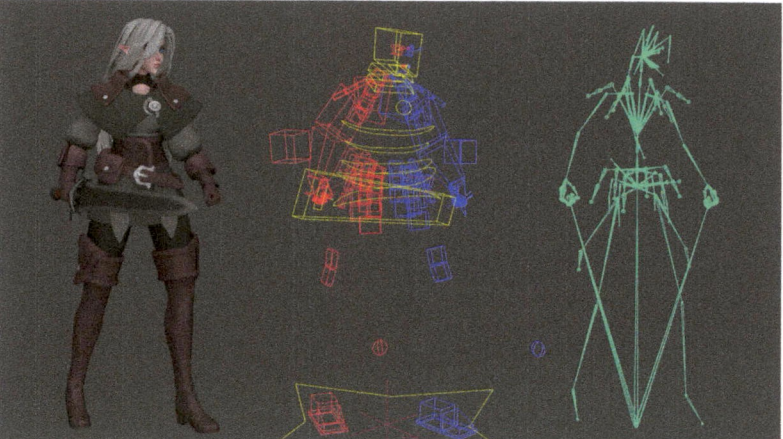

The character mesh, rig, and export skeleton.

Nonplayer Characters

While generally aesthetically similar, the demands of player animations differ greatly from those of nonplayer characters (NPCs). Depending on the goals and design requirements of the game, they bring their own challenges, primarily with supporting artificial intelligence (AI) such as decision-making and moving through the world. Failing to realize NPCs to a convincing degree of quality can leave the player confused as to their virtual comrades' and enemies' intentions and believability.

Cameras

The camera is the window through which the game world is viewed. Primarily concerning player character animation in 3D games, a bad camera can undermine the most fluidly animated character. A good game animator, while perhaps not directly controlling the implementation, should take a healthy interest in the various aspects of camera design: how it reacts to the environment (colliding with walls, etc.), the rotation speed and general rigidity with which it follows player input, and the arc it takes as it pivots around the character in 3D games. It's no wonder a whole new input (joypad right-stick) was added in the last decade just to support the newly required ability to look around 3D environments.

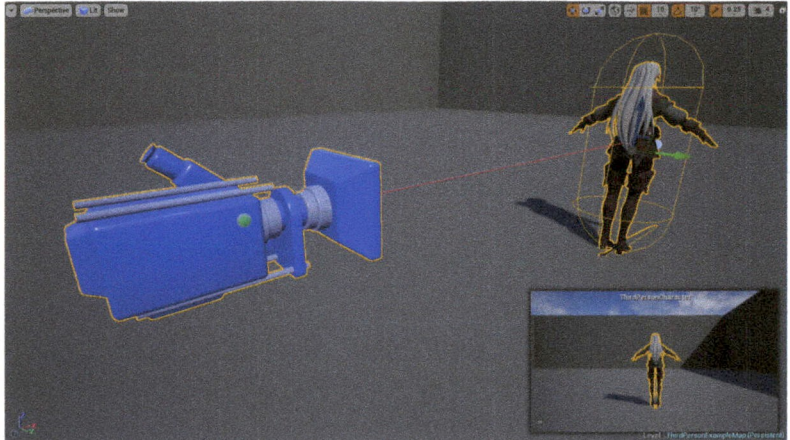

Gameplay camera setup.

Environmental & Prop Animation

While perhaps less glamorous than character animation, an animated environment can bring soulless locations to life. Moreover, a character's interaction with props and the environment with convincing contact points can place a character in the environment to an unparalleled degree.

Use of weapons, primarily guns and melee types, is a mainstay in games, and the knowledge required to efficiently and convincingly animate and maintain these types of animations is an essential part of most game animation pipelines. While doors, chests, and elevators might not be demo reel material, they are all essential in the player's discovery of a more interactive world.

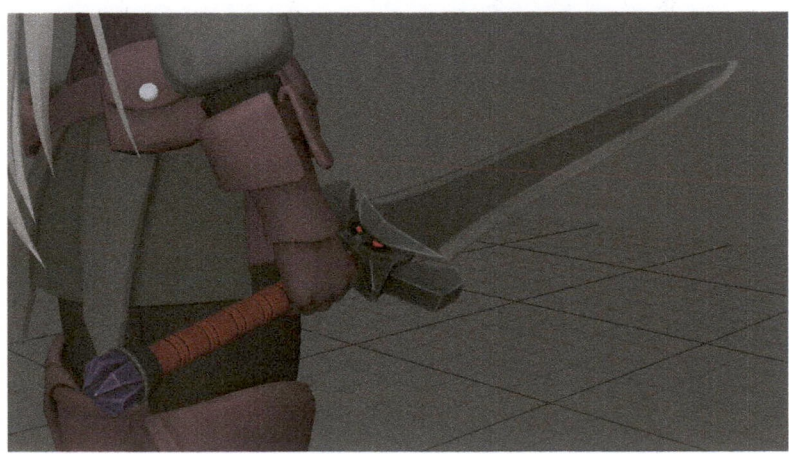

Many game characters require weapon props.

Required Software & Equipment

Digital Content Creation (DCC) Software

The primary method of animation content creation for video games has always been via expensive digital content creation packages such as Autodesk's Maya and Max, but now they are facing competition from free offerings such as Blender that increasingly support game development.

In the future, more and more of the creation aspect of game development is expected to take place within the game engine, but for now, we still rely upon the workflow of first creating, then exporting assets into the game.

A good game animator will have at least a basic knowledge of polygon modeling, rigging, and skinning, as well as an intimate knowledge of the animation export process and its various abilities and limitations. A good understanding of the many ways to break an animation on export can save time and increase iteration, making the difference between an acceptable and exceptionally polished animated game.

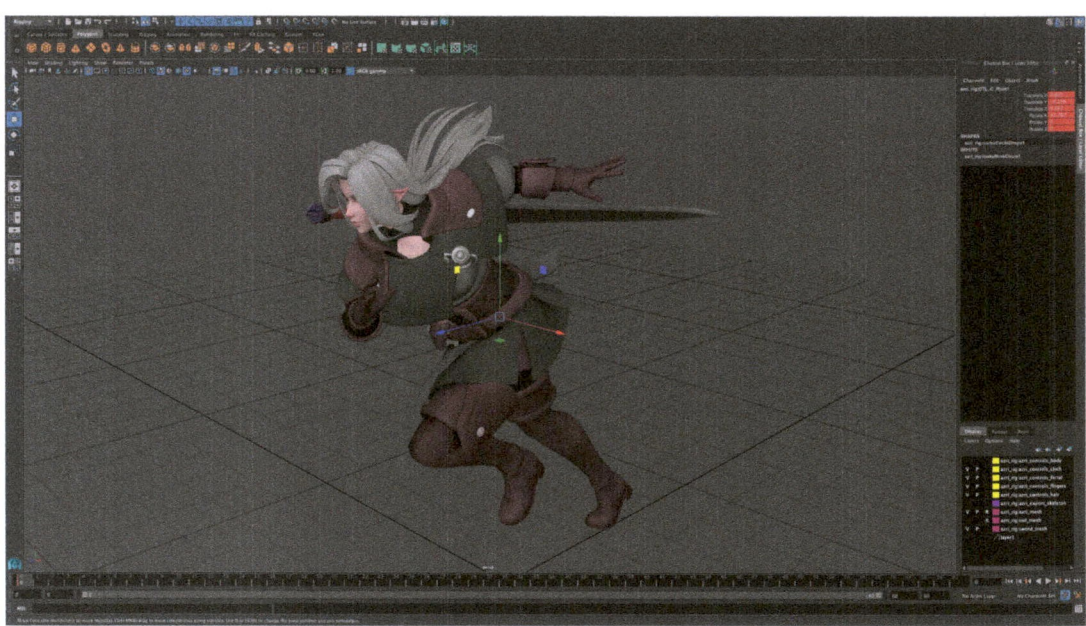

A character animated in Maya.

Game Engines

This is the software that wrangles together all the various game assets and data creation, from animation, art, and audio to level design and more, and spits out a complete video game.

While most studios use their own in-house engines that cater most efficiently to the type of game they make, in recent years a race to democratize game development for everyone has culminated in the two most popular game engines, Unreal and Unity, going free. Offering a suite of tools to create and integrate all aspects of game creation, these professional-grade game engines are now freely available to everyone reading this book!

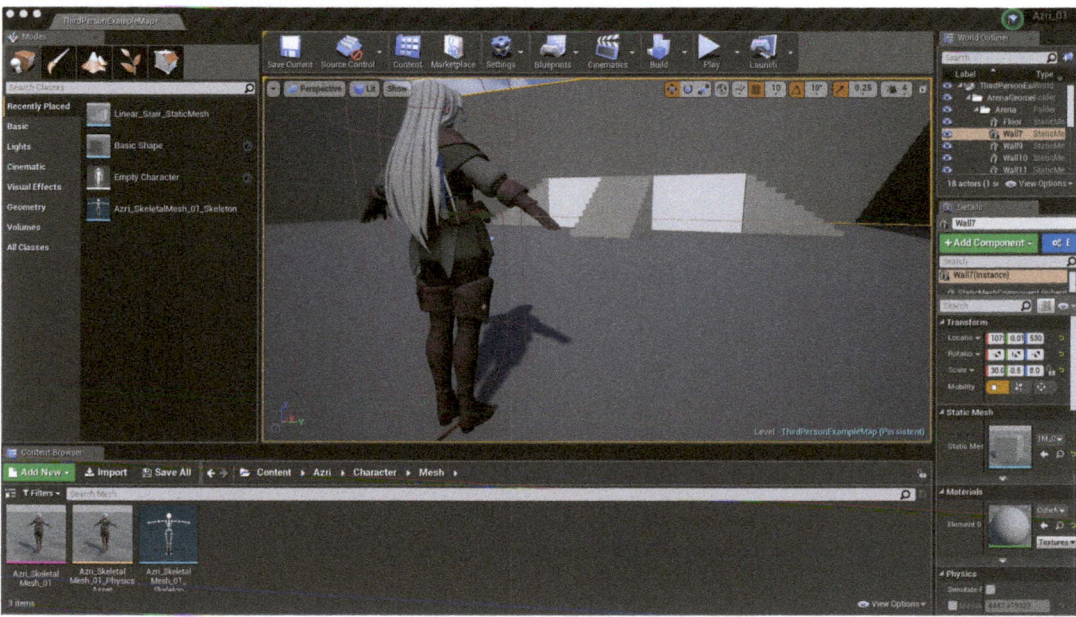

A typical game engine editor.

Reference Camera

Even the best animators work to video reference (this must be stated, as some juniors mistakenly see it as cheating), and these days every phone contains a video camera good enough to capture any actions you or your friends and colleagues can perform. Animating to video reference will not only save time by preventing basic mistakes in motion, it is the surest way to raise your animation quality as you better understand the physics and motion of the human body.

While you can source references from the internet, the only way to truly get exactly what you need is to have someone film you acting it out. Get outside if there's no room in the studio and get recording!

Video Playback Software

While these come as standard in your computer's operating system, it is important to use one that allows both scrubbing (easily moving the video forward and backward) and frame-stepping for detailed analysis of your chosen reference video.

While advanced functionality such as the ability to edit videos or choose a section to play on loop are ideal, the most robust free video player for scrubbing animation is Apple's Quicktime.

Notepad

Game animators do much more than just think about animation and must take notes on everything from design decisions to workload lists. Keeping a notepad handy helps you visually hash out ideas as you discuss with other team members—it's a visual medium, after all, and an agreed-upon diagram can speak a million more words than an easily misinterpreted idea aurally spoken.

Taking a notepad and pencil/pen to every meeting and creative exchange will make your life so much easier as you often come back to ideas and tasks some time after they have been decided upon.

CHAPTER 2

The Game Development Environment

Finding the Right Fit

We can choose our friends but not our family, and while we can't all choose where we work (at least initially), finding the right team will make a dramatic difference in your experience in game development.

Studio Culture

Just as a church is not the building but the community inside it, a game is not made by a monolithic studio but instead a collection of individuals who come together to create. Team makeup is fluid and will change from project to project, but generally individuals housed within a studio are drawn to a particular style of game or studio culture. It is the combined values of these individuals that make up a studio culture.

Different studios have different strengths, weaknesses, and priorities based on this team culture, and this often flows from the original founders (and therefore founding principles) upon which the studio is based. Some studios focus on storytelling, some on graphics and technology, some on fun gameplay over everything else. While none of these attributes are mutually exclusive, studios and teams within them will generally be stronger in one or a few areas depending on the team composition.

Beyond different discipline strengths, work ethic, attention to detail, perfectionism, production methods, and work/life balance all vary from studio to studio. Again, while not mutually exclusive, it is impossible to balance all different approaches to game development, so it is important to find a studio environment that matches your values to be happy and sustain a long career of game development.

For the ambitious game animator, it is important to find a team that values great characters and the desire to expend effort and resources bringing them to life. Thankfully, while strong animation was for years seen as a benefit or a "nice-to-have," it is all but becoming essential for studios with any kind of narrative ambitions. As such, recent years have seen an explosion of animation teams, whereas just a few years ago, the entire workload might have been assumed by a much smaller or single-person department.

Team Strengths

As said earlier, studios vary depending on the makeup of their team members, mostly depending on their initial founders. Studios and teams with a strong programming pedigree tend to favor technical excellence. Those with artists at the core instead often excel in incredible visuals and world building. Those with an animation background often place a desire to tell stories with memorable characters at the forefront.

All of the strengths above cannot come at the expense of good gameplay, so a strong design sense is essential to any team. While this rightfully falls on the shoulders of the designers, a game will only benefit from everyone, including game animators, knowing as much about game design as possible. Because there is no formula for good game design, due to the youth of the medium, there is no rich history of training to become a great game designer (unlike established avenues like animation, programming, and art). As such, many designers and creative directors come from backgrounds in other fields. This means that even individual game designers will typically approach a project with a bent toward art or programming and so on.

While junior animators are not yet in a position to choose, once established, a game animator seeking employment from various studios should consider if the team strengths match his or her own goals and aspirations.

Game Pillars

From the team strengths generally comes the desire to focus on the "pillars" of a project. Pillars form the basis of any project and allow a team to zero in on what is important and what is not. For every idea that arises throughout the development cycle, it can be held up as either supporting a pillar or not, and so can be endorsed and given priority, or, if not, then dismissed or given less priority.

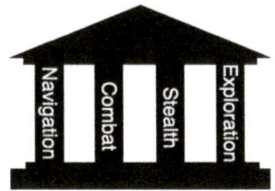

Every game has game design pillars upon which it is built.

In a game where animation-heavy melee combat or traversal of the world is a core gameplay pillar, then animation will be more supported than in a project where the core pillars do not depend so much on animation. Similarly, interacting and talking with a variety of high-fidelity characters will also require that facial animation quality become core to the experience, whereas a game about driving cars would naturally focus elsewhere.

Working on a team where animation quality is seen as a necessity is an entirely different experience from working on one that does not. Resources such as programmer time, hiring a commensurate number of animators for the workload (animation quality often rests on time allotted), and a willingness to listen to and take on the game animators' ideas and requests will be much more forthcoming on such a team. Naturally, it is not always possible to start a career in such a studio environment, but this is certainly something worth pursuing as an eventual goal.

While it is rare to be able to pick and choose, it is important when looking for different studios and teams to join that the kinds of games that studio makes resonate with you. As a game animator, it is highly likely that you prefer to play games with excellent animation quality, so this makes seeking out these teams and studios a natural fit.

Team Size

The type of team size you aim for should be the one you are comfortable with. Large teams generally afford greater programming support and resources, allowing game animators to push the envelope in terms of visuals and believable characters. However, starting your career in such a team means you will only have access to a small piece of the pie, sometimes leading to being pigeonholed or specializing in one specific area of game animation. As such, it might be hard to gain a grasp of the various areas that make up overall game development—something that can only help you grow as a game developer.

> A mismatch occurs when a smaller studio attempts to take on the big guns of AAA (Triple-A games are the biggest projects with often upwards of $100M budgets) without the means. Conversely, large teams with many moving parts have a hard time producing designs with the tight and concise visions of those from individual auteurs. Finding a team aware of its own limitations, and one that matches your own desires, is key.

Working on a small team and project allows for a much better overview of the entire game development process and will afford opportunities to try various aspects of not only game animation but likely character creation and rigging, visual effects, and so on. While this can make for a dynamic and varied career, you'll never be able to create the volume of work required to bring the most complex characters to life and will not have the tools, technology, or support that are afforded by a larger team. That said, some of the most delightful games and characters come from the smallest teams when animation and characters are a core focus.

Team Dynamics

Beyond strengths and weaknesses and a variable priority of animation as a focus, different studio and team makeups also vary in working practices. Time and time again, communication between team members is cited as a key area for improvement in project postmortems, but every team approaches this differently. While many focus on meetings, this can lead to too much time wasted that should be spent actually making the game. Some studios put the onus on individuals physically talking to one another, sometimes moving desks to work as close as possible to their most important contacts.

Some teams are spread across the globe, so they turn to technology such as video conferencing and other solutions to interact virtually. As team sizes grow, some adopt layers of middle management to facilitate communication between ever-spread-apart teams that cannot track all the moving parts of a giant project. Regardless of approach, one thing is certain—good games are made by real people with real emotions and interactions, and the more human an interaction can be made, the better and more soulful a game will be.

And yet, many great games have been made under conflict and extreme pressure, and some teams even work to reproduce this. While this is less than ideal (certainly no great game was ever created without at least a few heated disagreements and drama), such is the nature of different personalities working together creatively.

Game Animator Roles

Within animation (and especially on large teams where more structure and hierarchy are generally required), there are typically the following positions available with their respective responsibilities. Every studio has its own structure, so titles will vary, with many opting for further granularity with senior and junior/associate roles to provide a clear career progression path, but let's look at the different roles one can assume or aspire to as a game animator.

The path you take will be unique to your own skills and preferences, and it is recommended to cultivate as much as possible an overview of all areas of animation and game development as a whole to become as rounded and versatile as possible—maximizing opportunities for the full length of your career.

Gameplay Animator

The gameplay animator handles in-game animation, with responsibilities including player characters, nonplayer characters, and environmental animation such as doors and other props. The gameplay animator must have a keen design sense and, importantly, an awareness of the "feel" of the player character with regards to weight and responsiveness.

Cinematic Animator

Cinematic animators generally focus on storytelling more than game design, and should have a good understanding of acting, staging, composition (if required to handle cameras), pacing, and other elements of traditional cinematography—not to mention facial animation.

Lead Animator

Usually either gameplay or cinematic, a lead animator's primary responsibility is to make sure the team delivers the best-quality animation they can within the time allotted. A sense of organization and communication with other disciplines allows the lead animator to keep the animation team on track and up to date with the changes on the project.

A good lead will inspire and mentor animators that work under him or her, and, ultimately, the lead animator is at the service of the animation team—removing roadblocks to allow them to create their best work possible.

	Count	Character	Group	Sub-Group	Animation Name	Complexity	Priority
2	1	Elf	Navigation	Idle	elf_idle	2	1
3	2				elf_idle_combat	2	2
4	3			Walk	elf_walk_forward	3	1
5	4				elf_walk_backward	3	2
6	5				elf_walk_left	3	2
7	6				elf_walk_right	3	2
8	7			Run	elf_run_forward	3	1
9	8				elf_run_backward	3	2
10	9				elf_run_left	3	2
11	10				elf_run_right	3	2
12	11			Jump	elf_jump	1	1
13	12				elf_land	1	1
14	13			Climb	elf_climb_050cm	2	3
15	14				elf_climb_100cm	2	3
16	15				elf_climb_150cm	2	3
17	16				elf_climb_200cm	2	3
18	17			Vault	elf_vault_100cm	2	3
19	18				elf_vault_150cm	2	3
20	19		Combat	Sword	elf_attack_sword_a	3	1
21	20				elf_attack_sword_b	3	1
22	21				elf_attack_sword_c	3	1
23	22			Axe	elf_attack_axe_a	3	2
24	23				elf_attack_axe_b	3	2
25	24				elf_attack_axe_c	3	2

Expect to become familiar with workload spreadsheets as a lead.

Google Docs is a great way to manage information across a project, allowing multiple team members to update documents from a decentralized repository—and it's free!

Animation Director

While most teams have an art director, only the largest teams tend to require a specific animation direction role. This is to separate the organizational role of the lead from the purely aesthetic pursuit of the director. The animation director is expected to follow through on the artistic vision, continuity of style, and quality throughout the project while elevating individual animators' skills through mentorship, insightful critique, and most of all, example.

Principal Animator

Rarer even than animation directors are principals. In order to offer an alternative career path to just management or direction, some studios will also offer a principal animator role that recognizes a director-like seniority but keeps the animator animating. Many animators who reach management-only positions rightly miss animation—the reason they started in the first place, after all. Not to mention moving a senior from the team into a management-only role means less senior-level content is being created.

Technical Animator

A technical animator focuses more on the technical rather than the artistic side of game animation, though ideally, he or she should have an eye for both. They'll typically handle elements such as rigging, skinning, scripts, tools, and pipeline efficiency to support the animators, allowing them to focus on creating animations with minimal issues.

```python
def _snapXform(master, slave):
    pos = cmds.xform(master, q=1, ws=1, rp=1)
    rot = cmds.xform(master, q=1, ws=1, ro=1)
    cmds.setAttr('%s.t'%slave, pos[0],pos[1],pos[2])
    cmds.setAttr('%s.r'%slave, rot[0],rot[1],rot[2])

def _showHideAttrs(node, aAttr, mode):
    if node!=None:
        for attr in aAttr:
            nodeAttr = '%s.%s'%(node,attr)
            if mode=='show':
                cmds.setAttr(nodeAttr, k=1, l=0)
            if mode=='hide':
                cmds.setAttr(nodeAttr, k=0, l=1, cb=0)
            if mode=='unlock':
                cmds.setAttr(nodeAttr, k=0, l=0, cb=0)
            if mode=='nonKey':
                cmds.setAttr(nodeAttr, k=0, l=0, cb=1)

def doConstraint(offset, orient, *args):
    sel = cmds.ls(sl=1)
    time = cmds.currentTime(q=1)
    min = cmds.playbackOptions(q=1, minTime=1)
    isConnected = 0
    if (len(sel)==0 or len(sel)==1 or len(sel) > 2) :
        om.MGlobal.displayWarning('select two objects and try again. "driver -> driven".')
    else:
        checkNode = []
        if offset == 1:
            if orient == 1:
                spaceGrp = cmds.listRelatives(sel[1], p=1, pa=1)
                if spaceGrp==None:
                    return om.MGlobal.displayWarning('parent group is missing. create constraint space from "setup -> Setup Constraint Groups" and
                attrs = ['rx','ry','rz']
            else:
                attrs = ['tx','ty','tz','rx','ry','rz']
            checkNode.append(sel[1])
        else:
            parentSpace = None
            spaceGrp = cmds.listRelatives(sel[1], p=1, pa=1)
            if spaceGrp==None:
                parentSpace = cmds.listRelatives(spaceGrp[0], p=1, pa=1)
            if spaceGrp==None or parentSpace==None:
                return om.MGlobal.displayWarning('parent group is missing. create constraint space from "setup -> Setup Constraint Groups" and try
            else:
                attrs = ['tx','ty','tz','rx','ry','rz']
                checkNode.append(spaceGrp[0])
                checkNode.append(parentSpace[0])
```

Python is a popular scripting language for tool creation.

Animation Technical Director

Again, generally only on larger projects, the animation technical director (TD) oversees the technical animation team and has a more teamwide impact on the tools and processes used for any one project. An animation TD will also be expected to create new technologies and workflows that allow previously unseen animations and rigs to come to fruition.

Other Game Development Disciplines

Unless you're an indie developer flying solo or a remote worker separate from the core team, every day as a game animator you will be interacting with a variety of team members, each with their own expertise, personalities, priorities, and desires for their own work. Fortunately, they will all be working with you toward the same goal of making a great game!

Often, it's not about your own desires and sometimes not even about making the best animation, but what's best for the game. Here are how your daily interactions may differ with each discipline.

Programming

Gameplay animators interact with gameplay programmers on a daily basis to bring their playable characters and systems to life. While programmers are generally cut from a different cloth from animators (they prefer mathematics to motion), there is common ground when good programmers pursue the best character movement and control—especially those that focus on the end result the player experiences. You will be working together to determine which animations are required, and how they will work together for different gameplay mechanics and systems.

Other roles in programming range from gameplay, systems, tools, and graphics, with similar lead and director positions found in animation. As a project closes, the programmers will still be fixing bugs and stabilizing builds weeks after the animators have put down their pencils, so they should always have the team's respect. While coding is becoming a more popular and common career path in schools, the very best programmers are worth their weight in gold.

Art

Animators will mostly be interacting with the character art team with regards to character creation, with TDs and technical animators providing a bridge between the disciplines. Characters should be designed and created with the animator's input because it's difficult to bring appeal, (one of the 12 animation principles), to a character without any to start with, and, even at the concept phase, an animator's eye can catch potential rigging and skinning problems long before they make it into the game. It is essential for animators to make suggestions at the character-design stage that promote a strong silhouette, making the animators' job easier to achieve strong poses from all angles, as well as suggesting moving elements like hair and cloth that might provide overlap and follow-through (another animation principle, described in the following chapter), to add further visual interest to motions.

Cinematic animators must be in constant communication with not just the character artists for faces, but also with the level/environment artists where their cutscenes take place to minimize nasty surprises that affect the preset cameras and acting in cinematics. Mirroring the relationship between level designers and level artists (where artistic license is sometimes taken to the detriment of gameplay), artists can also negatively affect an already-created cutscene such as by dropping a tree in the middle of a scene where the characters might be walking. As ever, the only real solution is to ensure a healthy dialogue between departments. Other areas of art include user interface (UI), visual effects, and technical artists, all with a similar lead/senior hierarchy to animation.

> While it makes sense in smaller studios, some large studios wrap animation under art rather than it being its own department, with the lead animator reporting to the art director. Unfortunately, this rarely results in exceptional animation due to the differences in expertise, so it should be a warning sign to animators wishing to push the envelope.

Design

Design is heavily involved with player character movement and should always be pushing for the best "feel." Naturally, their initial inclination is always toward speed of response, which presents the game animator with the challenge of still providing weight and fluidity to a character.

In these types of trade-offs, response is king, but visual feedback is important, so it is the animator's job to provide the player with the correct visual tells both before and after an action—instantaneous visual feedback can supplant a noninstantaneous result. Just as player awareness is "better" with an extremely far and wide camera, the connection between the player and avatar will be weakened as a result. As such, animators and designers must strike a balance between what feels good and what looks good when the two are at odds.

Level design overlaps with both gameplay and cinematic animation.

In addition, gameplay animators on navigation-focused games must deliberate over metrics with level designers to ensure the player character's movement makes sense within a world that is built to a sensible scale. The design department usually features roles such as game, level, technical, and systems design, with a hierarchy encompassing leads and directors, with game and creative directors at the very top, usually emerging from their ranks. However, as mentioned earlier, creative directors need not come from a design background, though obviously they must have a strong design head to make well-considered decisions, and the makeup and style of the game will generally be a reflection of this.

Audio & Effects

As the saying goes, "sound is 50% of a game", and any animation that already looks good will be enhanced even more when the sound effects are added. The same can be said for the visual flair added to any attack by a visual swoosh that replicates the smearing or multiples (two classic effects akin to modern-day motion-blur) of traditional 2D animation. Generally, most of a project is spent with minimal effects and no music, so the difference is apparent when they're finally added in the later stages.

Due to being downstream in the pipeline (sound and effects can only come after the visuals are in place), the audio and effects teams often face an intense amount of work at the end of the project, making all others seem light by comparison. As such, animations and cinematics generally have deadlines that run ahead of the real end date to ensure time is allocated to add these essentials, and cinematics especially works toward a "timing lock" date after which the animation can still be polished but not retimed, as it will throw off the other teams.

It is a good idea for cinematic animators to maintain a healthy relationship with effects artists throughout development, as even while swamped at the end, they still desire to make the best work possible, so any suggestions the animator might have to improve an action or cinematic are welcomed, time permitting. Details added days before shipping can bring a scene together in a way that is just impossible without.

Quality Assurance

A strong quality assurance team is the vanguard in catching the multitude of bugs that will crop up over the course of a project, especially if tight schedules don't allow them to be fixed as the project goes on. Due to their often-temporary contractual work, some teams do not treat their QA with the respect they deserve. A good QA team is invaluable in preventing broken characters and animations becoming internet memes on launch, so they should be kept in the loop as new gameplay systems are implemented.

It is highly recommended to maintain your bug count throughout the project rather than leaving it all to the end because it'll allow you to focus on polish in those final weeks rather than just making your animations work. Techniques for efficient bug-fixing of animations will be detailed later.

Management

Be it your direct lead/supervisor or the project leadership, there is always some layer of management to handle the overall production schedule, vision for the project, and high-level studio decisions. The creative vision is often separated from the production schedule, as the two compete for time vs budget. The former would take all the time and money/resources in the world to complete a project to perfection, while the latter understands the reality that if projects go too far over budget and time, then the consequences can be severe, such as project cancellations or worse.

Creatively, animators have animation leads, animation leads have animation directors, and animation directors have game and creative directors—each with a higher level of oversight over the entire project so they can make decisions from those positions to maintain consistency. Schedulewise, animators have animation leads that may in turn have project managers and producers to oversee the project from a high level and ensure dependencies between other departments are maintained.

There is often conflict between production and creativity, and as animators we naturally tend to favor the latter, but the reality is that if the scope of a project isn't reined in, it simply won't ever see the light of day. The ideal situation is a kind of organized chaos that leaves enough room for experimentation and creative risks without blowing the scope or schedule— as such, managers who come up through the ranks and have a firm handle on the intricacies of their own field generally excel over those with a background only in organization and project management.

Public Relations & Marketing

You can animate the best game in the world, but it's all for naught if no one knows about it. The marketing department is an essential element of any team that actually wishes their game to be seen or played by anybody. Animators will likely have a lot of interaction with marketing later in the project as it becomes time to promote the game, and in the video-heavy internet age, animations and cutscenes are a natural part of any marketing and launch strategy.

No one knows the visual action of a game more than the animators, so be proactive and offer suggestions of the best scenes and moves to be included in any upcoming trailers to ensure they are flawlessly polished before going out to the world. There's nothing worse than seeing an unfinished animation you were planning on polishing show up front and center in a trailer when just a little extra work would have made it perfect.

A Video Game Project Overview

Now that we've covered the various types of roles that make up a game development team, let's look at how a full game production is typically structured and what the animator's role will likely be at each phase.

Phase 1: Conception

Before any characters are modeled and animated, before a line of code is written, a game starts with an idea. This stage can vary wildly by how that idea comes about. Is it a brand-new intellectual property (IP)? Is it a sequel? Does it center on a new and unique gameplay mechanic? Is it a personal story from the creative director just waiting to burst out?

From all of these birthplaces, an idea is only that until it gets written down outside the mind of the creator and begins to take shape, often with the input of a core team of creatives fortunate enough to be involved in the initial stages of what might be something enjoyed by millions of players around the world in the future. It may start with something as simple as an image scrawled on a napkin or a conversation over dinner, but as soon as it gets outside the head and into some tangible form, this stage of development is called "conception".

Monument Valley was born of this initial concept sketch. (Courtesy of Ustwo Games.)

What happens next, as more of the team becomes involved, is a series of visualizations of ideas. Artists conceptualize and build out locations, characters, and potential gameplay storyboards. Designers build simple prototypes in which they can begin experimenting with the most rudimentary of rules and controls. Writers can begin scrawling down high-level story and characters that might reside in the as-yet nonexistent world. Basically, anyone who can make something themselves can go off and begin investigating directions inspired by that initial idea. It is here that the animator has perhaps the most powerful ability with which to make something from nothing—previsualization.

With only a rudimentary knowledge of modeling and rigging (or temporarily using assets from a previous project), the animator should begin blocking out potential gameplay ideas with or without the help of input from design or other team members. Animating a camera to behave like a gameplay camera affords the animator the unique ability not only to make suggestions at this early stage but also show how it might look and play out as if it were under player control.

Conception can be an exciting time for an animator, as ideas generated here will provide the basis for mechanics built over the following years, though expect to throw away many more than will be kept. It's better to rapidly hash out a variety of "sketches" than hone in and polish any in this phase.

Ultimately, this stage will generally finish with a pitch to whomever makes the decision on future projects, be it the studio management or a potential publisher funding the project. At this stage, an incredibly persuasive tool in the team's arsenal will be a video mock-up of what the final game can look like, which naturally leans heavily on animation—only this time with a more finished look, illustrating things like setting, character, and, importantly, what the gameplay will be. Expect the creation of such a video to be tough, with input from all sides and many revisions as it coalesces into the team's vision.

Target footage gives an idea of gameplay in this early Rainbow Six pitch. (Courtesy of Ubisoft.)

This "target footage" video and other accompanying pitch materials like presentation slides can be invaluable throughout the project as new team members are brought on board, as well as being a reminder of the initial vision to make sure the project direction stays on track. The industry relies less and less on design documents to maintain vision, as design is fluid and will change throughout the project, rendering anything static like a document obsolete very quickly. Conversely, a target footage video loosely provides a vision and serves more as inspiration for the potential years of work that will follow.

Phase 2: Preproduction

If your team has successfully pitched and been given a "green light" to move forward with the project, the next phase, preproduction, is incredibly important in readying the team to build the full game. Preproduction generally encompasses the prototyping of mechanics to support the core gameplay, tools and pipelines to allow the team to work as efficiently as possible, rendering technology to achieve the visual result, and related artistic benchmarks for the team to hit, including the animation style.

Here, gameplay animators will be working with designers and animation programmers to get the player character up and running as quickly as possible so that prototyping within the actual game (rather than the independent tests) can take place, as well as basic movement through the game's world so designers can begin building it out. At this stage, it's likely that characters are in a high state of flux, so nothing here is expected to look finished beyond some key actions like idles and commonly seen walk and runs.

If your game features combat, there will likely be a lot of experimentation with how silhouettes and cameras work to aid gameplay and readability of the characters on screen, as well as a push to narrow down the stylization of the character movements. It is here that decisions will be made as to whether to adopt a keyframe or motion-capture pipeline depending on the visual look (and budget) of the animation direction.

Technical animators will be heavily involved in setting up file structures and naming conventions, as well as initial character rigging to be improved throughout the project or as new requests come in. An ideal pipeline allows the team to be flexible, never having to stick with a rig issue or slow workflow because of a misjudgment made at this early stage, but technical decisions made here will have an impact throughout production.

Cinematic animators will begin experimenting with the style of cinematography for any storytelling elements of the game and should be heavily involved in prototyping facial rigs. Any game with aspirations of storytelling with believable (not necessarily realistic) characters nowadays must focus heavily on getting the faces right, and that falls a lot on the facial rigging and ease of workflow for the animators. Too cumbersome and this already heavy workload will be impossible to create at any degree of quality, especially if the face has not been set up correctly for animation.

At the end of the preproduction phase, the team should have a section of the game up and running, and, importantly, must have answers to key questions surrounding the game before moving onto the next phase. Ideally, a playable demo of core gameplay that shows the game offers something fun and refreshing (called the core gameplay loop), with second-to-second gameplay, will be created. In addition, there should be a series of in-game visual benchmarks that give the art and animation teams the visual bar that they must achieve throughout the project. All these elements can be wrapped up in one demo, or as separate entities, but, importantly, should feature real working technology rather than fake "hacks," as questions remaining at this stage of the project can turn into real risks further down the road.

Phase 3: Production

Some animators prefer the idea-generation period, some prefer endlessly prototyping, but many prefer production most of all because they're no longer doing throwaway work and are instead building the real bulk of the game that players will eventually see. Easily the longest stretch of the entire project, by now many of the high-level questions such as story, characters, core gameplay, scheduling, and technology should have at least been figured out so the team can get on with the business of creating all the assets that make up the game.

Gameplay animators in this stage will mostly be working with finished character rigs to create the sometimes thousands of animations that make up their player and nonplayer characters. Cinematic animators will be hard at work assembling scenes, going through the various stages of previz to completion. If the project has opted for motion capture, shoots should be occurring as regularly as the budget allows, with animators fed enough mocap to keep them busy until the next shoot.

A schedule will set milestones and dates for certain stages of the project. Games are not linear entertainment, and neither are their productions. The first aim of any project's production phase should be to get the complete game playable from start to finish in any shape possible. This means inserting story scenes and events in as rough a form as possible. The player character(s), by now able to perform most actions in rudimentary form, will start shaping up as design hones in on the "feel" they are going for and new player abilities are added on a weekly basis. Animators will work with level designers to add relevant elements to the game as they come online, such as ladders to climb or chests to open up.

In the fast-paced production phase, it is beneficial for animators to always deliver a quick animation to whomever needs it (design or programming, usually), so they can begin implementing knowing that a more finished animation will be coming later.

As the production phase can sometimes last for years, with a team growing throughout, one of the biggest challenges is to remain focused on what is important and relevant to the original vision. Here, deadlines and demos are a great way to have the team pull together for a common goal. Often the bane of mismanaged projects when they are inserted without proper planning, having a target such as an external demo allows the whole team to coalesce on a shared deliverable where at least a portion of the game needs to look finished. Be it a demo for a publisher or to show to the public for marketing purposes, these slices of polish serve a similar purpose as the art benchmarks in the early stages by setting a standard for the rest of the game to aim for while forcing the team to iron out the last remaining pipeline and technology issues.

Demos are tough on the animation team, as they need to polish up every action the player will be expected to perform during the demo's playthrough, but this naturally reduces that work in the closing phases of the project. It is recommended to add unique details and "nice-to-have" features that give the game some extra personality at this stage, as there will be no time for it in the closing phase of mostly polish and bug-fixing. Similarly, don't let all the animation bugs pile up throughout production, as animators are better polishing in the closing phases rather than solely squashing bugs.

A game schedule is finite, but so large and flexible and containing so many moving parts that what actually goes into the game depends very much on what the team prioritizes throughout the production phase. You'll never get to everything you want, so make sure you do get in what is important to you as an animator to really bring your characters to life.

The ultimate goal of the production phase is to get the entire game to Alpha, whereby the game is content complete. This means every character, level, animation, and action is accounted for—regardless of quality level. Only then can the project leadership review the entire game and know what editing is still required to finish the project—making the correct cuts or additions to finish the game out to the vision set at the start. Sometimes hard choices must be made here, but failure to do so will make the closing phase even more difficult.

Phase 4: Shipping

Shipping, the closing phase of a project, is key to the quality of the final game players will get in their hands. Players will never bemoan a game that has fewer levels and characters or abilities than initially envisaged, mostly due to being unaware of the initial plans, but they *will* see when a game is lacking polish or, even worse, ships with a multitude of bugs.

Here, it is the animation director's (or lead's) responsibility to decide what to focus on when polishing. As time is running out, not every animation is of equal importance, so it is imperative to focus on what is going to be "player facing"—actions that are seen most often or are key to the experience. When deciding which cinematic cutscene to work on the most, oftentimes a "critical path" is referred to—the scenes the player *must* encounter to complete a game. Optional scenes or side content are generally less important, as they will be encountered less by the total player base.

Here, the animation team will take the game from Alpha to Beta, where everything in the game reaches shippable quality. This means replacing all temporary assets with final polished ones and locking timing on cinematics so that audio and visual effects can go in and add their respective elements to bring the story and entire game to life. Ideally, nothing new will be coming in at this phase, but the reality of post-Alpha editing means that there will still be changes. For every change, the animation lead needs to evaluate and argue the cost (in time) of that change and whether it adds to the overall quality of the game (commensurate with the work involved) vs using that time elsewhere.

The concept of "triage" comes into play in the final stages, as not all bugs or issues are given the same priority. It is important for the lead animator, along with other leads on the team, to focus on attacking the most serious bugs such as "progression stoppers" that prevent the player from continuing through the game first and work backward from there to issues that are purely aesthetic.

As the project winds up, different teams will finish at different points, usually with the animation team essentially being "locked out" of making changes to the game without approval to prevent the very real risk of breaking something else due to the interconnectedness of game assets. Programmers will likely be the last ones to finish up as they solidify the "release candidate" (to the publisher or similar), but other teams such as animation must still remain on hand to spot-fix anything essential that comes up relating to their field.

The absolute final stage of game development is sending the disc off to gold master for review by the platform holder (in the case of consoles) or uploading to the distribution channel (with a digital-only game). This time is perhaps the most focused of the entire project, with team members working intensely to avoid missing the ship date. Delays at this point can result in any accompanying marketing campaigns (usually prebought) being allocated elsewhere by the publisher or losing impact if the game ships too late.

Phase 5: Postrelease

The period after gold master approval usually results in the work easing up, with exhausted team members taking well-earned breaks and returning to a more relaxed schedule. The bug fixing may continue for patches and updates, and in this day and age, it is regular to expect some kind of postrelease downloadable content as a way of continuing revenue while maintaining the team momentum as the next project ideally ramps up.

It is rare to fix animation bugs postrelease, as the game is still highly fragile and any purely aesthetic change needs to be double- and triple-checked, so animators will likely be treating any DLC as a mini-project (very fun to do when you have a working game already) or starting the whole process again with conception and previz animations for the next project as the game-making process starts over.

CHAPTER 3

The 12 Animation Principles

Back when video games were still in the Pac Man era, Disney animators Frank Thomas and Ollie Johnston introduced (in their 1981 book, *The Illusion of Life: Disney Animation*)[1] what are now widely held to be the core tenets of all animation, the 12 basic principles of animation. They are:

1. Squash & stretch
2. Staging
3. Anticipation
4. Straight ahead & pose to pose
5. Follow-through & overlapping action
6. Slow in & slow out
7. Arcs
8. Secondary action
9. Appeal
10. Timing
11. Exaggeration
12. Solid drawing

While these fundamentals were written in the pre-computer graphics days of exclusively hand-drawn 2D animation, they translated perfectly for the later evolution to 3D animation, and while some of them less obviously correlate to the interactive medium, some light reinterpretation reveals their timeless value. Understanding these basics of animation is essential, so it's time to revisit them again through the lens of video game animation.

---

[1] F. Thomas and O. Johnston. 1981. *The Illusion of Life: Disney Animation*. Walt Disney Productions.

Principle 1: Squash & Stretch

This is the technique of squashing or stretching elements of a character or object (such as a bouncing ball) to exaggerate movement in the related direction. For example, a character jumping up can be stretched vertically during the fast portion of the jump to accentuate the vertical, but can squash at the apex of the jump arc and again on impact with the ground. Ideally, the overall volume of the object should be preserved, so if a ball is stretched vertically, it must correspondingly squash horizontally.

Many video game engines do not support scaling of bones unless specifically required to due to the extra memory overhead (saving position, rotation, *and* scale is more expensive) and relative infrequency of cartoony games. However, this principle is important even when posing nondeformable rigs, as the theory of characters stretching and squashing their poses comes into play whenever performing fast actions even if not actually scaling, by extending limbs to accentuate stretched poses such as during jump takeoffs and lands.

Squash & stretch was a key visual motif of the Jak & Daxter series. (Courtesy of Sony Interactive Entertainment.)

Principle 2: Staging

Only directly relevant to linear portions of games such as cinematics, where the camera and/or characters are authored by the animator (as opposed to gameplay where both are player controlled), staging is the principle of presenting "any idea so that it is completely and unmistakably clear." This involves the use of camera, lighting, or character composition to focus the viewer's attention on what is relevant to that scene while avoiding unnecessary detail and confusion.

Staging is relevant in gameplay when relating to level design, however, where certain layouts will funnel the player and direct him or her down a corridor or over a hill to reveal story elements laid out there, or the use of lighting to direct the player's attention. Here, the animator can work with design to best place scenes in the player's view by using techniques like these without resorting to fully commandeering the camera or characters.

Funneled into the doorway, Gears of War players encounter this gruesome sight on kicking open the door.
(Copyright Microsoft. All rights reserved. Used with permission from Microsoft Corporation.)

Principle 3: Anticipation

Anticipation is used to prepare the viewer for an action, such as a crouch before a jump or an arm pulling back for a punch. It occurs in the natural world because a person jumping must first crouch with bended knees to give enough energy to lift off the ground, so it is used similarly in animation to sell the energy transfer of an action in a way the action alone cannot.

Anticipation is a controversial topic in video games, with designers often requesting as little as possible and animators pushing for as many frames as possible. Too little and the desired move, such as a punch or sword-swing, will have little weight to it (a key component of player feedback, not just an aesthetic one). Too long and the move will feel unresponsive, removing agency from the player and reducing the feeling of directly controlling the avatar. Ultimately, it will depend on the goals of the project and the value placed on a more realistically weighted character, but there are many more techniques than just extra animation frames to help sell feedback that will be detailed later.

Designwise, anticipation in NPC actions or attacks (called telegraphing) is desirably longer, as it informs the player that they must block or dodge something incoming. There's not much fun in having to guess what an enemy might do with little warning, so the ability to read their attention is essential in creating satisfying back-and-forth gameplay. Both player and NPC actions tend to follow a balance of longer anticipations for bigger effect (higher damage) and vice versa to promote a risk-vs-reward scenario in performing actions with long anticipation that might leave the player vulnerable.

Principle 4: Straight Ahead & Pose to Pose

Referring purely to the process of animation creation, these two techniques describe the difference between working on frames contiguously (starting at frame 1, then onward) versus dropping in only key poses (called blocking) to quickly create a first pass and massage from there. Again, this has more relevance to linear animation (and especially 2D, where preservation of volume was key to the art of drawing) and essentially describes two philosophies.

In CG animation, there is no need to work in the former, and the realities of production almost demand that animations be done in multiple passes of increasing quality, so pose to pose is the preferable method for most game animation. This is due mostly to the high likelihood of animations being changed or even cut as the design progresses. Key gameplay animations will continuously require iteration, and doing so with a roughly key-posed animation is much easier than with a completely finished one, not to mention the time it wastes to finish an animation only to see it unused.

It is important never to be precious with one's own work because of this, so keeping something in a pose-to-pose or unfinished state as long as possible not only promotes minimal waste, but allows the animator to create rough versions of more animations in the same time—ultimately, many animations blending together creates a better and more fluid game character than a single beautifully animated animation.

This all goes out the window when motion-capture is employed, where the animator is essentially provided with the in-between motion as a starting point, then adds in key poses and re-times on top of the action from there. There is an entire breakdown of this process later in this book.

First blocking poses is the recommended method for gameplay animation.

Principle 5: Follow-Through & Overlapping Action

Overlapping action covers the notion that different parts of a character's body will move at different rates. During a punch, the head and torso will lead the action, with the bent arm dragging behind and the arm snapping forward just before impact to deliver the blow. A common mistake most junior animators make is to have all elements of a character start or arrive at the same time, which looks unnatural and draws the eye to clearly defined key frames.

Follow-through, while related, instead describes what takes place after an action (the inverse of anticipation). This can cover actions such as a landing recovery from a jump or a heavy sword or axe embedding in the ground and being heavily lifted back over the character's shoulder, and also includes the motion of secondary items such as cloth and hair catching up with the initial action. Follow-through is a great way to sell the weight of an object or character, and holding strong poses in this phase of an action will really help the player read the action better than the earlier fast movements. Follow-through has fewer gameplay restrictions than anticipation, as the action has already taken place, though too long a follow-through before returning control to the player can again result in an unresponsive character.

To maintain responsiveness, the animator should be able to control when the player is able to perform a follow-up action by specifying a frame where the player regains control before the end, allowing the follow-through to play out fully if no new input is given by the player rather than having to cut the follow-through short in the animation itself. Game engines that do not incorporate such a feature force animators to finish their actions earlier than desired to maintain responsiveness, losing out on a key tool in the game animator's belt to provide both great-feeling and great-looking characters.

Related to overlapping action and follow-through is the concept of "drag," where looser objects and soft parts such as hair or weak limbs can drag behind the main mass of a character to help sell the relative weight of one object or body part to another. Follow-through, overlapping action, and drag on nonanimated objects such as cloth cloaks or fat bellies can be performed procedurally in the game engine by real-time rigging that causes these elements to move with physics. Adding rigging elements such as these, especially those that visibly change or enhance a character's silhouette, are a fantastic way to increase the quality of a character's animation with little extra work, not least because their motion will continue whatever the following animation the player performs.

Principle 6: Slow In & Slow Out

This principle describes the visual result of acceleration and deceleration on moving elements whereby actions generally have slower movements at the start and end as the action begins and is completed, often due to the weight of the object or character body part.

This notion can be visualized very easily by a sphere traveling across a distance. Uniform/linear movement would see the sphere travel the same distance every frame, while slow ins and outs would see the positions gradually closer toward the start and end as the sphere's speed is ramping up and down, respectively.

Importantly, not everything requires a slow in and out, but it is a good concept to grasp when they are required. For example, a rock falling off a beach cliff will have a slow in as it starts at rest, then gains speed during the fall, but will finish with an immediate stop as it embeds in the sand below. Were this to be animated, the rock would feature a slow in and fast out with a steep tangent at the end. Conversely, a cannonball fired high in the air from a cannon would display a fast in and a slower (yet still fast) out if its target were far away and it slowed due to air resistance.

Objects that burst into full speed immediately can look weightless and unrealistic, so it is here again that there is conflict between the gameplay desire to give players immediate response versus the artistic desire to give weight to a character. A sword that swings immediately might look light, so it is the game animator's task to add that weight at the end in the follow-through, giving the action a fast in but a slow out as the character and sword return to idle.

Despite taking the same number of frames, the top sphere travels uniformly, while the bottom one moves slowly at the start and end, speeding up then down in the middle.

In the cannonball example, the sense of weight could be displayed by animating a follow-through on the cannon itself as it kicks back, much like a game animator will often exaggerate the kickback of a pistol to show its relative power and damage as a weapon in gameplay, all the while maintaining the instant response and feedback of firing.

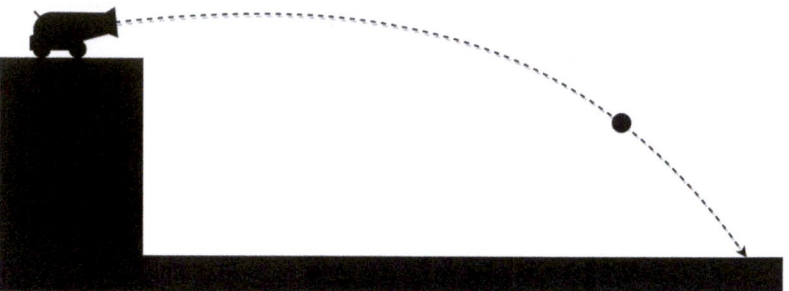

A cannonball creates a fast/slow trajectory in different axes.

Principle 7: Arcs

Most actions naturally follow arcs as elements of the object or character move, such as arms and legs swinging while walking. Body parts that deviate from a natural curve will be picked up by the eye and can look unnatural, so arcs are a great way of honing in on the polish and correctness of an action. Much of the cleanup of making motion-capture work within a game is removing egregious breaks from arcs that naturally occur in human motion, but might look too noticeable and "wrong" when seen over and over in a video game.

Contrary to this, though, animating every element of a character to follow clean arcs can look light or floaty when nothing catches the eye. Much like employing overlapping actions, like most general rules, knowing when to break a smooth arc will add a further level of detail to animation and make it that little bit more realistic. Due to its weight compared to the rest of the body, the head will often snap after the rest of the body comes to a stop following a punch. Having the head break from the arc of the rest of the body is one of many observable traits that extensively working in mocap can reveal, adding an extra level of detail to animation required to look realistic.

Principle 8: Secondary Action

Secondary actions are used to complement and emphasize the primary action of the character, adding extra detail and visual appeal to the base action. While it can be difficult to incorporate more than one action in many gameplay animations due to their brevity, (secondary actions must support and not muddy the look of the primary action), it is these little details that can take a good animation to great.

Examples of secondary actions range from facial expression changes to accompany combat or damage animations to tired responses that play atop long stretches of running. Technologies detailed later in this book such as additive and partial animations allow actions to be combined on top of base actions to afford secondary motions that are longer than the individual animations required for player control.

Principle 9: Appeal

Appeal should be the goal of every animator when bringing a character to life, but is ineffable enough to make it hard to describe. It is the difference between an animated face that can portray real emotion and one that looks terrifying and creepy. It is the sum of an animator's skill in selling the force of a combat action versus a movement that comes across as weak. It is the believability in a character's performance compared to one that appears robotic and unnatural.

Appeal is the magic element that causes players to believe in the character they are interacting with regardless of where they lie on the stylized vs realistic spectrum, and is not to be confused with likeability or attractiveness, as even the player's enemies must look aesthetically pleasing and show appeal. This is owed as much to character design as it is the animators' manipulation of them, where proportions and color blocking are the first steps in a multistage creation process that passes through animation and eventual rendering to make a character as appealing as possible. Simplicity in visual design and posing on the animator's part help the readability of a move, and clear silhouettes distinguish different characters from one another.

Principle 10: Timing

Timing is the centerpiece of the "feel" of an animation and is generally invoked to convey the weight of a character or object. Intrinsically linked to speed, the time it takes for an object or individual limb to move or rotate a distance or angle will give the viewer an impression of how weighted or powerful that motion is.

In 3D animation, this is best explained in basic mathematics:

$$\text{time} = \text{distance/speed, therefore, speed} = \text{distance/time}$$

That is why every animation curve editor available shows the axes of both distance and time as the main input for animators to visualize the speed of the manipulations they are performing. If we move an object 10 m over 2 seconds, that is faster than doing so over 5 seconds. Similarly, posing a character with arm recoiled then outstretched gives a faster punch over 2 frames than it does over 5.

Referencing slow ins and outs, appropriate timing ensures a character or object obeys the laws of physics. The faster a move, the less weight, and vice versa, which refers back to the game animator's dilemma of offering gameplay response while still maintaining weight. Having a character immediately ramp up to a full-speed run when the player pushes on the stick will make the character appear weightless without the correct visual feedback of leaning into the move and pushing off with a foot.

Moreover, timing of reactions gives individual movements time to breathe, such as holding a pose after a sword swing before the next so the player sees it; or, during a cinematic moment, the delay before a character's next movement can illustrate a thought process at work as he or she pauses.

The slow movement of the colossi in Shadow of the Colossus is juxtaposed with the nimble climbing of the hero. (Shadow of the Colossus (PS3) Copyright 2005–2011 Sony Interactive Entertainment Inc.)

Principle 11: Exaggeration

Real life never looks real enough. If you were to watch a real person perform an action, such as jumping from a height and landing on the floor, and copy it exactly into your animation, the character would likely look slow and aesthetically imperfect. Real movements do not follow perfect arcs or create appealing or powerful silhouettes.

In animation, we are looking to create the hyper-real, a better presentation of what exists in real life. In games, especially, we more often than not must create actions that look great from all angles, not just from the fixed camera perspective of traditional linear media. That is why one of the best tools in an animator's kit is to exaggerate what already exists. When referencing actions, the animator must reinterpret the movements in a "hyper-real" way, with poses accentuated and held a little longer than in reality.

Obeying the laws of physics completely, a bouncing ball causes a smooth parabola as it reaches the apex, then falls back to the ground with a constant gravity. An animator, however, may choose to hold longer at the apex (creating anticipation in the process) before zooming back to the ground, much like a martial-arts character thundering down with a flying kick.

Similarly, a real boxer might uppercut for an opponent-crumpling KO, whereas the game animator would launch the opponent off his or her feet and into the air to "sell" the action more and make it readable for the player. "Selling" actions via "plusing" them is an excellent technique to ensure a player understands what is happening, especially when the camera might be further away for gameplay (situational awareness) purposes.

Care must be taken to ensure all levels of exaggeration are consistent throughout a project, and it will mostly fall on the animation lead or director to maintain this, as the level of exaggeration is a stylistic choice and inconsistency between actions (or across animators) will stand out and appear unappealing when the player plays through the entire game.

Fantastic exaggeration of facial expressions in Cuphead. (Courtesy of Studio MDHR.)

Principle 12: Solid Drawings

While at first seemingly less relevant in the age of 3D animation, one must remember that drawing is an essential method of conveying information between team members, and the use of thumbnails to explain a problem or find a solution is an almost daily occurrence when working with game design. All the best animators can draw to a degree that can easily support or give a direction, and the skill is especially useful in the early stages when working on character designs to illustrate the pros and cons of particular visual elements.

Nevertheless, the "solid" part was essential in the age of 2D animation to retain the volume of characters as they moved and rotated on the page, so a lot of focus was placed on an animators' skills in life drawing and the ability to visualize a character in three dimensions as they translate to the two-dimensional page. While no longer done on a page, an understanding of volume and three dimensions is still essential for an animator when animating a character in 3D to aid with posing and knowing the limits and workings of body mechanics.

Solid drawings can be reinterpreted as a solid understanding of body mechanics, which covers everything from center of mass and balance to the chains of reaction down a limb or spine as a foot hits the floor. Understanding how bodies move is a core competency of a good game animator, and knowing how they should look from any angle means cheating is out of the question.

CHAPTER 4

The Five Fundamentals of Game Animation

The 12 animation principles are a great foundation for any animator to understand, and failure to do so will result in missing some of the underlying fundamentals of animation—visible in many a junior's work. Ultimately, however, they were written with the concept of linear entertainment like TV and film in mind, and the move to 3D kept all of these elements intact due to the purely aesthetic change in the medium. Three-dimensional animated cartoons and visual effects are still part of a linear medium, so they will translate only to certain elements of video game animation—often only if the game is cartoony in style.

As such, it's time to propose an additional set of principles unique to game animation that don't replace but instead complement the originals. These are what I have come to know as the core tenets of our new nonlinear entertainment medium, which, when taken into consideration, form the basis of video game characters that not only look good, but feel good under player control—something the original 12 didn't have to consider. Many elements are essential in order to create great game animation, and they group under five fundamental areas:

1. Feel
2. Fluidity
3. Readability
4. Context
5. Elegance

Feel

The single biggest element that separates video game animation from traditional linear animation is interactivity. The very act of the player controlling and modifying avatars, making second-to-second choices, ensures that the animator must relinquish complete authorship of the experience. As such, any uninterrupted animation that plays start to finish is a period of time the player is essentially locked out of the decision-making process, rendered impotent while waiting for the animation to complete (or reach the desired result, such as landing a punch).

The time taken between a player's input and the desired reaction can make the difference between creating the illusion that the player is embodying the avatar or becoming just a passive viewer on the sidelines. That is why cutscenes are the only element in video games that for years have consistently featured a "skip" option—because they most reflect traditional noninteractive media, which is antithetical to the medium.

Response

Game animation must always consider the response time between player input and response as an intrinsic part of how the character or interaction will "feel" to the player. While generally the desire is to have the response be as quick as possible (fewer frames), that is dependent on the context of the action. For example, heavy/stronger actions are expected to be slower, and enemy attacks must be slow enough to be seen by the player to give enough time to respond.

It will be the game animator's challenge, often working in concert with a designer and/or programmer, to offer the correct level of response to provide the best "feel," while also retaining a level of visual fidelity that satisfies all the intentions of the action and the character. It is important not to sacrifice the weight of the character or the force of an action for the desire to make everything as responsive as possible, so a careful balancing act and as many tricks as available must be employed.

Ultimately, though, the best mantra is that "gameplay wins." The most fluid and beautiful animation will always be cut or scaled back if it interferes too much with gameplay, so it is important for the game animator to have a player's eye when creating response-critical animations, and, most importantly, play the game!

Inertia & Momentum

Inertia is a great way to not only provide a sense of feel to player characters, but also to make things fun. While some characters will be required to turn on a dime and immediately hit a run at full speed, driving a car around a track that could do the same would not only feel unrealistic but mean there would be no joy to be had in approaching a corner at the correct speed for the minimum lap time. The little moments when you are nudging an avatar because you understand their controls are where mastery of a game is to be found, and much of this is provided via inertia.

Judging death-defying jumps in a platform game is most fun when the character must be controlled in an analogue manner, whereby they take some time to reach full speed and continue slightly after the input is released. This is as much a design/programming challenge as it is animation, but the animator often controls the initial inertia boost and slowdown in stop/start animations.

Original sketches from Sonic the Hedgehog (circa 1990). The animation frames are already heavily displaying inertia. (Courtesy of SEGA of America.)

Momentum is often conveyed by how long it takes a character to change from current to newly desired directions and headings. The general principle is that the faster a character is moving, the longer it takes to change direction via larger turn-circles at higher speeds or longer plant-and-turn animations in the case of turning 180°.

Larger turn-circles can be made to feel better by immediately showing the intent of the avatar, such as having the character lean into the turn and/or look with his or her head, but ultimately we are again balancing within a very small window of time lest we render our characters unresponsive.

A classic example is the difference between the early Mario and Sonic the Hedgehog series. Both classic Mario and Sonic's run animations rely heavily on inertia and have similar long ramp-ups to full speed. While Mario immediately starts cartoonishly running at full speed as his legs spin on the ground to gain traction, Sonic slowly transitions from a walk to a run to a sprint. While Mario subjectively feels better, this is by design, as Sonic's gameplay centers on high speeds and "flow," so stopping or slowing down is punitive for not maintaining momentum.

Visual Feedback

A key component of the "feel" of any action the player and avatar perform is the visual representation of that action. A simple punch can be made to feel stronger with a variety of techniques related to animation, beginning with the follow-through following the action. A long, lingering held pose will do wonders for telling the player he or she just performed a powerful action. The damage animation on the attacked enemy is a key factor in informing the player just how much damage has been suffered, with exaggeration being a key component here.

In addition, employing extra tricks such as camera-shake will help further sell the impact of landing the punch or gunshot, not to mention visual effects of blood or flashes to further register the impact in the player's mind. Many fighting games employ a technique named "hit-stop" that freezes the characters for a single frame whenever a hit is registered. This further breaks the flow of clean arcs in the animations and reinforces the frame on which the impact took place.

As many moves are performed quickly so as to be responsive, they might get lost on the player, especially during hectic actions. Attacking actions can be reinforced by additional effects that draw the arc of the punch, kick, or sword-swipe on top of the character in a similar fashion to the "smears" and "multiples" of old. When a sword swipe takes only 2 frames to create its arc, the player benefits mostly from the arcing effect it leaves behind.

Slower actions can be made to feel responsive simply by showing the player that at least part of their character is responding to their commands. A rider avatar on a horse can be seen to immediately turn the horse's head with the reins even if the horse itself takes some time to respond and traces a wide circle as it turns. This visual feedback will feel entirely more responsive than a slowly turning horse alone would following the exact same wide turn.

Much of the delay in visual feedback comes not from the animation alone, but the way different game engines handle inputs from the joypad in the player's hands. Games like the Call of Duty series place an onus on having their characters and weapons instantly respond to the player's inputs with minimal lag and high frame rates, whereas other game engines focused more on graphics postprocessing will have noticeably longer delays (measured in milliseconds) between a jump button-press and the character even beginning the jump animation, for example. This issue is further exacerbated by modern HDTVs that have lag built in and so often feature "Game Mode" settings to minimize the effect. All this said, it is still primarily an animator's goal to make characters as responsive as possible within reason.

Fluidity

Rather than long flowing animations, games are instead made of lots of shorter animations playing in sequence. As such, they are often stopping, starting, overlapping, and moving between them. It is a video game animator's charge to be involved in how these animations flow together so as to maintain the same fluidity put into the individual animations themselves, and there are a variety of techniques to achieve this, with the ultimate goal being to reduce any unsightly movement that can take a player out of the experience by highlighting where one animation starts and another ends.

Blending and Transitions

In classic 2D game sprites, an animation either played or it didn't. This binary approach carried into 3D animation until developers realized that, due to characters essentially being animated by poses recorded as numerical values, they could manipulate those values in a variety of ways. The first such improvement that arrived was the ability to blend across (essentially cross-fading animations during a transitory stage) every frame, taking an increasing percentage of the next animation's value and a decreasing percentage of the current as one animation ended and another began. While more calculation intensive, this opened up opportunities for increasing the fluidity between individual animations and removing unsightly pops between them.

Prince of Persia: Sands of Time was the first game to really focus on small transitions for fluidity. (Copyright 2003 Ubisoft Entertainment. Based on Prince of Persia®, created by Jordan Mechner. Prince of Persia is a trademark of Waterwheel Licensing LLC in the US and/or other countries used under license.)

A basic example of this would be an idle and a run. Having the idle immediately cancel and the run immediately play on initial player input will cause the character to break into a run at full speed, but the character will unsightly pop as he or she starts and stops due to the potential repeated nature of the player's input. This action can be made more visually appealing by blending between the idle and run over several frames, causing the character to more gradually move between the different poses. Animators should have some degree of control over the length of blends between any two animations to make them as visually appealing as possible, though always with an eye on the gameplay response of the action.

The situation above can be improved further (albeit with more work) by creating brief bespoke animations between idle and run (starting) and back again (stopping), with blends between all of them. What if the player started running in the opposite direction he or she is facing? An animator could create a transition for each direction that turned the character as he or she began running in order to completely control the character's weight-shift as he or she leans into the desired direction and pushes off with his or her feet.

What if the character isn't running but only walking? Again, the animator could also create multiple directional transitions for that speed. As you can see, the number of animations can quickly spiral in number, so a balance must be found among budget, team size, and the desired level of fluidity.

Seamless Cycles

Even within a single animation, it is essential to maintain fluidity of motion, and that includes when a cycling animation stops and restarts. A large percentage of game animations repeat back on themselves, so it is important to again ensure the player cannot detect when this transition occurs. As such, care must be taken to maintain momentum through actions so the end of the animation perfectly matches the start.

It is not simply enough to ensure the last frame of a cycle identically matches the first; the game animator must also preserve momentum on each body part to make the join invisible. This can be achieved by modifying the curves before and after the last frame to ensure they create clean arcs and continue in the same direction. For motion-capture, where curves are mostly unworkable, there are techniques that can automatically provide a preservation of momentum as a cycle restarts that are described later in this book.

Care should also be taken to maintain momentum when creating an animation that transitions into a cycle, such as how the stopping animation should seamlessly match the idle. For maximum fluidity, the best approach in this case is to copy the approved idle animation and stopping transition into the same scene to manually match the curves leading into the idle, exporting only the stopping transition from that scene.

Settling

This kind of approach should generally be employed whenever a pose must be assumed at the end of an animation, time willing. It is rather unsightly to have a large movement like an attack animation end abruptly in the combat idle pose, especially with all of the character's body parts arriving simultaneously. Offsetting individual elements such as the arms and root are key to a more visually pleasing settle.

Notably, however, games often suffer from too quickly resuming the idle pose at the end of an animation in order to return control to the player to promote response, but this can be avoided by animating a long tail on the end of an animation and, importantly, allowing the player to exit out at a predetermined frame before the end if new input is provided. This ability to interrupt an animation before finishing allows the animator to use the desired number of frames required for a smooth and fluid settle into the following animation.

Settling is generally achieved by first copying the desired end pose to the end of an animation but ensuring some elements like limbs (even divided

Uncharted 4: A Thief's End makes heavy use of "abort frames" to exit gameplay animations and cinematics before completion for fluidity. (Courtesy of Sony Interactive Entertainment.)

into shoulder and forearms) arrive at their final position at different times, with earlier elements hitting, then overshooting, their goal, creating overlapping animation. Settling the character's root (perhaps the single most important element, as it moves everything not planted) is best achieved by having it arrive at the final pose with different axes at different times. Perhaps it achieves its desired height (Y-axis) first as it is still moving left to right (X-axis), causing the root to hit, then bounce past the final height and back again. Offsetting in the order of character root, head, and limbs lessens the harshness of a character fully assuming the end pose on a single frame—though care must be taken to not overdo overlap such that it results in limbs appearing weak and floppy.

Readability

After interactivity, the next biggest differentiator between game and traditional animation, in 3D games at least, is that game animations will more often than not be viewed from all angles. This bears similarity to the traditional principle "staging," but animators cannot cheat or animate to the camera, nor can they control the composition of a scene, so actions must be created to be appealing from all angles. What this means is when working on an animation, it is not enough to simply get it right from a front or side view. Game animators must take care to always be rotating and approving their motion from all angles, much like a sculptor walking around a work.

Posing for Game Cameras

To aid the appeal and readability of any given action, it is best to avoid keeping a movement all in one axis. For example, a combo of three punches should not only move the whole character forward as he or she attacks, but also slightly to the left and right, twisting as they do so.

Similarly, the poses the character ends in after every punch should avoid body parts aligning with any axes, such as arms and legs that appear to bend only when viewed from the side. Each pose must be dynamic, with lines of action drawn through the character that are not in line with any axes.

> Lines of action are simplified lines that can be drawn through any single pose to clearly illustrate the overall motion for the viewer. Strong poses can be illustrated in this way with a single arcing or straight line, whereas weaker and badly thought-out poses will generally have less-discernible lines that meander and are not instantly readable to the viewer. Lines that contrast greatly between one pose and the next (contrasting actions) promote a more readable motion for the viewer than multiple similar or weak poses.

For the motions themselves, swiping actions always read better than stabbing motions, as they cover an arc that will be seen by the player regardless of camera angle. Even without the aid of a trail effect, a swipe passes through multiple axes (and therefore camera angles), so even if players are viewing from a less-than-ideal angle, they should still have an idea of what happened, especially if the character dramatically changes the line of action during poses throughout the action.

All this said, work to the game being made. If the camera is fixed to the side, such as in a one-on-one fighting game, then actions should be created to be most readable from that angle. Similarly, if you are creating a run animation for a game mostly viewed from the rear, then ensure the cycle looks best from that angle before polishing for others.

League of Legends pushes animation incredibly far due to the far overhead cameras and frenetic onscreen action. (Courtesy of Riot Games.)

Silhouettes

At the character design/concept stage, the animator should get involved in helping guide how a character might look, not just to avoid issues such as hard, armorlike clothing at key versatile joints such as shoulders or waists. The animator should also help guide the design so as to help provide the best silhouettes when posed. A character with an appealing silhouette makes the job of animating far easier when attempting to create appeal than one composed entirely of unimaginative blobs or shapeless tubes for limbs.

Team Fortress 2 uses distinct character silhouettes for gameplay, making the animator's job of bringing appeal much easier. (Used with permission from Valve Corp.)

It is advisable to request "proxy" versions of characters at early stages of development so they can be roughly animated and viewed in the context of the gameplay camera, which, due to wide fields of view (for spatial awareness gameplay purposes), often warps the extremities of character as they reach the screen's edge. Generally, the most appealing characters look chunkier and thicker than they might in real life, due to them being warped and stretched once viewed from the wide-angle game camera.

Collision & Center of Mass/Balance

As with all animation, consideration must be given to the center of mass (COM; or center of balance) of a character at any given frame, especially as multiple animations transition between one another so as to avoid unnatural movements when blending. The COM is generally found over the leg that is currently taking the full weight of the character's root when in motion or between both feet if they are planted on the ground when static. Understanding this basic concept of balance will not only greatly aid posing but also avoid many instances of motions looking wrong to players without them knowing the exact issue.

This is especially true when considering the character's collision (location) in the game world. This is the single point where a character will pivot when rotated (while moving) and, more importantly, where the character will be considered to exist in the game at any given time. The game animator will always animate the character's position in the world when animating away from the 3D scene origin, though not so if cycles are exported in place. Importantly, animations are always considered to be exported relative to this prescribed location, so characters should end in poses that match others (such as idles) relative to this position. This will be covered in full in the following chapter.

Context

Whereas in linear animation, the context of any given action is defined by the scene in which it plays and what has happened in the story up to that point and afterward, the same is impossible in game animation. Oftentimes, the animator has no idea which action the player performed beforehand or the setting in which the character is currently performing the action. More often than not, the animation is to be used repeatedly throughout the game in a variety of settings, and even on a variety of different characters.

Distinction vs Homogeneity

Due to the unknown setting of most game animations, the animator must look for opportunities to give character to the player and nonplayer characters whenever possible, and must also consider when he or she should avoid it.

If, for example, the animator knows that a particular run cycle is only to be performed on that character being animated, then he or she can imbue it with as much personality as matches the character description. It's even better if the animator can create a variety of run cycles for that character in different situations. Is the character strong and confident initially, but later suffers loss or failure and becomes despondent? Is the character chasing after someone or perhaps running away from a rolling boulder about to crush him or her? The level of distinction the animator should put into the animation depends on how much control he or she has over the context in which it will be seen.

The player character generally moves at a much higher fidelity and with more distinction than NPCs. (Copyright 2007–2017 Ubisoft Entertainment. All Rights Reserved. Assassin's Creed, Ubisoft, and the Ubisoft logo are trademarks of Ubisoft Entertainment in the US and/or other countries.)

If an animation is not designed for the player character but instead to be used on multiple nonplayer characters, then the level of distinction and notability should generally be dialed down so as to not stand out. Walks and runs must instead be created to look much more generic, unless the animation is shared by a group of NPCs only (all soldiers might run differently from all civilians). Almost always, the player character is unique among a game world's inhabitants, so this should be reflected in his or her animations.

Repetition

Similarly, within a cycling animation, if the action is expected to be repeated endlessly, such as an idle or run cycle, then care must be taken to avoid any individual step or arm swing standing out against the rest, lest it render the rhythm of repetition too apparent to the player—such as every fourth step having a noticeably larger bounce for example.

Stand-out personality can instead be added to on-off actions or within cycles via "cycle breakers" such as the character shifting his or her footing after standing still too long, performing a slight stumble to break up a tired run, or even by modifying the underlying animation with additive actions—covered in more detail in the following chapter.

Uncharted: Drake's Fortune utilized additive poses to avoid repetition when in cover.

Onscreen Placement

A key factor in setting the exaggeration of movement is the relative size on the screen of the character as defined by the camera distance and field of view. While cameras have gotten closer and closer as the fidelity of characters has risen, players still need to see a lot of the environment on screen for awareness purposes, so many games may show characters that are quite small. Far cameras require actions to be much larger than life so as to be read by the player.

The same is true of enemy actions that are far off in the distance, such as damage animations to tell the player he or she landed a shot. Conversely, only really close cameras such as those employed in cutscenes afford subtleties like facial expressions—here, overly theatrical gestures will generally look out of place. It is important as a game animator to be aware of the camera for any particular action you are animating and to animate accordingly within the style of the project. The wide field of view of the gameplay camera will even distort the character enough to affect the look of your animation, so, as ever, the best way to evaluate the final look of your animation is in the game.

Elegance

Game animations rarely just play alone, instead requiring underlying systems within which they are triggered, allowing them to flow in and out of one another at the player's input—often blending seamlessly, overlapping one another, and combining multiple actions at once to ensure the player is unaware of the individual animations affording their avatar motion.

If not designing them outright, it is the game animator's duty to work with others to bring these systems and characters to life, and the efficiency of any system can have a dramatic impact on the production and the team's ability to make changes further down the line toward the end of a project. Just as a well-animated character displays efficiency of movement, a good, clean, and efficient system to play them can work wonders for the end result.

Simplicity of Design

Industrial designer Dieter Rams, as the last of his 10 principles of good design, stated that good design involves "as little design as possible," concentrating only on the essential aspects. A good game animation system should similarly involve no more design than required, as bloated systems can quickly become unworkable as the project scales to the oft-required hundreds or thousands of animations.

Every unique aspect of character-based gameplay will require a system to play back animations, from the navigation around the world to combat to jumping and climbing to conversation and dialogue and many more. Here, the game animator must aid in creating systems to play back all the varied animation required to bring each element of character control to life, and often the desire to create many animations will come into conflict with the realities of production such as project length and budget.

DOOM opted for full-body damage animations over body parts alone for visual control. (DOOM® Copyright 2016 id Software LLC, a ZeniMax Media company. All Rights Reserved.)

Thankfully, there are many tricks that a team can employ to maximize their animation potential, such as reuse and sharing, layering and combining animations to create multiple combinations, or ingenious blending solutions to increase the fluidity without having to account for absolutely every possible transition outcome. While the simplest solution is to do nothing more than play animations in sequence, this will rarely produce the best and most fluid visuals, so the smartest approach is to manipulate animations at runtime in the game engine to get the most out of the animations the team has the time to create. Again, we'll cover some of the potential systemic solutions in the following chapter.

Bang for the Buck

Just as we look to share animations, being smart about choices at the design stage should create a workable method of combining animations throughout production. This will in turn prevent unique solutions being required for every new system. For example, a well-thought-out system for opening doors in a game could be expanded to interacting with and opening crates if made efficiently. When building any one system, anticipating uses beyond the current requirements should always be considered.

A good approach to system design will produce the maximum quality of motion for the minimum amount of overhead (work). It must be stressed that every new animation required not only involves the initial creation but later modification over multiple iterations, as well as debugging toward the end of the project. Every stage of development is multiplied by every asset created, so avoiding adding 20 new animations for each object type is not only cost effective but allows more objects to be added to the game. (All that said, sometimes the solution to a system is just to brute-force create lots of animations if your budget allows it.)

Sharing & Standardization

As mentioned earlier, it is important to know when to keep animations generic and when to make unique ones for each example. If the game requires the player character interact with many objects in a game, then it would be wise to standardize the objects' sizes so one animation accommodates all objects of a particular size.

The same goes for world dimensions, where if a character can vault over objects throughout the game, then it makes sense to standardize the height of vaultable objects in the environment so the same animation will work anywhere—not least so the player can better read the level layout and know where the character can and cannot vault.

Gears of War featured high and low cover heights supported by different sets of animations. (Copyright Microsoft. All rights reserved. Used with permission from Microsoft Corporation.)

That said, if your gameplay is primarily about picking up objects or vaulting over things, then it may be worth creating more unique animations to really highlight that area and spend less effort elsewhere. This, again, feeds back into the idea of bang for the buck and knowing what is important to your particular game.

All these decisions must come into play when designing systems for your game, as very few teams can afford unique and bespoke animations for each and every situation. Nevertheless, beautiful game animation can come from even single-person teams that focus on one thing and do it very very well. This is the crux of what good design is, and every aspect of game development benefits from clever and elegant design, regardless of game type.

CHAPTER 5

What You Need to Know

Basic Game Animation Concepts

Every game animator should know about the basics of creating and getting a character into the game, opening up the first stages of video game animation creation, and enabling the sheer joy of controlling a character you helped bring to life.

Common Types of Game Animation

To understand how game animations generally fit together, it is essential to understand how each is played on a character and for what purpose. There are essentially three primary types of animation required to make a character move fluidly, determined as much by how they start and end as by the action within.

Cycles

Perhaps the most commonly used, cycles are named such because the start and end poses and velocities must match to create a seamlessly looping motion that can be played indefinitely until another animation interrupts. The most common examples are idles (where a character stands relatively still doing nothing) or walks/runs (where the player gives a movement input on the controller, causing the character to move through the game world at speed).

A good video game cycle smoothly loops back to its original starting movement such that the viewer is unaware of the exact start and end of the loop. More than simply matching the pose at both ends, it requires the movement to flow in such a manner as to prevent any noticeable hitch in momentum on any body part. To achieve this, animation curves must contain no harsh steps, and curve tangents must match at the start and end.

Similarly, it is imperative actions do not all arrive at a noticeable end pose on the same frame, however smoothly, as this too will detract from the seamlessness of a loop. It is essential to build in overlap in as many body parts or elements like clothing as possible to mask the exported end frame.

Last of all, care must be taken to avoid any one part of a cycle that stands out too much over the rest, causing the player to recognize the repetition in a cycle such as a single gesture being much larger than the rest. Ultimately, this falls under considerations around homogenization over distinction, the style of your project, and the particular character you're animating.

Linear Actions

A linear action is a one-off animation that has a distinct start and end, and usually goes to and from the "idle pose" with less requirement to smoothly play on repeat due to its one-off nature. Animations on joypad inputs such as jumps, punches, or sword-swings are the most commonly required and basic examples, essentially interrupting the character from the current state for the duration of the animation, returning him or her to the prior state once completed.

A sword-swipe attack animation has a definitive start and end.

Emphasis should be placed on a clean transition to and from the cycle pose this animation is interrupting, often with a fast transition due to the desired responsiveness by the player via an instant state-change related to input. Importantly, the player has often committed to this move with no ability to interrupt or change decision midway, so that must be considered when marking out the timing of any kind of linear move.

Transitions

These types of animations are often superfluous but add to the fluidity of character movement by allowing artistic authorship of how the character moves from one action to another. Transitions are typically short and serve mostly to display proper weight-shifting between moves and keep feet planted when doing so.

For example, the most basic games, on detecting a movement input from the player, will simply interrupt the idle cycle with the walk/run cycle by quickly blending across from one animation to another, whereas a better look can be achieved by creating a transition animation from the idle pose to the first frame of the walk/run cycle due to the animator's desire to control how the character leans into the initial acceleration.

Even higher fidelity can be achieved by creating a variety of directional transitions that cater to each direction the character can start moving relative to the current facing direction, with the animator able to control every facet of the turning and momentum shift during the transition. As you can start to see, the number of transitions required to give fluidity to a character can quickly explode, so only the biggest-budget games dedicate lots of resources to this area.

Skeletons, Rigs, & Exporting to Game

Much like the traditional medium of stop-motion animation involving models with rigid skeletons inside them allowing for articulation, 3D character animation (and now a lot of 2D packages, too) primarily involves binding elements of a character to an underlying skeleton placed inside to allow articulation. In its most basic form, the rotational and positional values of these bones are exported, per frame, into the game engine and played back to allow the animation to be replayed on your character in game.

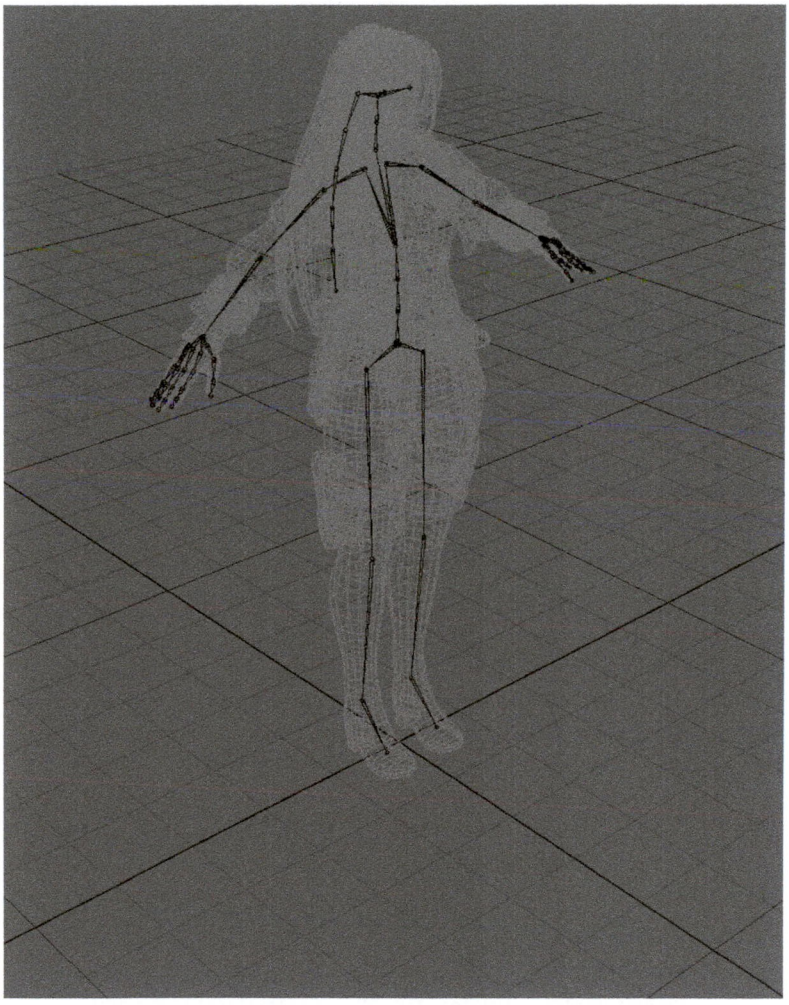

Often, only the export skeleton is read by the game engine.

As such, 3D character animation is at its core a set of rotation and translation values on joints that in turn move polygons, (or more precisely, their vertices) around in 3D space to give the illusion of a living character. After animating long enough, you may one day have the revelation that all motion in the world around you can be described in these numbers—which opens up tremendous opportunities. Once this curtain is peeled back and you view game characters this way, there is much that can be done with these numbers beyond simple manipulation in a 3D package.

- Cross-fading the numbers when moving from one animation to the next will produce blending, creating smoother transitions between bespoke actions.
- Adding the numbers together will produce additive animation, allowing you to play the same breathing animation on top of multiple other animations. This should already be familiar to anyone animating via DCC layers, as the concept is identical.
- Subtract these numbers and you'll be able to remove poses from an animation, required for additive animations where you wish to combine multiple complex animations.
- Export and/or play back only values for certain body parts and you'll get partial animations such as upper body or arms only. This allows your characters to carry, shoot, and reload a pistol while using the same running animation as if they are empty handed.
- Gradually vary the percentages of animations playing down a joint chain to produce feather blends, allowing an animation to be more visible farther down arms or up a spine for example.

While all of these calculations will be handled by the game engine, understanding what is being done with the values on and between your animations is key to unlocking the true potential of real-time video game animation. This allows resourceful game animators to find ways to produce more animations at a high quality by combining and reusing animations in smart ways.

Regardless of the keys used in your animation scene file, the animation is exported to the game every frame at your project's framerate—most commonly 30 frames per second. The game then linearly interpolates between these key values at runtime. While playing an animation back at full framerate offers best results, animations are often compressed to save memory (albeit less radically nowadays as memory budgets grow) by saving only every second frame or less depending on the compression algorithm's rules. Compressing too much can cause the animation in game to be visibly less fluid than the animation you created in the DCC, so caution should be taken to not overcompress.

An important aspect to understand when exporting skeleton values to the game is that animators typically don't directly manipulate the skeletons but instead a rig on top of the skeleton. This allows animators to take advantage of all the tricks and tools a DCC like Maya can offer to get the result they want, such as simple switches between local and global rotation, and work with complex tools like Inverse Kinematics (IK).

Despite 3D animation generally being created by animators manipulating rotations via X-, Y-, and Z-axes called Euler values (pronounced "Oiler" after their mathematician creator), animations are actually read by the game engine as "quaternions." The math involved requires four values, with every rotational value described instead by yaw, pitch, and roll relative to a plane, but this is too complex for an animator to work with, so keys are instead described via the human-readable Eulers.

The dreaded downside of this translation is "Gimbal lock." This occurs when an animated object such as a skeleton bone is rotated on one axis such that the remaining two axes match up and make them unworkable, highlighting a limitations of Eulers.

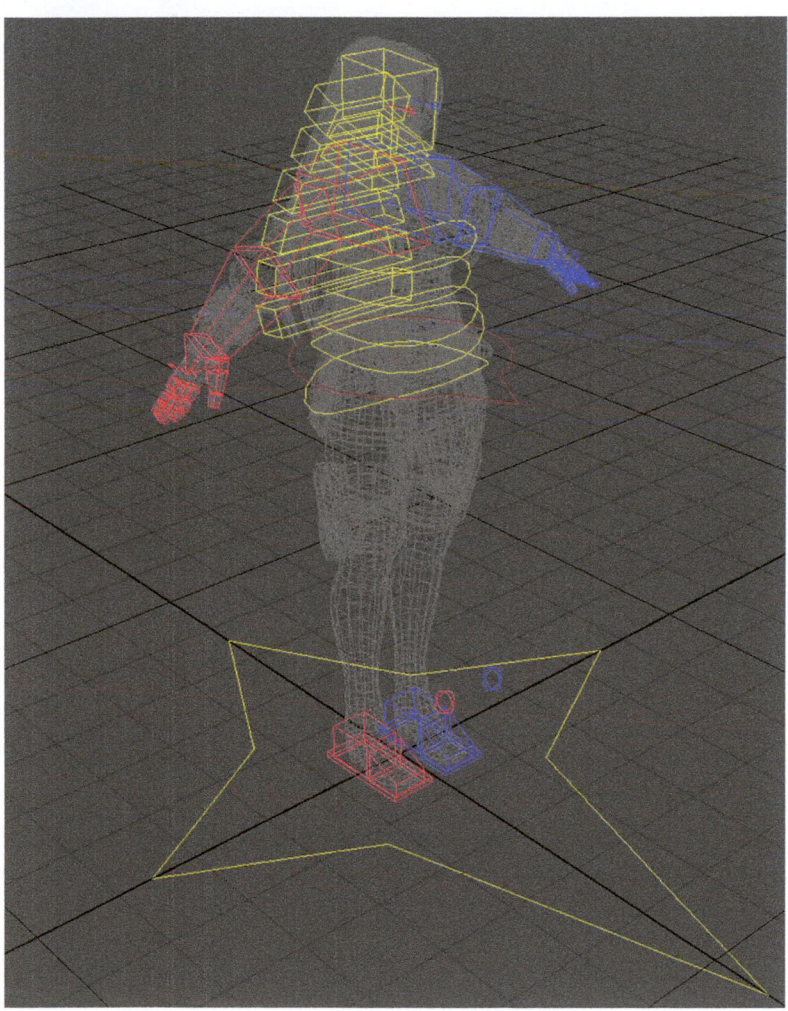

The animation rig sits on top of the skeleton.

These aspects are covered in detail in Chapter 8, "Our Project: Technical Animation," but it is handy to know the limits of your particular game engine and how the skeleton animation values are read into your game. Armed with this knowledge, you can greatly modify any animation scene or character you're working on to get the best results depending on the complexity.

How Spline Curves Work

Back in the days of traditional 2D animation, an animator would draw the important key poses in the same manner as we might nowadays block in key poses to initially sell the action's movement. Once happy with the overall action, either the animator or (depending on the team size) one of many "in-betweeners" (an intermediary role under the animator) would draw the frames in between, allowing the more senior animator to more quickly move on to the next shot.

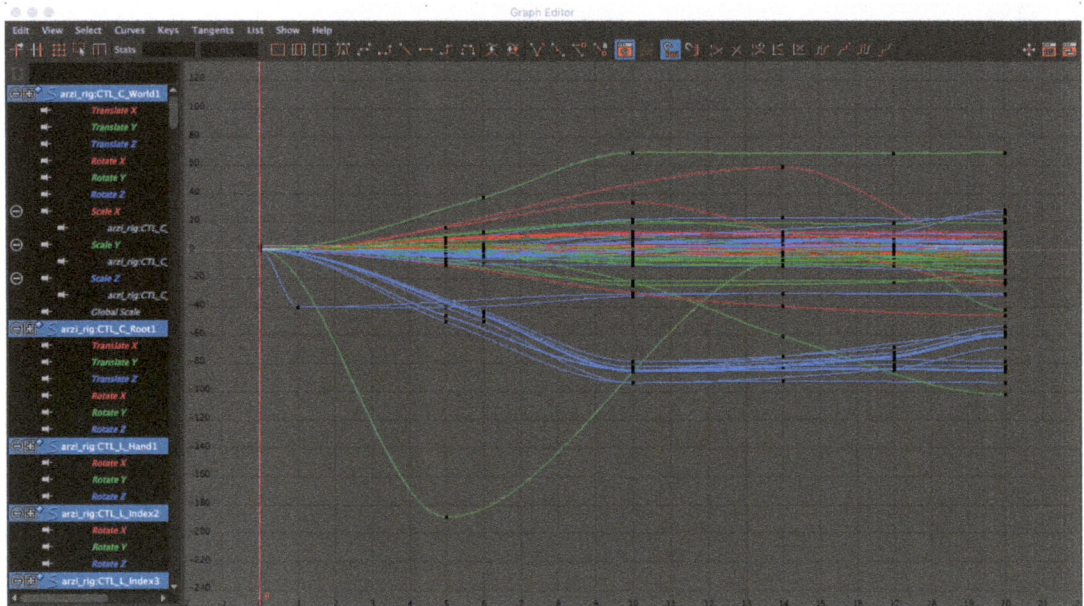

The curve editor is how the animator modifies motion between keyframes.

With the advent of 3D animation, the computer now calculates all frames between key poses, with the animator able to modify how the 3D character moves between them by way of inserting more keys and, crucially, modifying the curves to promote the classic principles of slow-in slow-out (often called ease-in/out when referring to curve shapes).

As with everything in motion, speed is denoted by distance over time. Regardless of the 3D software used, curves will be plotted on a graph with one axis in distance (often centimeters or meters) and the other in time (frames). An object keyed at 0 m on frame 0, then at 1 m at frame 30 (assuming a 30 frames per second animation) will have traveled 1 m in those 30 frames. In this example, the curves are linear (straight), so we can say the object traveled at a speed of 1 m per second throughout.

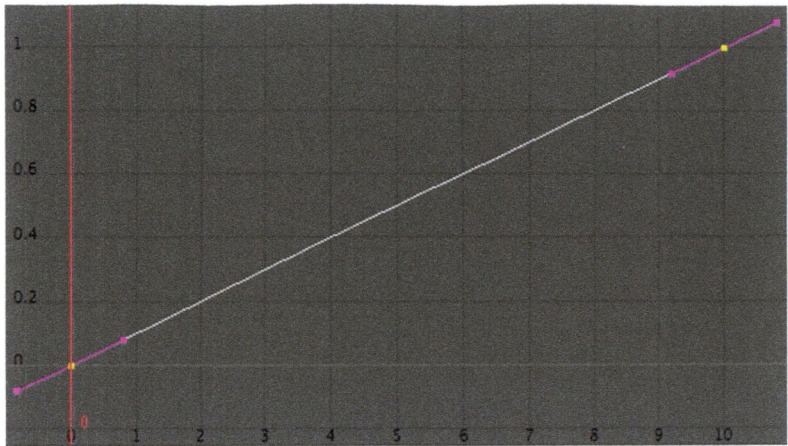

A linear tangent.

However, animators more often than not do not animate linearly, so a more likely scenario would be that the object traveled at an overall speed of 1 m per second, but was slower at the start and end and faster in the middle. This is because the spline handles around the keys are flat rather than linear, causing the curve to display a slow-in and slow-out. The steeper the curve, the faster the object travels, and vice versa.

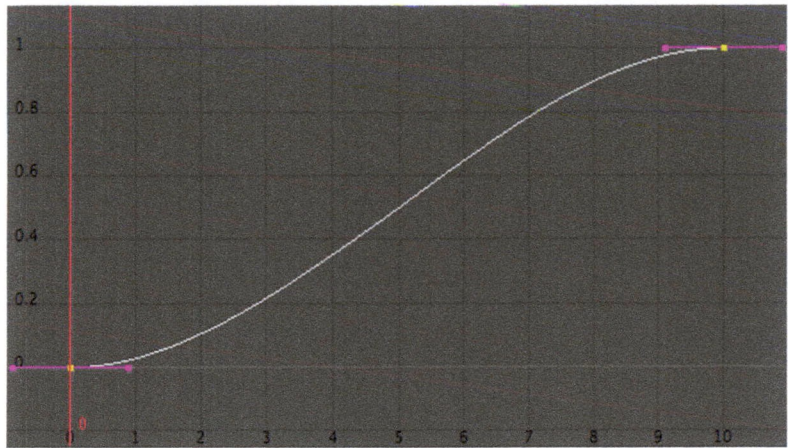

An ease-in/out tangent.

Not to be confused with the curve editor's axes, this curve refers to the distance in one of the three axes (X, Y, and Z) in 3D space. Any object that moves in all three axes will have three such curves described by different colors. (In Maya, X is red, Y is green, and Z is blue.) Manipulation of these three curves will describe the object's motion in a manner that allows the object to be given more personality than simply moving linearly, with a variety of possibilities.

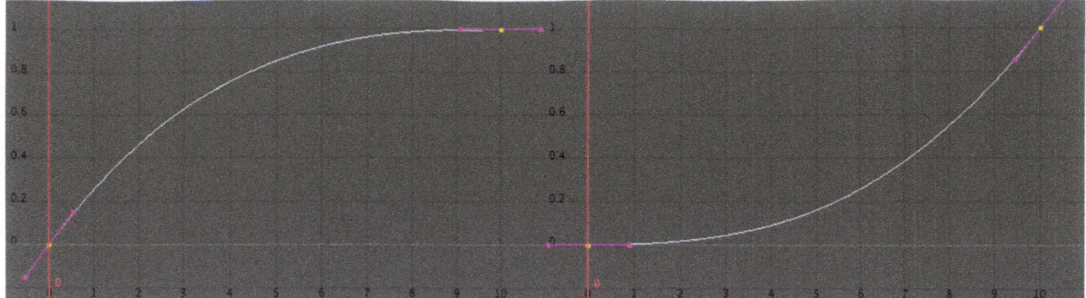

Curve variations. Fast-in/slow-out and vice-versa.

Importantly, curves can be better bent to an animator's whims by inserting additional keys in between key poses. Traditionally, this was done by inserting whole new poses (called breakdowns) in between key poses to aid the in-betweener in making decisions about the fast/slow-in/outs, and the same can be done in 3D animation by inserting whole breakdown poses. Another advantage 3D animation has, though, is the ability to add keys only on certain parts of a character, so, for example, an animator can delay only an arm as the rest of the body winds up to throw a punch.

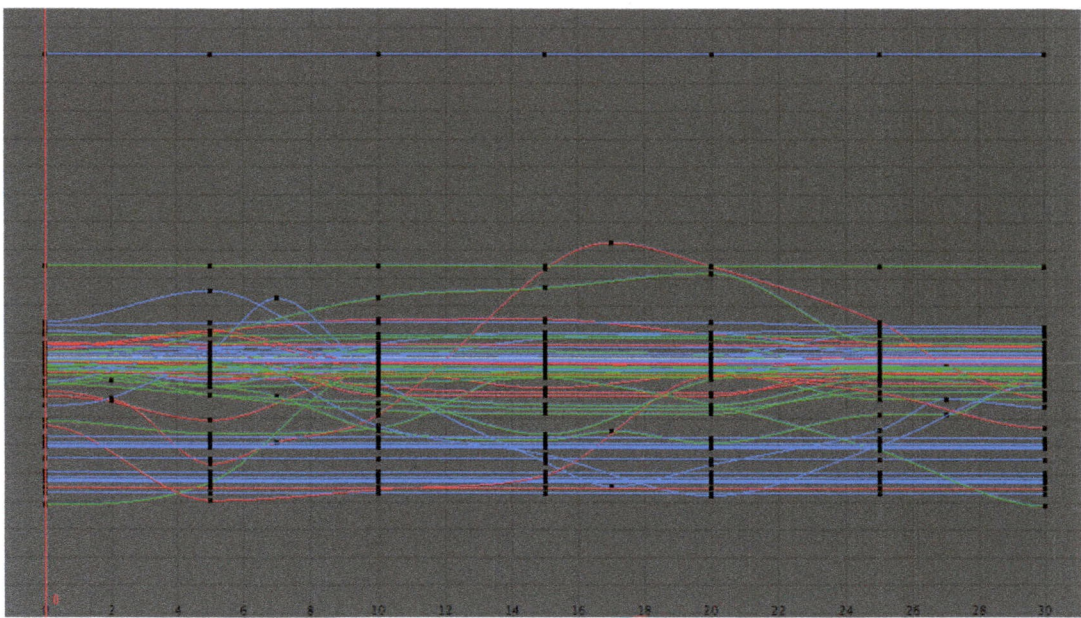

Whole body keys with limb breakdowns in-between.

This has the benefit of making a curve editor less dense and more easily readable by the animator as well as allowing easy manipulation and retiming of individual components of a character. Generally, it is good practice, however, to key on a full character throughout the early blocking phase of an animation so as to easily retime an entire body pose/action, only going in to key more detail such as individual limbs, head, and so on once happy with the overall timing. Doing so allows the animator to easily apply offsets and overlapping actions, but it can make retiming messy, as many of the keys in the curve editor will now be offset and less easily read.

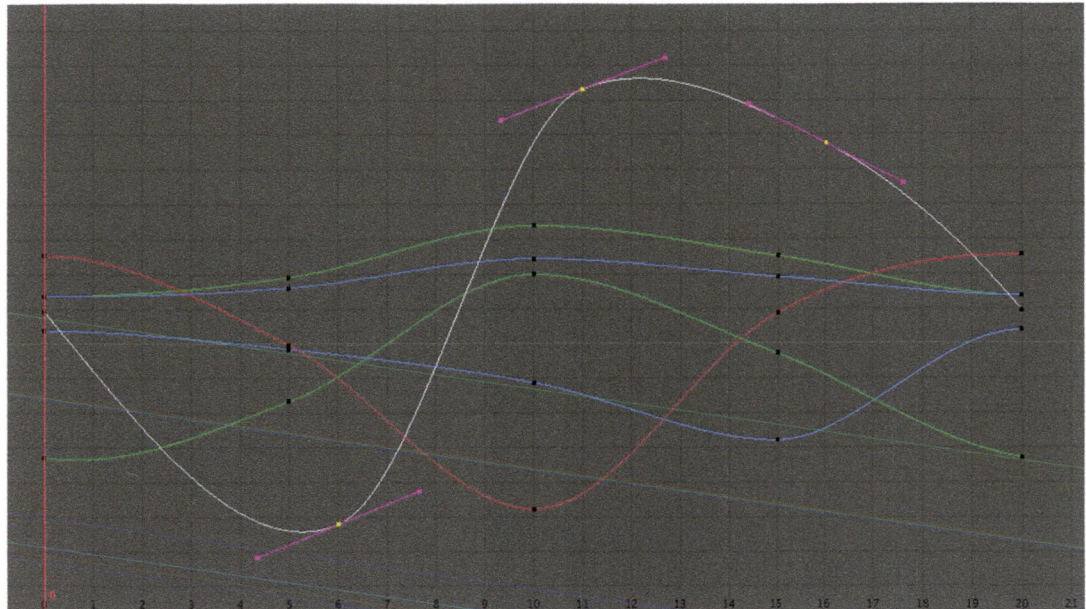

Individual body-part curves offset from the rest of the body.

It is important to bear in mind that animation should not be done primarily by looking at the curves, and instead in the 3D view. Some animators focus on creating clean curves when rarely do these have as much personality as curves full of steep spikes and a mess of offset keys. As such, it is best to refer to the curve editor mostly when looking to debug or better understand why the inbetweens may be misbehaving.

A speedy way of retiming an animation can be done via the timeline editor, which allows fast manipulation of the timing (not values) of keys only, without the need to work in the curve editor. In Maya, shift-middle-clicking allows you to select and then move a single or group of keys. In addition, hotkeys can be set up to allow for quick copy, cut, and paste functionality. Hotkeys are essential for fast workflows and can be tailored to an animator's whims – set these up by following the DCC's "help" functionality.

Maya timeline with keys easily retimed.

Collision Movement

For the game to know where the character is expected to be in any given frame, the animator typically animates the character's collision. This is an exported bone, either at the top of the skeleton's hierarchy or altogether separate, that tells the game where the player is.

This serves the purpose of updating the character's collision (typically a cylindrical or pill-shaped volume), enveloping the character to facilitate the calculation of impacts from weapon and bullet hits, but most importantly preventing the character from running through walls or falling through the ground. While collision shapes can become more complex depending on the nature of the game (shooting games, e.g., require more precision for bullet hits and attacks to make it fair and readable, better hugging the animating limbs of the character, for example), a cylinder provides the best feel when traversing the environment, with its circular shape lessening the likelihood of getting stuck on edges in the environment.

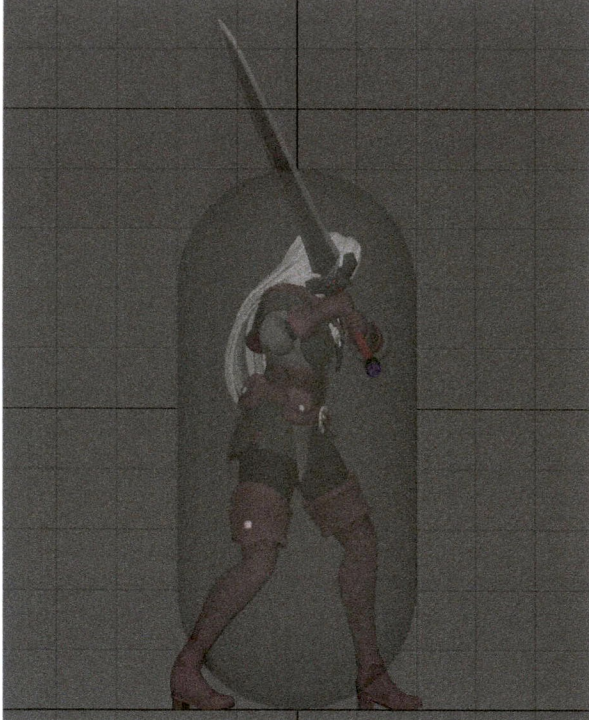

The invisible collision cylinder moves with the character.

Depending on the particular engine, the requirements for the exported animations may involve animating the collision forward with a character to provide forward movement in the game. This means the player's forward trajectory (or any other direction depending on the animation) is read from the animation itself. Other engines instead export animations on the spot and are given their forward movement through the world from code alone. This approach makes it difficult for an animator to match exactly the position in the world and causes foot-sliding (skating), but may be of higher importance for your particular project. Ultimately a hybrid provides best results, using animated collision only when required for precise movement, most commonly when requiring precise contact with the game world.

Foot-sliding issues commonly occur when the movement of a character through the game world does not match the speed of the animation. This is more often than not the result of the design requirements for a character's movement being sped up without the animation being updated, or just to such an unrealistic speed that the animation can never match without completely being redone. Take heart, though, as while this is painfully obvious when viewing enemy characters from a static position, it is possible to greatly cheat the sliding of player characters that move through the world as long as the camera is moving too, because the player cannot determine the mismatch as the ground zooms past. To best avoid this issue, however, always try to prototype gameplay as much as possible before committing to final animations, and know that designers rarely slow characters down, instead often speeding them up for gameplay purposes.

While some games simply always set the collision at the base of the character by default, it is important for animators to have control on actions related to complex navigation such as climbing, vaulting, or using cover due to the nature of the character interacting with the environment. It is never advisable to turn off collision to solve an issue (it might turn back on again with the character inside an object), so the position of the collision always must be carefully managed when touching walls or cover objects, for example.

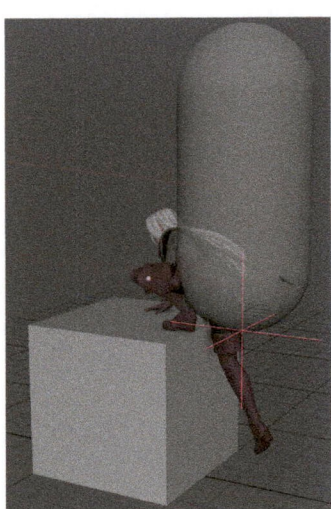

Collision can be animated independently of the character.

Careful management of collision is also essential when transitioning between one animation and the next. It means nothing if your idle poses match when the collision is in a different position/orientation between animations, as this will cause the character to slide or rotate as the character blends from one animation to the next. This is because the pose is always read by the game as relative to the collision, so care must be taken to ensure an animation that ends rotated 180° must also have the collision rotated 180° underneath.

Ultimately, incorrect animation of collision is the cause of a lot of animation pops, bugs, and imperfections, so a good understanding of how it behaves for your particular project and game engine is essential. At the very least, your animation team should have the ability to copy and paste poses relative to a character's new position in the world. The most common tools required for a good game animation pipeline are detailed in Chapter 8, "Our Project: Technical Animation."

For third-person player animations, the camera will typically follow an offset from the collision to maintain the character onscreen, with the offset required to pivot around the body of the character. As such, it is important for the collision to generally have a smooth trajectory to avoid jerky camera movements, compared to the center of the character's body that will have more accentuated movement. Were a camera to be directly attached to a character's body, the body part to which it is attached will always appear to remain static on screen as it moves in lockstep with the camera.

As an example, for a run cycle, the collision must move in a linear forward motion under the feet rather than matching the position of the center of mass or root of the character every frame. To achieve this, ensure that the collision is placed relative to the character at only the start and end of a cycle, with linear movement in between. If the run cycle involves multiple pairs of steps, then match the collision under the character at the end of each pair rather than just at the extremes to avoid the character moving too far outside the collision when running if the run speed is not exactly constant.

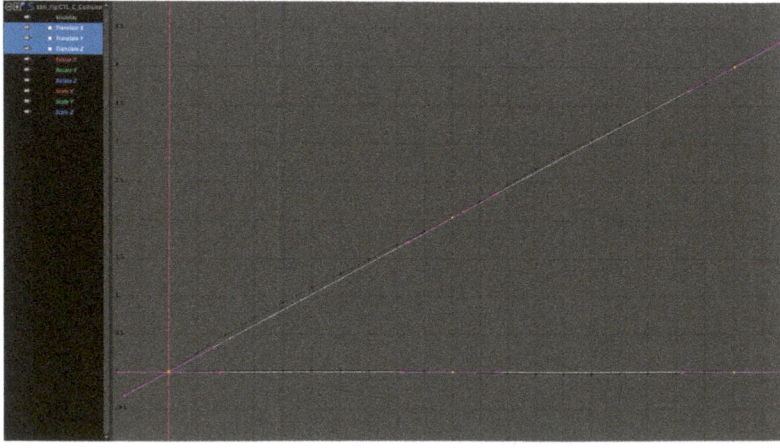

The collision position keyed per step pair.

Forward vs Inverse Kinematics

Three-dimensional animation, or specifically posing that when sequenced creates animation, is primarily done by moving and rotating bones for a desired result. Posing bones higher in a joint chain typically affects those lower down, such that the rotation of a shoulder will naturally affect the position of the elbow and wrist. This process describes forward kinematics and is desirable when animating an arm swinging while walking or legs when swimming or jumping—not when touching the ground.

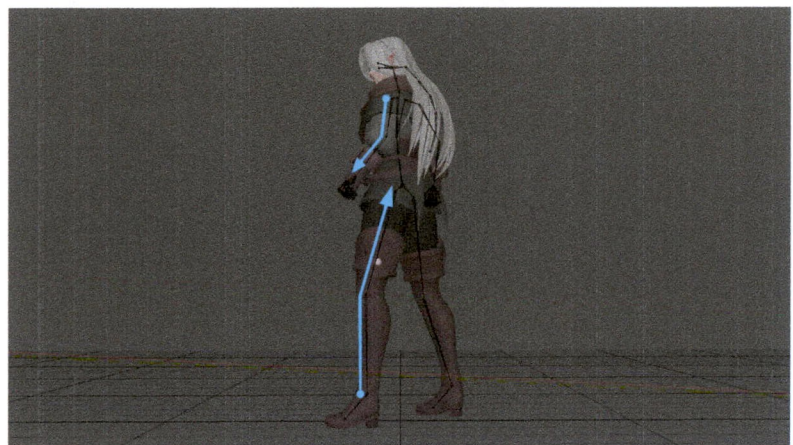

Forward vs inverse kinematics.

For the most part, feet are planted firmly on the ground and we expect them to stay in place unless the animator moves them, so we require a different approach. This is where IK comes into play. When we have a desired end position/rotation for a bone like the heel, calculations are performed to rotate the hips and knees to maintain this result. The additional calculations required as compared to FK for this type of animation make this effect more expensive in game, so while it rarely has an impact on the pre-exported animation in the DCC, it can prove expensive if desired inside the game engine, especially on multiple characters. (Animations are almost always exported as fully FK, regardless of whether IK is used in the DCC.)

As such, real-time IK is generally best only used when absolutely required or on important characters like the player only. It is primarily used in two instances:

1. As a real-time modifier to conform feet to uneven terrain in the game, adding to the realism of a character planted in the world, as the feet are matched to the ground despite animations being authored on a flat plane.
2. To maintain visual fidelity when blending between animations that would cause undesirable results with FK, such as when a driver's hands need to remain in place on a steering wheel or similar attachment.

Intermediate Game Animation Concepts

Once you understand the basics of how video game animation is created and played back in the engine, understanding these intermediary areas will expand your utility as a game animator by knowing about established tools and workflow opportunities out there to increase quality and output.

State Machines

Also referred to as finite-state machines or state graphs, and similar to blend trees, state machines are a visual editor that describes and controls the various states (actions) animated characters can be in and how they transition between states, as well as the various blending that can occur within a single state, such as when aiming a weapon. Inputs such as joystick angle and button presses can be directly mapped to trigger or blend between animations, allowing animators to do much more than simply animate but also implement and adjust blending once they've exported their work to the game engine. A good game animator can make beautiful flowing animations, but a great game animator can find clever and novel ways for them to flow together inside the game engine when controlled by the player.

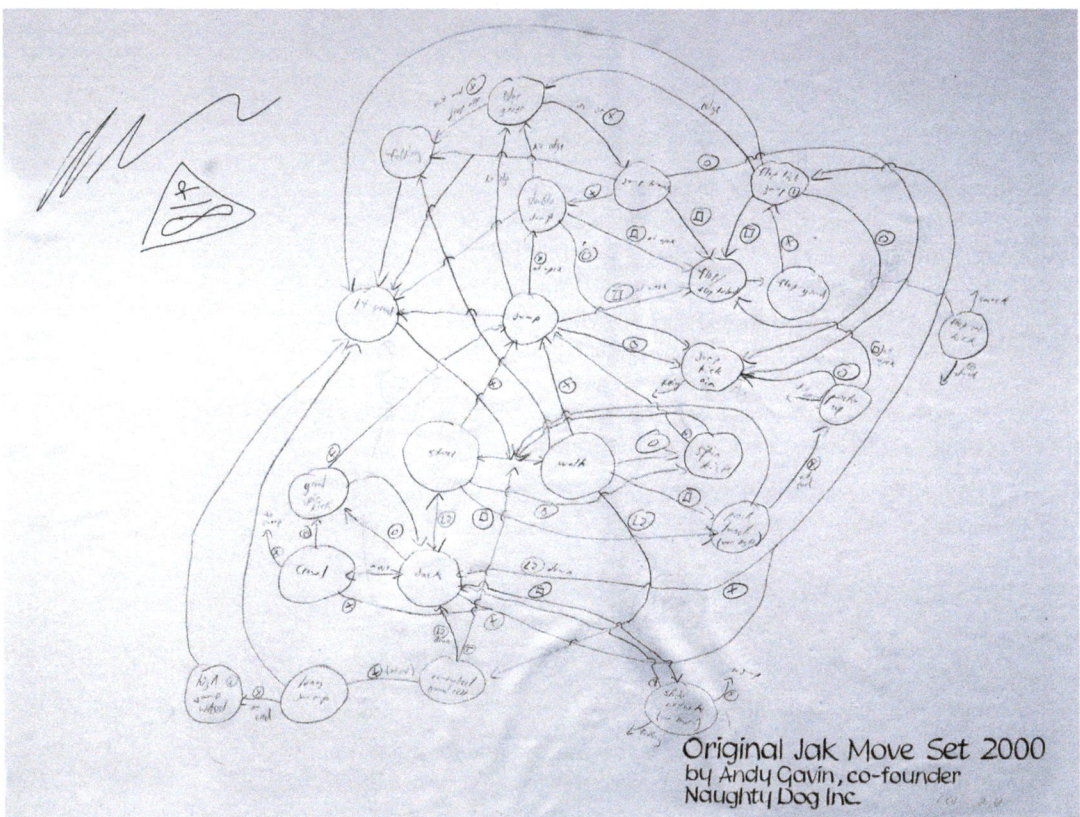

Original Jak & Daxter animation state graph on paper. (Courtesy of Sony Interactive Entertainment.)

Traditionally, when first designing or evaluating the requirements for a given character, the game animator would draw out on paper the various states the proposed character could be in (such as idle, walk, run, etc.) as nodes in a flowchart with lines connecting the states that could be moved between. This helped not only list all the animations that would be needed to get the full functionality of the character up and running, but also highlighted where transition animations might have been required to smooth over commonly used transitions between states. The animator or designer would then work with the programmer to implement the character, using the state chart as reference.

As game character animation grew more complex, these state charts became incredibly complex spider webs containing hundreds of animations with difficult maintenance. Computer software to draw them is still employed, and from that came the most natural interface when a visual editor was desired to not only illustrate but also control the various states. Nowadays, finite-state machines are included with many game engines, so they should be learned and employed by game animators to allow them to get characters up and running with little to no programmer support.

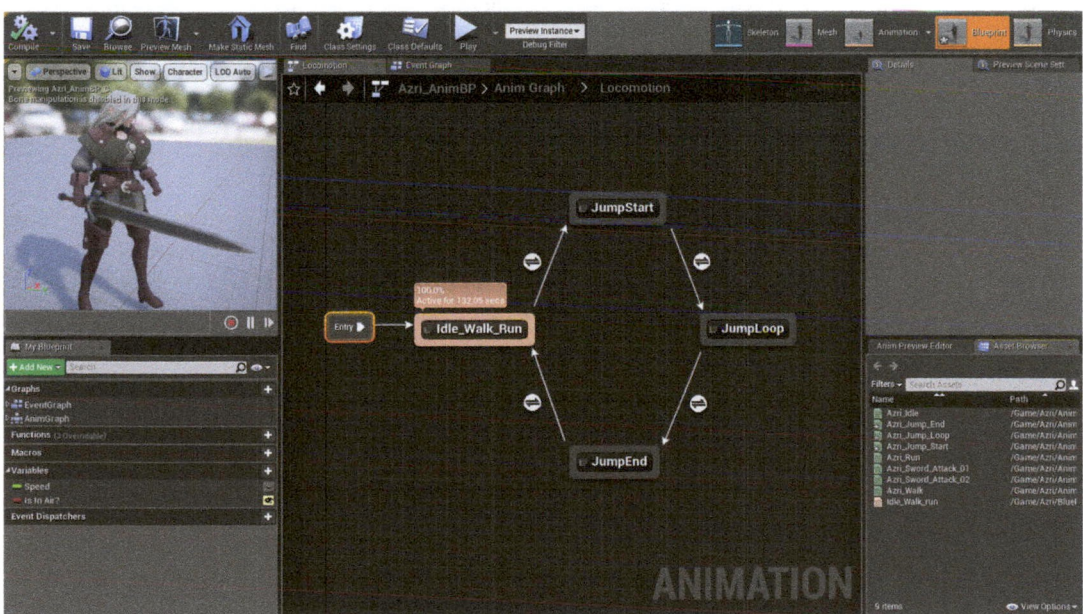

State machine in a game engine editor.

Parametric Blending

While the most basic implementation of animation on a character is to play one animation at a time and blend across to a new animation when required, many games these days play several animations at once. Blending between multiple animations is required to give the character a constant illusion of life and pull away from singularly authored actions, instead running complex systems of animations on top of each other for fluidity.

The primary reason for blending between multiple animations is to perform varying actions depending on parameters in the game. For example, an incline/ decline angle detected on the ground beneath the character's feet can be utilized to blend between flat, ascending, and descending walk/run cycles, making the character appear to use more or less effort on slopes. This helps give the impression the character is "aware" of the surrounding environments and reacts accordingly—further grounding the character inside the virtual world.

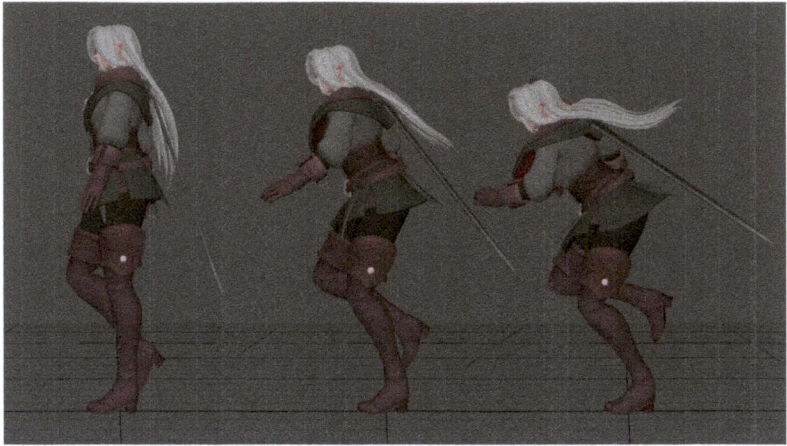

Parametric blending between synced walk and run animations depending on player speed.

Other common parameters that can be set up to influence blend values between multiple animations are things like speed, rotation angle or jump height, and so on. The faster a run, the tighter a turn, or the higher and longer a jump, the more the character will play a percentage (weight) of a number of animations created for each individual action.

Partial Animations

In order to enable multiple actions playing on a character at once, one method is to break the character into multiple body part groups such as left/ right arm, upper/lower body, head and neck, and so on and fully play unique animations on each. This is most commonly used to allow a character to move through the world via walk/run animations on the lower body while simultaneously playing combat animations like sword-swinging or shooting on the upper body, but another common use for this technique is to cleverly maximize animation reuse. In this instance, one set of walk and run strafing animations can be used for a variety of different gun weapons if playing unique upper-body weapon animations on top for each weapon type.

The biggest drawback of this approach is the visual nastiness with a noticeable disconnect between the upper and lower body, but this harsh effect can be lessened somewhat by applying a "feather blend" up the chain of bones (e.g., the arm or spine) between the two disconnected animations.

This means an upper-body animation of holding a gun may receive more weight the further up the spine, with the lower spine joints playing a larger amount of the movement driven by the walk or run.

Additive Layers

A step up from blending between both full-body and partial body-part animations is the process of blending multiple animations on top of one another in any number of layers. Much like the ability to have layers in the DCC, this approach requires different actions to be authored individually, then recombined at runtime on the in-game character. Often, this approach requires some amount of guesswork, as the animator can only see the final result in game, but as every animation should ultimately be evaluated and approved in the game, this fits into the workflow.

Importantly, for additive animations to work correctly, the second "additive" animation almost always requires a pose to be subtracted from it before it can be overlaid. This is because we only want the *difference* between the additive animation and a selected (usually idle) pose to be applied to the underlying animation (two full animations overlaid would cause the character to explode, as it doubles all the position and rotation values).

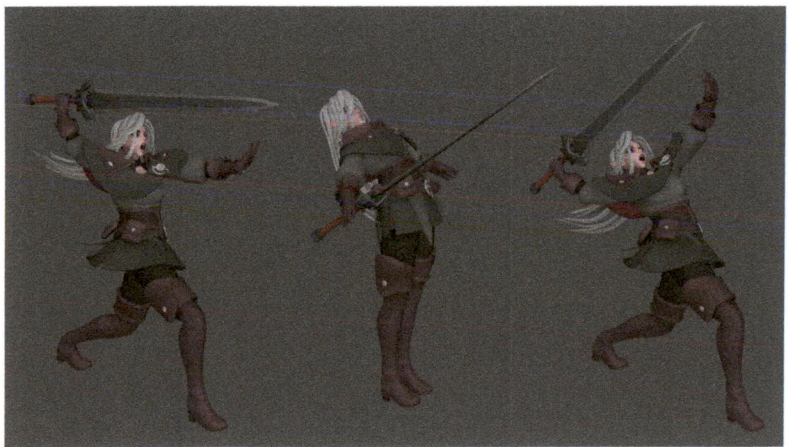

Original animation + Offset Pose = Modified Animation.

The way additive animations work is to combine/add the position and rotation values of two animations together to create the desired result, therefore allowing the underlying action to remain visible underneath the added animation. This creates a much more fluid result than partial animations that essentially overwrite one another, but comes with some degree of risk. If an underlying walk animation, for example, causes the forearm to swing a lot and we attempt to add an attack animation on top that also contains the forearm bending at some point, then it is possible the two combined animations will cause the forearm to bend past the limits of what are physically possible and break the arm.

Physics, Dynamics, & Ragdoll

One benefit of animating characters in real time is that we can use the game engine's processing power to improve animations further via physics motion, with next to no additional work required on the animator's part. Setting up elements on characters such as clothing or long flowing hair to move via physics at runtime can do wonders for animations—especially with regards to making them flow fluidly into one another as the physics motion straddles all blends and transitions, no matter how harsh. The more physics motion the better, with body parts that affect the character's silhouette, like a long cloak, working the best to mask the jumps between animations from the player's eye.

Some of the first implementations of full physics on game characters focused primarily on "ragdoll," used for death reactions by switching characters from animated to fully physicalized motion to enable characters to flop down dead wherever they expired. In recent years, however, physics has become a much more integral part of motion. Like additive layers, games now combine physics on top of animated motion to show characters flinching from attacks or being buffeted around in moving vehicles, and deaths are now a combination of premade animations with physics layered on top to react to the environment—allowing a performance to play out in the character's death throes.

Red Dead Redemption put emphasis on physics-driven deaths. (Courtesy of Rockstar Games.)

Physical simulations are also used to generate destruction of objects and the environment that would otherwise be difficult and time consuming to animate by hand in a convincing manner. They can be done at runtime (in the case of objects affected randomly by the player's actions) or as prebaked animations that exist like any other animation, with the simulation being run in the DCC and exported as a regular animation. Destruction is a great way to make the game world feel much more reactive to the player and can add lots of drama and movement to an action scene.

Physical simulations are often applied not to the full character but to certain movable clothing elements like cloaks and jackets, as well as softer areas of fat and muscle. This causes additional follow-through and overlapping motion to be created on the fly whenever a character transitions between animations or comes to rest, blurring the start and end of each animation. After initial setup on the rig and maintenance to ensure things do not break, this affords a higher visual quality with next to no additional work. The two approaches to this involve installing and calculating dynamic elements either in the DCC or at runtime in the game—each with its own pros and cons:

1. At runtime, physics are calculated by the game, creating a calculation load on the game that might otherwise be spent elsewhere. The benefit of this approach is that settings can easily be tweaked across the board instantly, and physics causes motion to naturally flow between any actions performed by the player.
2. In the DCC is where all simulations are run on export of the animation to game, meaning all overlapping movement is prebaked into the animation file, adding to the memory footprint of each animation. Any tweaks to settings must be done in the DCC and all animations re-exported, taking time. Without the benefit of runtime application of overlapping movement to aid with fluidity between actions, the main reason for this approach is to save on runtime calculations—especially important if applying to many characters such as a crowd or aiming for less-powerful systems like mobile.

Batman's cloak physics greatly aids transitions in the Arkham series. Batman Arkham Knight image used. (Courtesy of Warner Bros. Entertainment Inc. and DC Comics.)

Advanced Game Animation Concepts

Advanced concepts are mostly technology-based opportunities usually reserved for animation teams with larger budgets to support the technology and tools required, but still useful to understand regardless because game development is often about finding workarounds and cheaper alternatives.

Procedural Motion & Systems

In video game parlance, "procedural" animation means anything made by computer algorithms instead of an animator. This covers motion generated by an algorithm by feeding it data, such as behavioral rules as to how a character might move that will allow the algorithm to make decisions on the fly to generate the required motion. This approach requires minimal animation, so it can be a great time-saver in terms of asset creation, though it greatly adds to the complexity of a character's setup and has yet to produce convincing results on realistic humanoids.

The Last Guardian employed a suite of procedural movement systems on Trico.
(The Last Guardian: Copyright 2016 Sony Interactive Entertainment Inc.)

Doing these calculations at runtime allows for characters to respond naturally to the player's actions and the environment that playing back preset animations alone can never achieve. Regardless of the level of procedural influence used on a character, an animator's eye is essential to guide the visual result toward something that is acceptable.

Procedural systems are also beneficial in game development when generating numbers of assets that might otherwise be beyond the scope of the project budget or team size. Using algorithms, essentially sets of rules, to generate content can open up opportunities to new game experiences that rely on quantity—but almost always at the cost of quality when compared to motion hand-authored by an animator. Examples are systems to sequence animations together for natural gestures when speaking, or procedural lip-sync based on the audio and text of dialogue.

Full-Body IK

While it can be used in the DCC when animating, the best use of full-body IK is to manipulate animations at runtime in order to modify precreated animations to match contact points in the game world. Commonly used for climbing systems, full-body IK will not only move the hands and feet to correctly attach to the desired surface, such as a wall or ladder, but will also manipulate the position of the body via the root so as to avoid hyperextension of arms or legs when attempting to reach these targets.

The UFC series utilizes IK to enable complex character connections. (Courtesy of Electronic Arts.)

This solution is also used to ensure characters of differing sizes from those the animator used to author the animations can interact with one another effectively, such as during grappling or throwing moves in a fight, or even to adjust attacks between the player and enemies while on variable terrain such as slopes or while standing on objects of varying heights.

Full-body IK can also be used to reach and interact with objects, such as accurately grabbing a door handle when the position of the player character is variable. Full-body IK is a postprocess that requires a set of tweakable variables on the character setup or for each action, making it time-consuming so is usually used sparingly.

Look-Ats

Look-ats are an invaluable tool in the game animator's book for adding the illusion of "awareness" to a character in the game world. Look-ats will utilize IK to rotate a bone or chain of bones, most commonly the spine, neck, and/ or head, to aim toward a target as if the character were looking at it. This rotation can completely override or be overlaid on top of animation on the underlying animation, with the latter preferable so as to not lose the animator's work underneath when activated. Most look-at systems in games also require the placement of targets in the world for the character to look at, as well as potentially requiring a priority so the character appears to switch between them in a logical fashion.

The equivalent of a look-at can be created inside the DCC by way of an aim constraint that contains certain parameters such as aim axis, up-vector, strength, and rotation limits, as well as blend times in and out—the same as will be required in a game system. For best results, when a look-at is activated, the eyes then head should lead and the body should follow down the chain, as is the case in real life when someone's attention is caught.

Blend Shapes

Primarily used for facial animation, while most facial animations are exported to the game as regular bone animation (or, more accurately, as pose values driving those bones), the best visual quality in video game facial animations is via blend shapes. This is the process of uniquely modeling the face mesh for each pose, sometimes in the hundreds, rather than simply repositioning the facial bones.

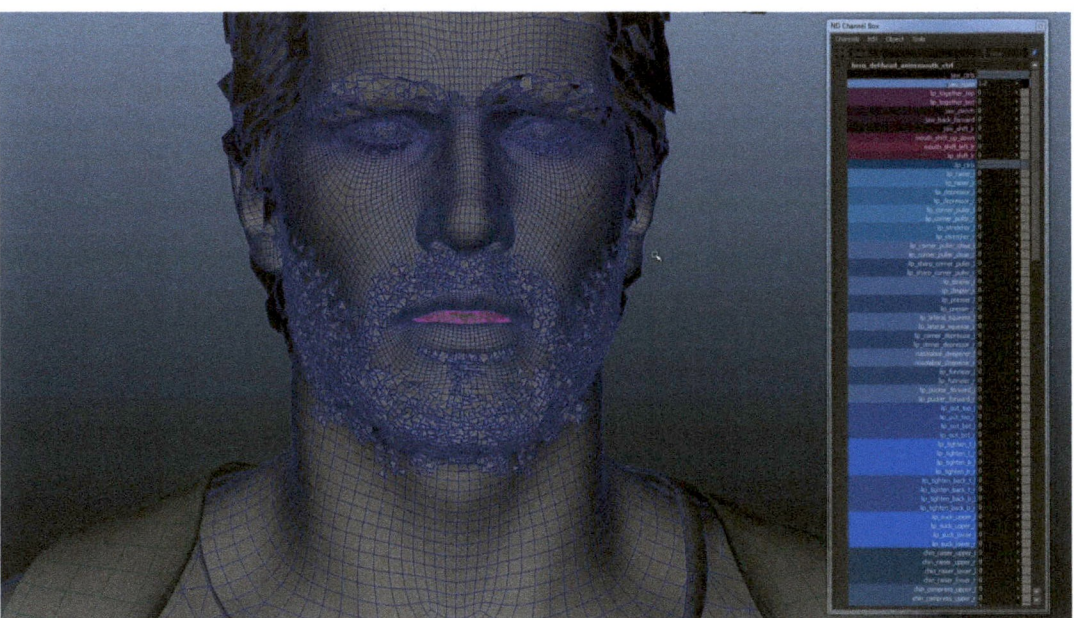

Uncharted 4: A Thief's End drives bone-based faces with blend-shapes. (Courtesy of Sony Interactive Entertainment.)

Uniquely modeling the face allows for individual deformation to best recreate the shapes of highly detailed areas such as the lips, fixing creases that unnaturally occur when simply moving underlying bones, or maintaining volume in the mouth when lips are pursed. Blend shapes also enable mesh-deforming details such as muscles as the neck tightens and individually modeled wrinkles around the forehead and eyes rather than using shortcuts such as animated textures/shaders.

Blend shapes are still expensive computationally and production time–wise, so they are an unlikely solution for games with many characters, but a middle ground can be found by using blend shapes in conjunction with bone poses as a corrective measure for facial issues arising from a bone-only solution.

Muscle Simulation

While standard animation involves deforming a mesh around a skeleton's pivot points, with weighting adjusting how much each joint affects every individual vertex on the model, muscle simulation creates a mass of "muscle" underneath the mesh that performs additional corrective deformations on top.

Muscle deformation in the Fight Night series. (Courtesy of Electronic Arts.)

While real muscle simulation is a rare occurrence in video games due to the additional computation required, there are solutions that approximate the same results. They include corrective blend-shape deformation of key body parts, additional helper bones that float atop the export skeleton to maintain mass at pinch-points like the shoulders, elbows, wrists, pelvis, and knees, and physics bones that can be driven to approximate muscle contraction when moved by the bones around them.

Animated Textures/Shaders

While primarily a tool for visual effects artists, it is useful to have an understanding of any game engine's ability to animate textures on characters and other objects. One classic example is simple UV animation that moves a texture across a surface (where U and V represent horizontal and vertical coordinates across a texture). Others can include playing a flip book (a number of frames of precreated animation rendered out, then played back in 3D space or on a character).

Normal maps, the technique used to provide extra detail on flat surfaces via textures that contain depth/height and directional "normal" information to give the illusion of a 3D surface, are now commonly used to create the impression of creases on faces and clothing. Rather than animating a high-detail rig that manipulates wrinkles and creases in the mesh itself, normal maps are simply faded in and out when required. Most often (in the case of facial wrinkles), blend values are automatically driven by the poses an animator manipulates for facial animation. For example, raising the eyebrows will fade in the forehead wrinkle automatically without the animator having to animate them independently.

Artificial Intelligence

While a game animator will not be expected to create or implement AI behaviors, some knowledge of them helps complement the programmer(s) tasked with doing so. Working together, this collaboration will result in not only more believable movement through the world but also the visible decision-making process of when NPCs make choices.

It should be noted that artificial intelligence is one of the hottest and most rapidly improving fields within all programming, so the below examples are tried and tested generalities rather than the latest cutting-edge methods, which are evolving daily.

Decision-Making

The aspect of AI that "decides" when to carry out an action, what to do, where to move to, and how to get there. These decisions are usually in response to the player's actions, such as taking cover when fired upon or, more commonly, moving to a better vantage point for engaging in combat scenarios. Typically, AI uses a combination of:

1. Points-based systems that assign values or weights to various possible outcomes to emulate priorities
2. Rules that govern what situation will trigger an AI event, such as "when NPC health is below 50%, cause them to retreat"

Programming typically requires animation to create highly visible animations that illustrate decision changes, such as starting, stopping, or being surprised.

Pathfinding

A common result of changes in decision-making is that NPCs will make their way toward a new location such as a cover object or the player. For pathfinding to work on all but the most basic of level layouts, NPCs must have a degree of awareness of their environment so as to find the optimum path while navigating obstacles. Paths are determined by priorities given to the AI, such as "engage or avoid player," "fastest route," "maintain momentum," or "avoid turning 180°."

Similar to the decision-making points/weights system, preset path points within a level (either hand placed or procedurally generated) will often have values assigned to them, with the NPC looking for the lowest value possible (most efficient path) to reach a goal. More than simply allowing running to the target, path priority calculations can include bespoke traversal actions such as points designated as appropriate to vault over a wall that will also be assigned a value and entered into the calculation.

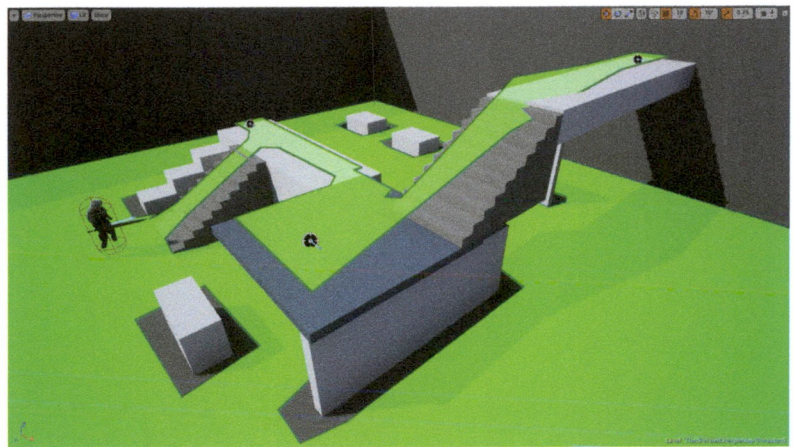

A level layout with marked-up AI path nodes and the navigation path (navmesh) in green.

An important rule to remember is that good video game AI is not about making characters display the most realistic responses, but instead the most readable and enjoyable that fit within the gameplay systems. Clever decision-making is all for naught if invisible to the player, so it must be supported by readable animations that clearly show what an NPC is "thinking." The job of video game AI is not to be smart, but to be entertaining.

CHAPTER 6

The Game Animation Workflow

Being a great game animator means more than just creating beautiful animations. When each individual animation is only one of potentially hundreds of assets required to bring your character to life, being productive and efficient with your time is also an invaluable skill to cultivate. While every animator must discover his or her own unique techniques in bringing ideas to life, below are some invaluable practices to start with so as to ensure you maximize your output while minimizing wasted effort.

Reference Gathering

For starters, more often than not, the secret behind an animation that stands out as exceptional is the animator's use of reference, regardless of their skill or experience. A good video reference can bring in subtleties and detail that may be missed when creating purely from imagination and can make the difference between a good animation and a great one.

Sometimes wrongly confused with cheating or copying by juniors, most experienced animators spend time sourcing video reference or shooting their own before tackling any significant or demanding animation task. If the very best animators out there rely on obtaining good reference, then so should you.

No video can compare to real-life observation, but often it's the only way we can observe motions that are not easily found or recreated within a studio environment. When real-life reference is not possible because of time or budget constraints, a good Google search will suffice.

If you can recreate the action yourself, you will greatly benefit from recording either yourself or a friend/colleague performing the action, not least because you can control camera angles and recreate the exact action you wish to animate. The ubiquity of phone cameras means virtually everyone has the power to easily obtain self-shot reference, and nowadays there is no need to cable-transfer to your work computer when simply emailing the file(s) will suffice.

When you and/or a teammate cannot re-enact the motions, or something more exotic like animal reference is required, a field trip to the zoo or a gym equivalent is next up on the list. Unfortunately, game studios can sometimes be reticent to spend money or devote resources (your time) to send team members out to gather reference. As such, the idea can be better sold by combining animation, audio, and other disciplinary trips so as to maximize their value to the team, with a smaller group recording the material to be shared among the whole team on their return.

A reference-gathering field trip to the zoo.

In the case where you'll be required to animate a fantasy creature that does not exist, look for the closest real-life counterpart (or combination of animals) that most closely resembles the creature. For example, an alien tentacled creature would benefit greatly from reference of a squid, cuttlefish, or octopus. The same can be done for human characters that require elements of animalistic behavior. A monster chasing the player may have some qualities of a raging bull, such as the blind determination to catch and attack the target, from which bull reference can provide timing and attitude, if not the exact motions.

> While exaggerating movements and timing in your self-shoots can aid with reference-gathering for stylistic purposes, be careful when shooting your own reference that you don't overact movements. Too often, animators will act out the motion as they see the final animation in their head, when this kind of stylization should really only be interpreted when it comes time to animate—essentially negating the purpose of using reference in the first place.

Once you have the video you require, you need to view it in a format that is easy to scrub (move forward and backward) to compare to your animation by viewing it alongside. This depends on the player you view it in. It is possible to embed video reference into the background of the DCC to facilitate one-to-one timing and posing, but that really takes the fun out of animating, and, just like mocap, timing should be the first thing to be enhanced compared to real-life reference, with posing the second. As such, it's best to keep your reference separate in a viewer.

Reference video can be embedded in the DCC's background.

Recommended free video players are QuickTime and VLC, while paid ones are RV and Keyframe MP.

Don't Be Precious

One of the worst feelings you can experience as a game animator is having an animation or system you poured your heart into cut from the game after days or weeks of hard work. While there are few certainties in the dynamic and nonlinear whirlwind of game development, one thing you can count on is that this *will* happen. You can either fight it, try to avoid it, or just accept the inevitable.

All are valid paths, but one way of avoiding heartache is never to have loved at all, though this is impossible to convince an artist of entirely. While it will always hurt to lose work you cared about, something that helps is to know that each cut asset and every discarded prototype was ultimately useful in helping the team arrive at the final game. Whether it be a better animation, a more efficient system, or a more focused game in the end, no work is truly wasted when it was essential to explore in the first place only to arrive at a different but better final result.

To this end, never be overly precious with an individual animation or gameplay mechanic. Something that may be great standing on its own might just not fit in the grand scheme of the game, (plus every great idea can be saved for future projects). The following steps should help minimize the impact of cut work.

Animate Pose to Pose over Straight Ahead

A key traditional principle—there are generally two main approaches to animation creation. Straight-ahead animation is done in a linear manner, with the animator progressing chronologically over the animation from start to finish, whereas pose to pose takes the approach of initially "blocking in" a rough version of the entire animation, then modifying and working from there.

The former, mostly a leftover from traditional 2D animation, is said to be generally freer in terms of animators beginning unaware of where the action might end up as they discover the motion themselves during the creation process. The latter is much more controlled right from the start, with animators able to edit posing and timing from the start as they mold the action into the final result. More often than not, pose to pose is the preferred method for game animation, as we generally know our start and end poses already, with the ability to modify and tweak posing and timing relatively easy in 3D, as well as being incredibly beneficial to the proceeding workflow described below.

Rough It In

Using a pose-to-pose approach allows rough "proxy" versions of any required animation to be created very quickly, with minimal commitment from the animator. Long before focusing on the kinds of details that really bring an

Lab Zero's Skullgirls previews 2D animations in game before balancing and polish. (Courtesy of Autumn Games.)

animation to life, the animator should aim to create a quick "blocking" pass of the animation that can then be used by other team members who may be waiting on something to get their own work started.

Keeping an animation rough like this for as long as possible means there is minimal wasted work should the requirements change or the action itself be cut, and in the event that it is still used, it makes it far easier to modify the timing (important for response) and posing (making the action readable) when there are minimal keys involved. Maintaining a minimal amount of keys on a rough animation (avoiding visual niceties like overlap and offsets) will allow individual frames or complete sections to be more easily reposed and retimed.

> There can be instances when animators will be judged on the quality of quick and dirty temporary animations by other team disciplines unfamiliar with the process, so it is important for the animation team to clearly communicate with and educate other disciplines as to this aspect of the workflow should they have concerns. The penalty of holding back work until an "acceptable" quality is reached so as to not raise concerns is simply not worth the cost vs benefit of working rapidly with a fast and loose approach.

Get It In Game!

It cannot be stressed enough that by far the best way to evaluate an animation, even in its early stages, is to review it the game under the correct camera FOV on the actual characters at 30–60 fps (seeing it *in context*). The most desirable workflow, therefore, is to get the animation hooked up and playable ASAP (sometimes worth pointing the game to an empty or T-posed scene even before creation), so as to make iteration of the action as fast as possible.

Often the animator will be ahead of the programmers required to get an actual gameplay system up and running due to their many commitments, so it is desirable to create test levels to review animations that aren't fully viewable in their correct gameplay situation. Even better, you can temporarily replace an animation that already exists if required to see it on the player character—just be careful not to submit your changes to the game lest you break a system someone else is working on or requires for his or her own work.

Iteration Is the Key to Quality

If there is one single aspect of the game animation workflow that fastest drives your work toward quality, it is reducing the time it takes to iterate.

You will never get an animation working in one shot, as it's impossible to judge how it will look and play until it's fully in context with all the related gameplay elements working in concert. Knowing that it is important to iterate on the animation once in game should help you zero in on the final result faster.

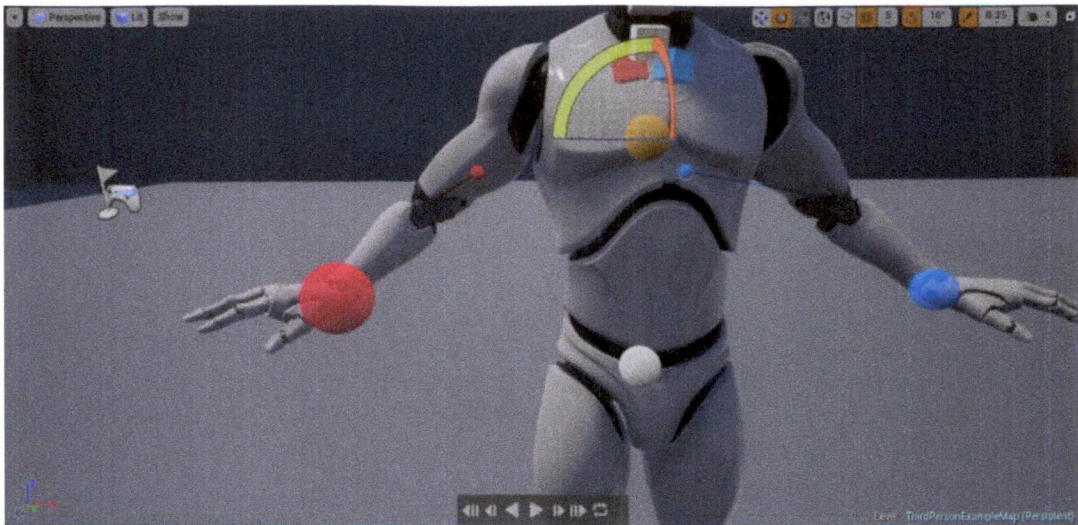

Animating in real time within Unreal Engine 4. (Copyright 2018 Epic Games, Inc.) (Courtesy of Autumn Games.)

With an animation hooked up in game, the amount of time it takes to see changes on that animation should be reduced as much as possible, with the ultimate goal being a 1:1 real-time update. Ultimately, this is often beyond the animator's control but should nonetheless be something to strive for with the engine programmers if improvements can be made in this area.

Blocking from Inside to Out

The root of your character affects every other element, so it makes sense as the place to start your rough blocking pass. It can give you a good idea for timing before you've even done your posing. Once happy with the "rhythm" of your action from start to finish, then begin to assemble the relevant poses around this action with the head and limbs (in the case of a humanoid), modifying the timing and adding more poses as required.

When you begin to see a human as only a few elements (a root, head, and four limbs), the process of blocking in a sequence becomes much less daunting. Only once these aspects have been posed out should you then finish the blocking pass with smaller details like hand poses, clavicles, and improved spine and pelvis orientations. Taking this approach affords the animator the fastest way to block in with more visibility on the entire animation with each new quality pass.

Begin by animating the main body mass only for timing.

Pose-Sharing Libraries

No animator has time to repeatedly make the same facial or hand poses over and over again, so a library of precreated poses is an essential tool in any workflow for rapid creation of assets. Access to the poses should be centralized on a network so that every animator can share the same assets, allowing for pose standardization and stylistic consistency across the team. Because many game animations come to and from poses such as the idle (or several different idles), a way of quickly copying and pasting oft-used full-body poses like these across many individual animation scenes is essential.

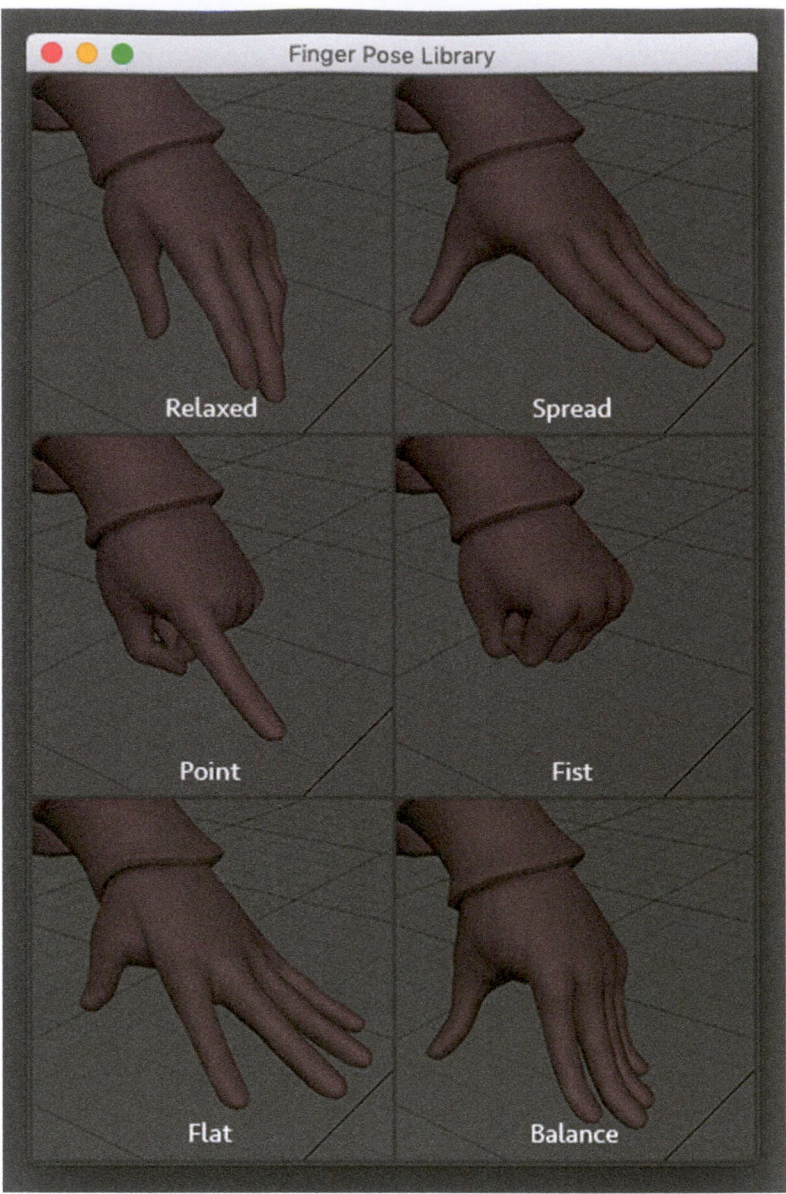

A hand-pose library can be an invaluable time-saver.

Keep Your Options Open

Anticipating the potential changes to an animation is a skill that will come with time as you work with designers more and more, so why not make it as easy as possible to make the quick modifications that you expect will come? A good way to facilitate this is to animate certain potentially variable elements (such as the overall arc height of a jump) on a second layer so that the entire animation can be changed with only one key. Just remember to commit at one point, or your animations can quickly become difficult to parse, especially for any other poor animator who must make edits later as he or she struggles to decipher your complex layered scene setup.

> Game animators on teams should not expect to be the sole owner of any aspect of development, and that too includes individual animation scenes, as finishing a game often requires an all-hands-on-deck approach. It is essential to maintain clean animation scenes whenever possible in the likely event they will be opened by multiple animators.
>
> Additional animation layers should be correctly named (and minimal at best). Use of constraints to drive aspects of motion should be sparse, but, when used, should ideally be visually obvious and correctly named. Version-control submission comments work best when clearly stating the major revisions in each check-in, written in a manner that can be understood by someone new to your scene. Essentially, anyone left to pick up after you should find a clean house so they can get straight to work.

A bad habit is retaining animation layers for the purpose of allowing you to undo changes, when the cleanest and best way to leave yourself options is to go back to previous versions of a file via the project's version-control software. It is imperative to write submission comments that reflect any changes that you may wish to revert back to at a later stage. Submit versions several times a day (on top of local automated backups enabled from your DCC preferences) so as to prevent work loss in the instance of a crash or power outage. Submitting *before* a major change is highly recommended.

Use Prefab Scenes

Throughout the project, the game animator will likely be creating hundreds of animations, so any opportunity to automate repetitive tasks, however small, can be an invaluable time-saver. One such task is setting up your scene to be ready to animate. Rather than starting every new animation from an empty DCC scene, take your scene as far as is required, then save it as a prefab from which you will start all others. For example:

- If you're primarily working on one character, reference them into the scene.
- Set visual layers to display only the ones you prefer to work with for that character.
- Add any additional animation layers you often end up adding.
- Add cameras and/or other cinematic elements required.
- Add any additional elements required for the export process.
- Save this scene in an easily accessible folder.

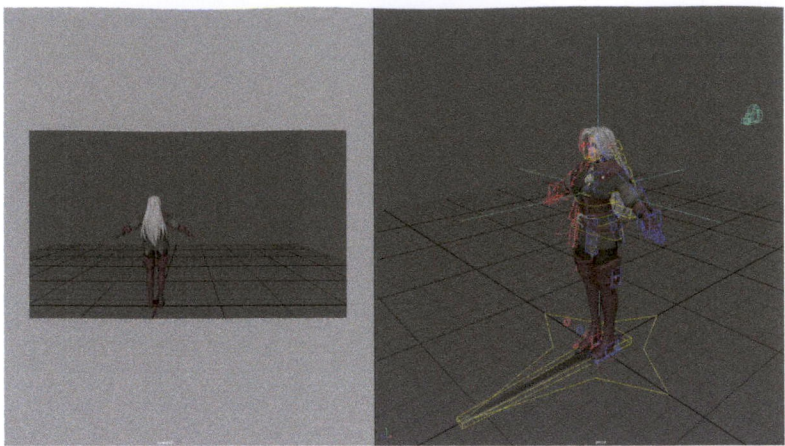

Start new animations from a prefab scene set up to your liking.

Going through this process will enable you to get started animating as quickly as possible for each new animation.

> Window layouts you commonly use are another version of setting up your prefab that can save lots of time over a project's life cycle. If you have a different setup for animating a single-character gameplay animation than you do a cutscene with cameras, be sure to save them, clearly named, in the DCC so you can easily switch depending on the task at hand.

Avoiding Data Loss

One of the worst fears of any animator is losing work due to a crashing DCC or, worse yet, accidental file deletion. Thankfully, there are a variety of best practices to adhere to that can minimize the potential risk of data loss without slowing down a workflow, listed below in order of risk-vs-reward should you be unlucky enough to lose or choose to revert work.

Set Undo Queue to Max

Experimenting with a new pose or series of poses only to find it doesn't work is one of the great advantages of 3D animation over the traditional hand-drawn approach; however, the more you go down one path, the more you run the risk of being unable to fully undo the experiment, frustratingly requiring a full reload of the file. Take the guesswork out of the undo limitation by setting it to the maximum possible.

Configure Auto-Save

A one-time setup when first opening your DCC, ensure that auto-saving and auto-backups are set to regular intervals. While auto-saving, you'll generally be locked out of your work, which can prove frustrating, especially when working on heavy scenes that take some time to save. As a rule of thumb, set the auto-save interval to the maximum amount of work that you are prepared to redo in the unfortunate circumstance you lose your work at that point.

Save Often

Why only rely on auto-backups? Make sure to save your file often, especially before you are about to perform a difficult task or one that you may wish to revert. Remember that saving overwrites your previous save, so you must be confident you are committing to all your most recent decisions since the last version submission.

Incremental local saves (when the DCC automatically saves a new file with an incrementally increasing numerical suffix such as 01, 02, 03 and so on…) are generally less desirable than relying on version control, primarily because there is no opportunity to comment on what changes were made for the benefit of other users. In addition, only those with access to your machine can return to previous versions—especially risky should the hard drive fail.

Version Control

The most robust form of saving your work, whereby a snapshot of your current scene is saved and submitted to a database that is then duplicated (or physically stored) off site for maximum safety in the event of the studio burning down or similar. This is the choice of most studios that cannot risk work and time being lost, as well as protecting against disastrous occurrences like fire and theft. The biggest advantage of version control is the decentralized access to all versions of a file, allowing other team members access to submitted files (as well as making files inaccessible while in use to prevent two people working on the same thing), with each submission requiring notes that describe the important changes.

Get into the habit of clearly describing important changes in each version, not only for others but also for yourself should you wish to revert a scene to before a significant change. Submissions to version control should be almost as common as you choose to save locally to ensure you have the maximum amount of options when reverting to a previous animation direction or to debug something technical that went wrong in an earlier version of the scene.

CHAPTER 7

Our Project: Preproduction

For this section of this book, we're going to look at the video game production process from an animator's standpoint in a more sequential manner to better help understand what challenges you'll face if you're fortunate enough to find yourself on a project from the very beginning, on a hypothetical new intellectual property. In the games industry, that is perhaps the rarest and most sought-after role—to be given a blank slate on which to make your mark on the gaming landscape. For our purposes, we're going to assume a third-person story-based action game, as that is perhaps the most comprehensive project one can imagine from an animation standpoint.

While small studios and single-person indie teams offer more opportunity to land this enviable position due to the one-team-one-project nature of their productions, large AAA games typically begin with a small "core" team that lays the groundwork for the rest of the team as they roll onto the project after completing others within the studio. Multiteam studios typically stagger development so that as one game ships and the team has a well-earned break, they can return to ramp up on a game already underway.

If you find yourself on a core team as an animator, you will be expected to begin researching animation styles, working closely with your teammates to define not only who the player character is, but how he or she moves. Long in advance of actually getting a character playable in the game, animators have a unique set of skills that allow them to mock up or "previsualize" how this might look in video form—creating a visual blueprint for motion and even design and gameplay ideas. Think of previz as the moving equivalent of concept art, which can contain elements like motion style, speed, camerawork, and unique gameplay features.

Importantly, as with much of game development in the experimental phase, expect none of this exploratory work to make it into the game. As such, polished art and animation should be furthest from your thoughts. Mock-ups will instead feature temporary characters with temporary blocked-in animation only. Remember, you're not only experimenting with animation but also game design ideas that should come about from discussion with designers. Keeping everything rough and loose will allow the animator to work fast and make changes on the fly—such is the exciting and exploratory nature of game design at this stage in a project.

Style References

You wouldn't start a difficult animation without reference, and there's nothing more open (or terrifying) than a blank Maya scene on a game that doesn't even exist yet. Before jumping straight into creating, discuss with the team leadership and your teammates what references and tent-poles you wish to draw upon for the game you'll be envisioning. Oftentimes, this will involve the core team watching relevant movies, playing inspirational games together, and sharing related images and websites so you all have the same experiences upon which to draw and refer to later.

At this stage, you're looking to create a common language when discussing the vision of the game, so it's a good idea to collect your reference videos and Google searches into a central folder structure or wiki that can be easily shared not only among the current team but future members as they join the project. For example, you may have separate wiki pages for the various elements (combat, navigation, etc.) of your game with videos embedded in each, or a folder for animation reference that contains folders for combat, navigation videos, and so on. The importance of this reference library being assembled is so that you can easily link to or pull up a video in a discussion about a feature when you wish to have a great example of how it might look, or for how your character might move overall.

Brütal Legend's rapid pose-to-pose style made sense for the volume of work. (Courtesy of Electronic Arts.)

As a reminder, however, the worst art is based on other art. Make sure your entire vision is not based on other fictional or artistic references, or your animation (and entire game) is doomed to be limited by the original work. If you want your weapon-handling to be exceptional, then only looking at other shooting games means your first-person weapon animations will likely be no better than theirs. Look for unique video examples. Try to find uncommon actions or military styles you haven't seen elsewhere. Even better, meet with weapon experts or go through basic training yourself. If your game relies heavily on weapons, then you should always have dummy weapons in the studio to illustrate and try out ideas throughout the project. Getting away from a screen as much as possible can only help at this tentative stage of the project.

Adding more reference to this library and more original, non-video game, movie, or comic-book reference upon which you can draw will stand you in great stead throughout the entire project. Reference gathering should continue throughout the game development cycle and should be an important first step in every new element you wish to add. This can only help in setting your animation apart from the crowd.

Defining a Style

Now that you have a variety of reference upon which to draw, the style in which you animate is an important artistic trait to lock down early, as it cannot easily be changed midway through production. A number of questions that arise might be:

- What kinds of characters make up your cast?
- Are the characters to move realistically or display superhuman actions?
- Can they jump around with abandon, or are they weighted and grounded in the world?
- Considering style and workload, might the project require mocap?
- If so, how will you treat it once delivered—shall it maintain a realistic style or only be used as a base for exaggerated posing?
- If the characters are cartoony, how does that translate into their movement?
- If the setting is heavy on violence, will the tone be helped or hindered by unbelievable character movements?
- Similarly, if the story is to carry some weight, then how seriously should actors be directed at the mocap shoots?
- If nonrealistic, which of a plethora of potential styles will be assumed?

Comparisons

The easiest way to discuss options like those above is to draw comparisons to other works. Is it more or less gory than game X? We like the cartoony style of game Y, but we want to exaggerate the characters even further. Is it a mash-up between the visuals of movies A and B with a little of C? These are quick ways to ensure the team is on a similar page with regards to visuals before anything has even been created. If looking for something entirely original, then, again, looking outside the world of movies and games will yield better results. A puzzle game in the style of M.C. Escher is something most can understand with a single image, while taking character design cues from *Cirque du Soleil* will require everyone unfamiliar with their performances to be introduced.

Realism vs Stylized

Again, comparisons are the best vernacular to agree upon directions to investigate, but can only be arrived at with iteration. It's easy to state we want 35% realistic and 65% cartoony, but that means nothing until the character is moving in a digestible previsualization and able to be modified.

Who Is the Character?

Familiar characters from movies and television are the easiest way to explain a character to those unfamiliar with the project, but if you want something original, it's best to also investigate historical and nonfictional characters of notability and imagine who they would be as people. Many great real-life stories and people involved in them are the inspirations for the best books and movies, so a wider range of experience on which to draw will only help inform not only your character creation process but acting choices, too.

Previz

Previsualization is the single best tool animators have at their disposal in the early stages of a project when there are minimal assets to work with and the possibilities of what the game might be are wide open. Animators are in the best position to mock up what any gameplay scenario might play like in visual form by using any means at their disposal to grab temporary assets and animate to a faux gameplay camera to illustrate ideas.

Gameplay Mock-Ups

Animators, with a basic understanding of simple modeling techniques, can create basic blocky environments and gameplay situations that, while looking rough, can create moving concepts of any given idea they and anyone on the team can imagine. This serves not only to begin to answer questions about how the game might look and play, but also motivate and excite others on the team before a single line of code is written.

Animators can mock up gameplay to prove ideas.

This can be something as simple as how a series of jumps might look for different height/distance variations, to a complex combat system, to a brand new gameplay mechanic never before seen in video games—anything is possible! If set up efficiently with an eye for reuse, these temporary assets can be the basis of the first pass of actual animations exported into the game to begin prototyping with. At the very least, they will inform the animator how to best create and export these animations when required.

As for available characters to animate, these can be work-in-progress proxy meshes built by the character artists or completely throwaway assets from previous projects. A sequel benefits from directly starting from where the previous iteration left off, and similarly, in the case of a new IP, older assets are generally phased out over time as new character art comes online, with only initial prototypes and previz created with the last project's assets as a starting point.

The more projects a studio successfully makes, the more it becomes valuable to create asset libraries to be shared across not just team members on the same project, but across multiple projects, especially given their similarities or whether they're sequels. Asset libraries are a boon, especially when beginning a new project, whereby characters, props, or even mocap from previous projects are incredibly useful in the prototype phase so animators can begin previzing immediately. Libraries of mocap (ideally raw and untouched) speed up prototyping times and can also reduce the budget on sequels by avoiding having to recapture similar actions repeatedly.

A standard camera setup that mimics that of a third-person gameplay camera involves parenting a camera to an object to be used as a pivot (usually a simple locator) that is itself point/position constrained to the player character so it moves, but does not rotate, with the character. This not only recreates the behavior of a third-person gameplay camera as it pivots around the character, but also moves with the character as he or she moves through the environment. Be sure to set up the wider camera angle (field of view) and position as close to the actual/desired gameplay camera as possible for accurate gamelike visuals. Find more on camera settings later in Chapter 10, "Our Project: Cinematics & Facial."

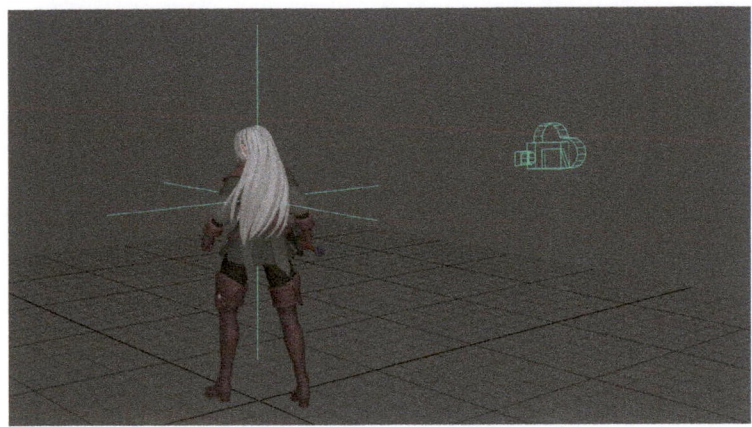

Previz gameplay camera rig setup.

Target Footage

Once enough work has been done to visually describe individual gameplay ideas, a single long take of prerendered target footage that mocks up a typical exciting few minutes of gameplay works wonders for galvanizing the early core team and coalesces them on how the eventual game might look. Working with other team members to make decisions on early character designs and environments takes the team one step closer to the finished look of the game and provides not only great motivation early on in the project but also something to onboard new hires as they arrive later by quickly getting them up to speed.

As this is purely an art/design task (nothing is expected to be playable in the game, though it *can* be rendered in the game engine if it's easier), it frees up programming and other more technical disciplines to make headway on getting the basics of the actual game up and running in concert with the target footage, with the goal of being ready to begin real prototyping once done. Note that as with most of game development, the nonlinear nature of production means that the order of these early tasks as described in this book (or whether they are done at all) is very fluid and dependent on budget and staffing schedules.

The Last of Us was in part pitched via this mockup gameplay footage. (Courtesy of Sony Interactive Entertainment.)

A key visual element of the target footage is that in order to be successful, it must not look like a movie or cutscene, but instead, as much as possible, camerawork should aim to mimic that of gameplay cameras. Gameplay actions, especially those of the player, must strive to at least look possible in a gameplay context, as they will be expected to be created in the final game. This is a great time for tough decisions to be made about designs as to their viability, as they will first be seen in the target footage. That said, no new game design idea was ever created without going out on a limb into the somewhat unknown, so this early concept phase is the time to dream big. It's desirable to push this target footage beyond standard conventions with a view to some questions being solved later, especially if the gameplay being shown has never been attempted before and so has no pre-existing counterpart.

One of the hardest technical aspects of the creation of target footage is whereas gameplay animations are typically made of many small cycles and transitions, this element of the project is one long animation from start to finish. This makes it very difficult to make changes and additions later on as the character moves through the environment, especially if those changes result in the character moving to a different location. As such, like all previz, it is imperative to keep the character's position in the world loose as long as possible until it can be locked down before polishing. While gameplay rarely has camera cuts, use any cuts available to divide the animation up into multiple scenes to be shared among animators whenever possible, using fast camera motions to mask seams in the absence of a cut.

Repeat cycles in the DCCs sequence editor.

One trick to reducing the complexity of one long animation that moves through a 3D space is to create versions of all the basic movement cycles and other animations that will be seen repeatedly in the target footage and play them on the characters while they are animated to move through the world. This naturally has the benefit of simultaneously building out the required animations to be put into the actual game during the prototyping phase.

Prototyping

Prototyping game systems is the next stage of game development following previz. While gameplay prototyping can begin with simply pen and paper, the game animator will come into play when it's time to get things into the engine. Importantly, when prototyping, it's important to move fast without getting too bogged down with technical and artistic constraints. Animations need not look any better than the previz stage—in fact, a game idea can often be proven out without characters or movement, using only primitive objects and on-screen text to describe actions, but proxy art and animations can only help. Elements can be imported into the engine without having to worry too much about cleanliness and organization of assets due to an expectation that all this work will be thrown away, though this is a good time to start establishing some initial file management.

Using any character or precreated animation assets from the previz stage, the game animator should aim to get a character up and running in the engine with basic movement to at least allow designers to move around the environment. This enables level designers to get an idea for the scale of spaces as tweaks are made to character size and speed. Being heavily involved at this stage affords the animator time to become more familiar with the engine, export, and character setup process if new to the tools.

Prototyping with the mannequin provided with Unreal Engine 4.
(Copyright 2018 Epic Games, Inc.)

From there, the real prototyping can begin for gameplay systems that are as yet unknown in terms of how exactly they'll work. Here, typically animation and design (though possibly animation programmers at this stage) will work hand in hand to add custom moves without real concern for scalability (a final system will likely require many more animations than a prototype), to get things playable as quickly as possible with minimal turnaround. At this stage, iteration is key, so systems ideally remain light with minimal asset requirements. The animator should expect to be making changes to the already-exported animations daily and at a rapid pace in order to work toward that elusive fun factor.

Because speed is of the essence, it may be worthwhile investigating prototyping outside of the game engine to be used for the final game, which can often be bloated and bogged down with legacy assets (from previous projects)—especially AAA engines. For example, one way of moving fast is to use a pre-existing framework such as Unreal's "Blueprints" to hit the ground running, temporarily using free online assets with basic systems such as movement already in place.

Pitching the Game

The primary goal of animation in preproduction is to answer as many of the major questions about the project that can arise via previz and prototypes. This leaves the team in the best position to begin drawing up realistic schedules and lists of required animations for all the various planned systems.

Toward the end of preproduction comes the project "greenlight" pitch to a prospective publisher, upper studio management, or even a crowdfunding site to be granted the necessary budget to start the project in earnest. Here the animators and their ability to previsualize a game before it starts can be an integral resource for convincing others to give the go-ahead (or part with their cash).

Gone are the days of static documentation and game ideas written on the back of a napkin (in the AAA space, at least). Now, in order to get a project green-lit, the team, after some time in the idea-generating conception phase, must lay out the entire high-level plan for a game's creation in which the target footage is the jewel in the crown. Nothing convinces executives like a moving visualization.

In addition, any additional previsualization and prototypes that are suitably explanatory will greatly support the typical pitch package consisting of PowerPoint presentations covering the team's high-level design aspirations as well as expected timeline, budgetary requirements, and sales goals. Time permitting, it is worth cleaning up the rendering of any useful rough previz videos for a consistent look to maximize the chances of success.

Early gameplay prototypes of Horizon: Zero Dawn's robot dinosaurs. (Courtesy of Sony Interactive Entertainment.)

Here, the animation director will be expected to set out the vision for the animation style and why he or she arrived at their artistic choices. Is the animation style realistic or not? How much will the game rely on mocap, if at all, and how is the animation director planning to manipulate it for the final look? What is the plan for storytelling and exposition? Without target footage, the animation portion of a pitch will at least be expected to have examples of fully polished sequences and vignettes that clearly illustrate the expectations to even the untrained eye.

This will all be accompanied by art concepts of key characters that back up the stylistic choices of the animation, with the art director or character lead presenting similar high-level goals for characters to be animated. All in all, the pitch is a snapshot of the entire game from the perspective of all disciplines that should excite anyone lucky enough to watch. Like the target footage, the pitch is useful throughout the project as new team members arrive, as well as a good anchor to remind the team of their original intent and steer them throughout the wild and wonderful ride of an entire game project.

Lab Zero's beautiful indivisible playable prototype proved out both visuals and gameplay systems. (Courtesy of 505 Games.)

If all goes well and the project is green-lit, the team will move into full production. At this point, the team size will very likely grow to accommodate the more specialized roles now required, not least because the volume of assets to be created necessitates many talented team members. But before this book moves onto that stage, there is one very important animation area whose team members will have been working simultaneously throughout preproduction to ensure the animation team can ramp up in size and begin creating real assets that will make it into the final game—that of technical animation.

Interview: Eric Chahi
Creator—Another World

(Courtesy of Eric Chahi.)

Another World was a standard-bearer for in-engine cutscenes with a lengthy intro and many inserts during gameplay long before the term "cinematic" became an overused adjective for cutscene-heavy games. What drew you in that direction when plotting out the story?

As strange as it may seem, the story came later because the game was made progressively, level by level. It was therefore an overall desire to create a game with a cinematic style that oriented me in that direction. My technological realization was when I played the Amiga port of the Dragon's Lair arcade game. This game was a faithful adaptation of the original LaserDisc game. The animations were huge, the characters took up three-quarters of the screen. Their technological genius was to stream on discs! Six discs! I told myself it would be possible to save an enormous amount of memory by drawing images with 2D polygons. After a few technical tests I realized that it was possible, though when I spoke with others they did not quite understand.

Another World is often assumed to be heavily rotoscoped like its contemporaries of the time, but while you started with that approach for the opening cinematic, you then transitioned to purely keyframe. What led you to drop rotoscopy (and yet still arrive at a very realistic result)?

Creating animations in perspective is difficult. Rotoscoping turned out to be very useful for complex animations like the car skidding in the intro. In practice, however, it was very laborious because I had to superimpose an image on the background of the Amiga's screen. Often, the VCR would unpause after a few minutes. I would then have to rewind and reposition the tape. This technique was far less useful for creating profile views or small animations, which meant working down to the pixel. I did that only for Lester's walking and running, and I had already acquired keyframe experience in previous projects.

Building your own editor for flat 2D polygonal animation over pixels was revolutionary in terms of allowing more frames of animation than other games of the time. Did that approach come about as a result of hitting memory limitations on prior projects, an aesthetic choice, or something else entirely?

Yes, the objective was to remove technological barriers while also achieving a specific aesthetic for the animated image, the rhythm and dynamics of the design pacing, and being able to cut immediately. Obviously, from a graphics perspective I had to change my pixel artist habits. Having a 2D polygonal expressive image with an angular structure was a big unknown at the start of the project. I inspired myself the same way black-and-white comic-book artists did to create volume with few traits, often only suggesting contours. Additionally, there were only 16 colors in the game. Hence in pixel art I would often use vague colors to create nuances. That was the challenge, to be able to find the right balance, allowing me to convert the character as well as the scenery. It took me one week to choose the color palette for the first level alone!

The gameplay often features custom animations created for protagonist Lester, when many games even now use one set of motions for the duration of a game. What led you to feature so many bespoke sequences over generic movement despite it naturally requiring more work?

I love diversity, especially when things renew. If there is a pattern, it must be broken in some way. So yes, surprising the player demands special animations. That's also why there so many kinds of death, too!

While a relatively short game overall, the universe created appears to extend beyond the scope of the story with the player merely being a temporary participant in a much larger tale. Why do you feel this "other" world still resonates with players decades later?

Probably because of the space left to the player's imagination. Indeed, the minimalism of the game gives the freedom to build your own world in your mind. In the same way reading a book description is only partial. We have this with the graphics of flat color shapes, and in narrative where the story is suggested by a flow of events without any text. The only dialogue is alien words where, again, you can imagine many things.

The other aspect is the pacing. How events happen, moments of acceleration, moments of surprise while playing. It structures all narrative and the gameplay experience. I think it is this nonverbal rhythm and tone that make Another World still resonate today. Especially the use of cinematics and how they are woven into gameplay. Cinematics are punctuations (not short films) in Another World. Even today, not many games are using short inserts like this.

CHAPTER 8

Our Project: Technical Animation

Video game animation is both an artistic and technical challenge. While animators on larger projects aren't always required to handle the technical side of animation (this instead falling to a department that straddles both animation and character modeling), it helps to understand why things are the way they are in order to see opportunities for improvement. On smaller projects and teams, the animator will likely be expected to handle all aspects of the technical implementation of animation.

Regardless of the level of technical responsibility placed on the game animator, an understanding of the entire pipeline transforms regular game animators into indispensable resources as they wear many hats and help solve technical problems. It is very rare nowadays to find roles that require artistic knowledge only, so becoming familiar with what happens to a game animation beyond its artistic creation will open up more opportunities for any animator and ultimately make him or her a more capable member of the team.

Character Setup

Before a single frame of animation can be created, first there must be a character to animate. A highly skilled discipline in its own right, there will be lots of communication between the animation and character teams during the creation phase of at least the initial characters on a project, often with technical animators mediating and deriving tasks from these conversations.

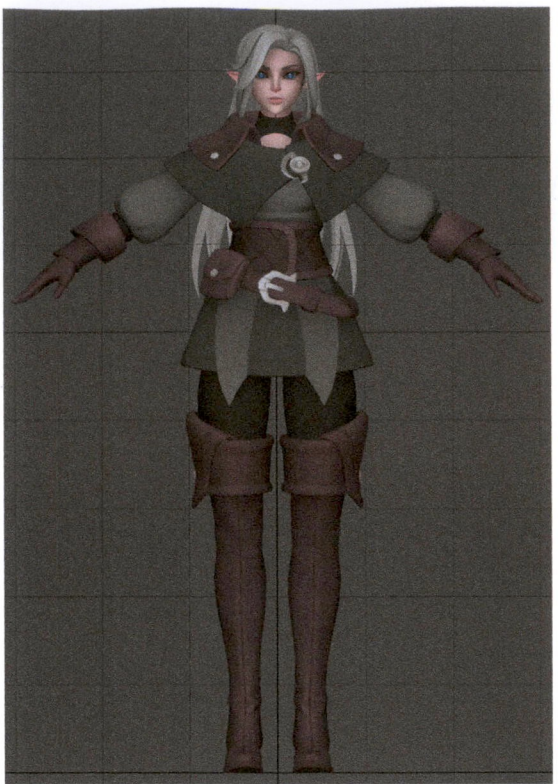

An unskinned character modeled in the "T-pose".

Modeling Considerations

Early considerations that animators should express, many of which can even be anticipated at the concept phase, typically revolve around how the character will deform once skinned and animated. For example:

- If they wear hard armor, this can be particularly difficult to maintain should it be placed at key points of articulation such as the shoulders, waist, and groin area.
- Can custom rigging be used to alleviate anticipated deformation issues?
- If they have high collars, will this restrict head movement without accepting some mesh intersection?
- Is there a visual difference between elements of a character's clothing that denote which areas are hard and soft (stretchable)?
- Will the character's arms intersect with the legs, body, or weapons when down by their side, and is this important for your project? (Especially relevant if characters are heavily customizable by the player.)
- Similarly, if animation is to be shared across multiple characters, what visual limitations should be placed on character design? For example, might there be an upper limit to girth, and should the back remain unobstructed for sword placement when holstered?

- Does the silhouette of the character lend itself to 3D? Models are often warped with the wide-angle gameplay camera, so chunky characters fare far better than slender ones. Are the limbs dynamic and anatomically interesting or simply pipes that look the same from all angles? Can the character type be read by the player in the often-frantic heat of gameplay?
- Are there opportunities for overlap and follow-through? Cloth and other moving parts can increase the visual quality of animation greatly, so any opportunities should be highly considered.

Beyond that, other considerations will likely relate to workflow, workload, and performance:

- What are the memory and performance limitations that might affect bone count, such as how many characters are expected to be onscreen at once?
- How many characters do we plan to uniquely animate?
- What are the plans for the level-of-detail (LOD) system with relation to bone count? (Bone counts can be reduced on more distant characters, along with their polygon counts.)

Ultimately, a variety of factors such as distance to camera, character customization, budget, and the priorities of the project will all play into decisions made around character deformation and visual integrity. Assuming we are always pushing for the best possible visual quality, there are many tricks available to the technical animator to achieve the best results.

When working with the different disciplines involved, the most efficient results can be achieved by utilizing a nonlinear workflow between character artists, technical animators, and animators to minimize issues that might lead to rework of the characters over and above what is expected.

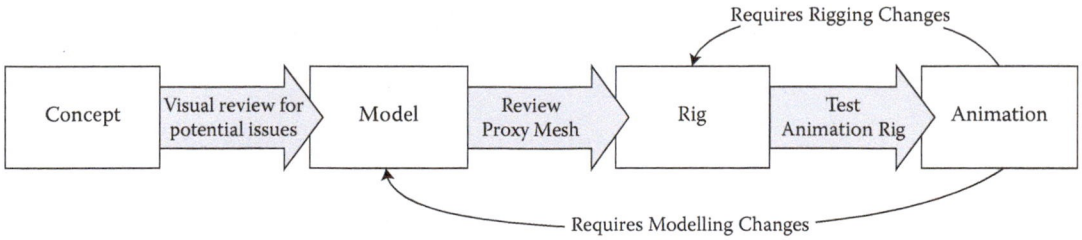

A recommended workflow process for character creation.

While this workflow is harder to schedule for because the amount of rework is variable, it is safe to assume there will be more at the start of the project and less at the end as the workflow stabilizes and most issues are avoided up front. The primary goal of such an iterative workflow is to avoid issues with the rig or character further down the pipeline that force a decision between potentially large amounts of rework or shipping with visual issues.

Skinning

So now we have a beautiful model waiting to be animated from the T-pose, but first it must be attached to the skeleton. This first step, called "skinning," is the long and thankless task of first attaching the mesh to the skeleton with a blanket pass, then working into the areas that deform undesirably.

The T-pose refers to the pose of characters as they are exported into the game engine, with no animation yet to bring them to life. We now rarely model characters in a T-pose with arms horizontal (despite the name sticking) and instead build them at 45 degrees down because we rarely lift the character's arms above the head, so it made little sense to continue using horizontal as a midway point to model for. Arms are down for the vast majority of animations, so modeling this way allows the skinning to be better polished for the most common poses.

Three-dimensional DCCs have greatly improved their default skinning over the years to minimize the amount of manual work required. There are shortcuts such as saving/loading presets and mesh wraps, where a precreated skinned character overlaid on a new asset will aid the auto-generated weights, especially the more closely the two meshes match, as well as third-party plug-ins that often do a better job than the built-in tools. The vertex weighting process may be done individually for low-poly characters, but high-resolution characters demand the use of envelopes (adjustable shapes that can more easily adjust large amounts of vertices at once) and painting tools due to the larger concentration of vertices.

Painting skin weights in Maya.

Nothing beats the visual eye of a dedicated technical animator making the final adjustments, so sufficient time for skinning each new character should always be included in the schedule. The technical animator will likely use a premade "range-of-motion" (ROM) animation that rotates each joint individually over the course of the timeline so that scrubbing back and forth will move the current area being skinned. If using mocap, then it is worth retaining the warmup range-of-motion data the actors perform to calibrate with the system when a shoot begins for this purpose in addition to a hand-keyed one to focus on difficult areas like the fingers.

Additional helper bones/joints that retain volume around pinch points such as elbows and knees may be added to the skeleton and skinned to if required, but must be driven by the rig (automated so the animator doesn't need to move them). As such, it benefits the technical animator to create the rig in concert with the export skeleton as part of the cyclical workflow mentioned earlier.

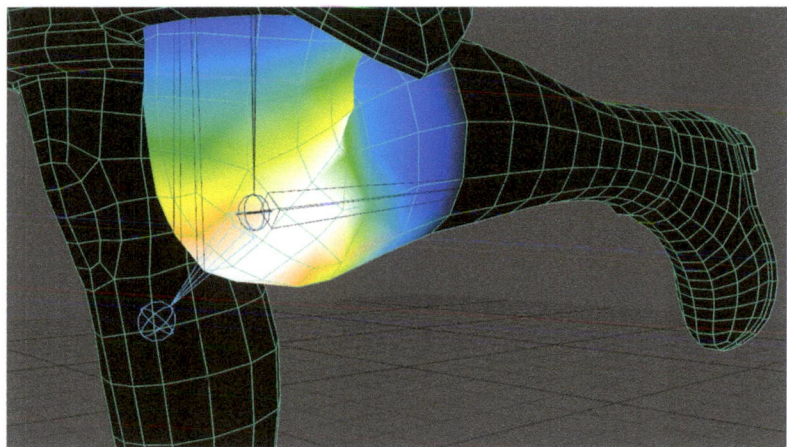

Volume-aiding helper joints.

Rigging

The final result of skinning should be a character that moves seamlessly with the underlying skeleton. However, while the position and rotation values of that skeleton are what gets exported into the game as animation, animators rarely animate it directly. Instead, they manipulate a rig on top that drives the skeleton, affording them more control, custom tricks, and settings. This has the benefit of not only making the animation controls more easily selectable in the DCC viewport, but the team can adjust the underlying export skeleton without breaking the animation (that resides on the rig). The skinned-to export skeleton almost always has a different hierarchy from the rig to utilize the DCC's various constraint setups for smart, animator-friendly control that would not be possible animating a skeleton alone.

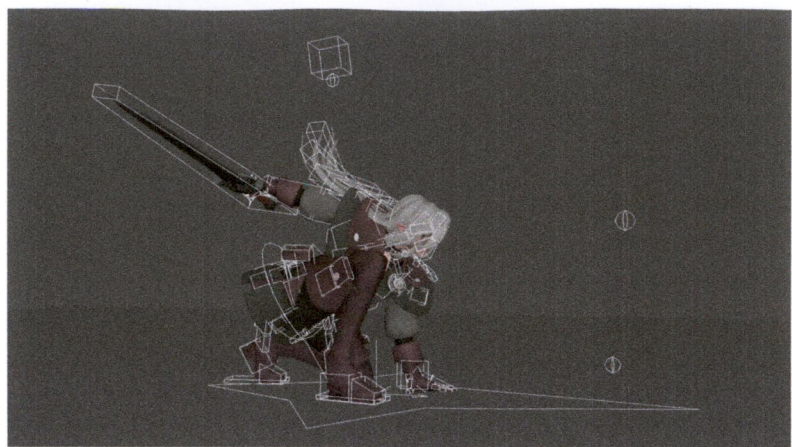

The animation rig.

To learn all about rigging requires a book unto itself, and many have been written on the subject. For the game animator, however, the most important thing to understand is how the unique aspects and attributes of rigs work to make animation creation as fast and frustration free as possible. Some standard elements that most game animation rigs include:

- *Animation controls*: The ability to select the desired body part is essential, and while some rigs are embedded inside the mesh, many float outside the character, making seeing and selecting them in the 3D viewport easier.
- *Root (collision) control with autopositioning*: A clearly marked control that drives the position of the character's collision relative to the scene origin. Should be switched between autofollowing the character's center of mass or animated independently.
- *Picker*: A 2D representation of the rig in a separate window, allowing even easier access to all controls and custom attributes.
- *IK/FK swapping*: The ability to animate controls between IK and FK is essential for animations requiring contact with an object or surface, with most animation placing feet on the ground making this a must-have.
- *Attach points*: Bones with controls to attach props such as weapons, allowing them to be animated independently of the character's hands (or passed between them) when required.
- *Attribute sliders*: Animating attributes on and off or via nonbinary values (usually anywhere between 0 and 1) allows for additional control to custom constraints or even individual facial elements that would be difficult to manipulate otherwise.
- *Deformation helper bones*: Semiautomated controls that maintain volume at key pinch points such as elbows or wrists, with the ability to be further controlled by the animator.
- *Fast framerate*: Game rigs are expected to run fast so as to avoid necessitating an animation be rendered for previewing, slowing down the workflow considerably.

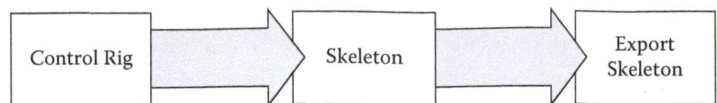

A hierarchy of controls for an even cleaner export separates the exported skeleton from a skeleton driven by the rig, which in turn drives the export skeleton.

Ultimately, games can still be made with little or none of the above depending on the game's simplicity, but complex rigs are essential for high-res characters to maintain a high level of fidelity and efficiency in animation creation.

Beyond the rigging associated with the character, it should be at the animator's discretion to make use of custom scene rigging to achieve the desired result as long as the animation still exports correctly. Tricks such as constraining characters to moving objects (such as moving vehicles or simple nonexported locators to allow additional control) are a viable method of achieving the desired result for the scene. This is most often the case because the export process typically ignores all custom constraints and hierarchy additions (at least those that don't break the skeleton), exporting only the world-space position of the character and the bone rotations, however they are achieved.

While rigs for prerendered footage like film and television can be broken by the animator to get the desired result, the integrity of real-time game animation rigs and skeletons must generally be maintained to prevent issues when exporting into the engine. At best, a broken rig will not display the animation correctly, and at worst, it will not export to the game at all.

By far the best way to attain the most robust and successful rigging for your characters is to ensure the technical animator is in constant contact with the animator(s) who will be using the rig throughout the process, and afterward when they are using it to ensure fixes/changes are swift.

Animation Sharing

Standardization and conformity of skeletons allow the easy sharing and reuse of animations across multiple characters inside the game, as the animations map exactly to one another. For this reason, many games share identical skeletons across multiple characters. Due to this, animation schedules typically consider the number/variety of skeletons rather than unique characters.

Even a minor difference between skeletons will require a non-negligible degree of additional work or specific technology (such as real-time retargeting animations) to account for the differences. While not real-time, so a memory hit rather than performance, shared rigs across differently-proportioned skeletons can allow animation to be easily copied between them, then exported individually as long as the skeletons are similar (same number of limbs, etc.). By conforming rig controls but not skeletons, a project can have a larger variety of character shapes and sizes without exploding the workload.

For near-identical skeletons such as male/female humanoids, one skeleton can be used for both sexes but skinned differently so as to appear to have different proportions. For example, a femenine character can look slimmer by skinning the limbs and shoulders and so on toward the inside edge of the relevant bones, while the masculine character may be skinned toward the outside to appear of different build but with an identical underlying skeleton. Ultimately, approaches such as these fall to the importance of character variety and fidelity on the project.

File Management

Perhaps the most important technical step in preparing for production is a clean file management setup due to the potentially massive number of files required when creating movement and other gameplay systems for a game.

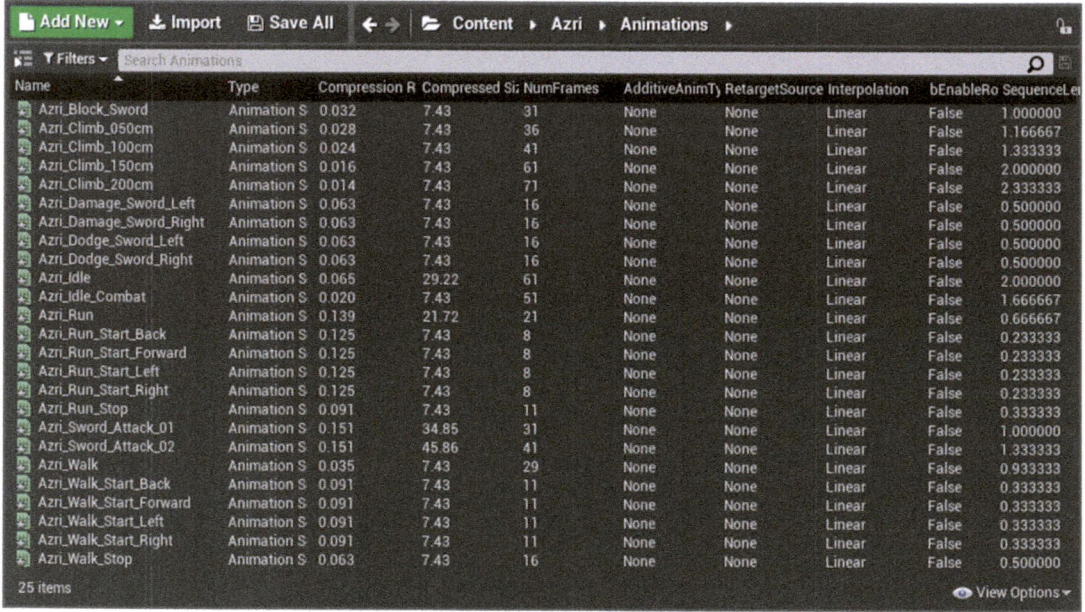

Exported animation files listed in engine.

File-Naming Conventions

First off, clear and consistent naming conventions for animation files are essential due to the large number, often requiring multiple animators, programmers, or designers to easily be able to find an animation from often huge alphabetically sorted lists, especially on larger projects. At its core, the purpose of any naming convention is to best order groups of related animations together under a convention that makes searching easy and the purpose of a given animation file clear to whomever is reading them.

The best way to achieve this is to group animations by character (skeleton type) first, then animation type, then individual animation, working your way from high-level general grouping to specific descriptors at the end. The following example of simple three-descriptor-deep filenames, when ordered alphabetically, groups animations together first by the skeleton, then by the action type, then by further details into the action type.

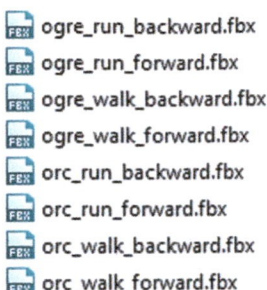

ogre_run_backward.fbx
ogre_run_forward.fbx
ogre_walk_backward.fbx
ogre_walk_forward.fbx
orc_run_backward.fbx
orc_run_forward.fbx
orc_walk_backward.fbx
orc_walk_forward.fbx

Animation naming conventions for alphabetic grouping.

Don't be tempted to use too many abbreviations (such as fw, bk, lt, and rt for directions) to shorten the names, as the purpose of naming is clarity, not brevity. When using numbers, apply a 0 before 1, 2, 3, and so on to avoid ordering issues after reaching 10 (1, 10, and 11 may come before 2, 3, 4, etc., plus it keeps them orderly by being of equal length in a list).

> The clearest and most popular method of separating descriptors is underscores "_" due to their clarity, while hyphens are similar but less legible. Another popular method is to use CamelCase (capitalization to separate words), though be wary due to the visual muddiness with letters featuring ascenders (t, d, f, h, k, l, b), not to mention the common confusion between lowercase L and uppercase i (l vs I). Never, ever use spaces in either animation scene files or exported file names due to their ability to break folder links.

Most engines do not accept all characters, usually excluding forms of punctuation, so it should be quickly established which characters are illegal when naming. In addition, engines sometimes have a seemingly arbitrary filename character limit. It is worth asking the engine programmer(s) what that may be and whether it can be extended, as long filenames that better describe the contents of the file or asset are preferable to abbreviations, so names should not be unnecessarily truncated.

Folder Organization

The next step after file naming is to begin organizing DCC scene files into a folder structure that should make sense for anybody looking to find them. Like naming conventions, folder structures will be unique to the kind of project you're making, so a good start is to ask how many individual files you expect, how might they be grouped, and, importantly, how many unique character animations you anticipate compared to animations being shared across multiple characters.

If, for example, all animations will be unique to each character and small in number, then it makes sense to simply group all animations under a character-named folder, likely shared with modeling.

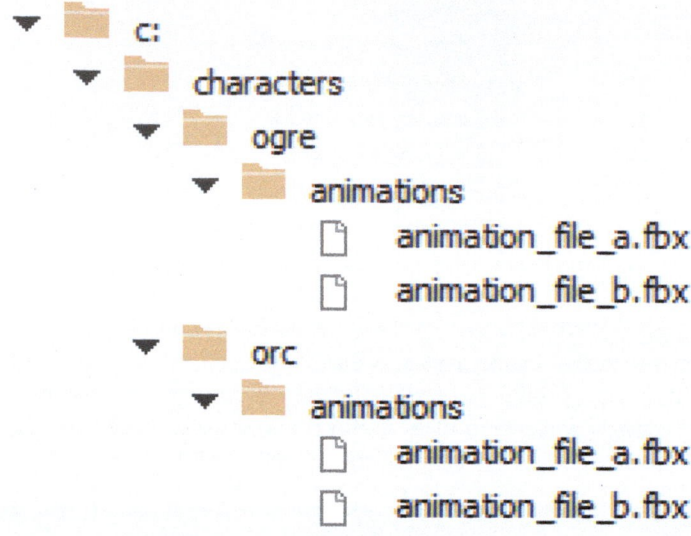

Recommended folder structures for animation DCC scene files.

However, as is more often the case, animations shared across multiple characters necessitate naming your top-level folders after the skeleton they are made for, so they would instead use the skeleton name as the top-level folder, with animations separated from models.

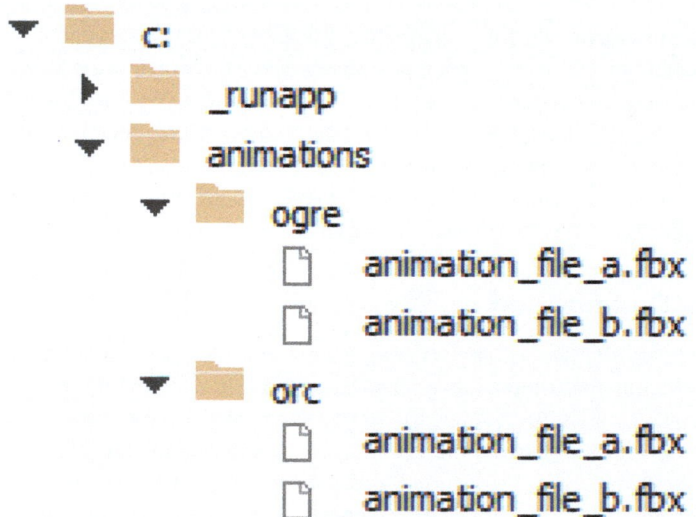

An alternative structure for animations shared across multiple characters.

Yet this is assuming there are multiple skeletons, still with very few animations. If every character shares one skeleton and/or if each skeleton or character has numerous animations, then a better folder structure would include grouping types of move, with the expectation that each type (combat, navigation, climbing, etc.) requires many animations to bring that particular system to life.

Subgroups of folders per system.

Ultimately, the process for deciding a folder structure will best mirror that of the file-naming convention whereby it must prioritize searching and listing. Importantly, however, it is better to err on the side of shallow rather than deep folder structures to reduce searching and lengthy file addresses.

> To ensure folders of animation files don't get clogged with temporary files that are not intended to stay in the game, it is worth saving such files in a folder named "_test" or something similar to reduce clutter. If, as is often the case, something was used in game and then later removed, it is worth moving to a folder named "_cut" or similar rather than deleting, allowing for easier access to reinstate rather than having to sift through version control. The underscore "_" prefix keeps these folders at the top of a list, visually separate from others.

Referencing

An important step to ready files for full production is to properly set up referencing. While not available in all DCCs, it is an essential feature of Maya to allow changes to be made to all animations without batch-processing individual files, which must otherwise be used. Referencing is essentially the ability to embed a reference to one file inside another, such that an animation file only contains a link to the model and rig rather than a unique copy of them.

Batch processing, or "batching", is the process of running a script to perform a repeated task across multiple files within a directory so as to vastly reduce the time and effort it would take to do so manually. Similarly, scripts can be used to automate repetitive tasks within a single scene the animator is working on, which can be as simple as snapping one object to another over a time range to cleaning an entire scene of excess elements that may be causing exporting issues. The more complex an automation process (usually requiring more variables), the more a full-blown tool may be required for the animator to interact with.

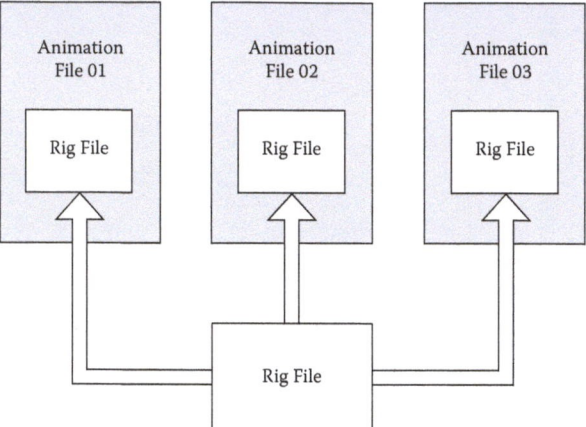

Rig file referenced inside multiple animation files.

This allows the technical animator to work in parallel with the animator, make any requisite changes to the rig, and see them automatically propagate to all animation files created thus far. The changed files will likely need to be re-exported, however, therefore still necessitating a batch export script.

As a result, the animation file contains only the animation keys and attributes, greatly reducing its file size on the network, which would quickly add up otherwise. This is a huge bonus when many animations are required, so the savings are exponential.

Not only limited to rigs, referencing can be used to bring any file into another, enabling multiple animation scenes to be updated by a master scene with elements relevant to the task such as referenced environment geometry. This is incredibly useful for long or complex scenes that may require more than one animator, for example, if one animator is animating a scene taking place aboard a ship that the characters are attached to, while the actual animation of the ship is done by another animator.

Exporting

Once some animation files referencing rigged characters have animation on them, even with a quick first pass or temporary animations, it's important for the technical animator to run at least one animation (and character) through the entire pipeline to see it in game. This is to ensure that not only are the rigs and animation being read correctly by the engine, but also to immediately highlight any individual time sinks in the process. Any overlong aspects at this stage can cripple a project as they multiply in the hundreds or thousands when iterating requires exporting thousands of times over the course of multiyear projects.

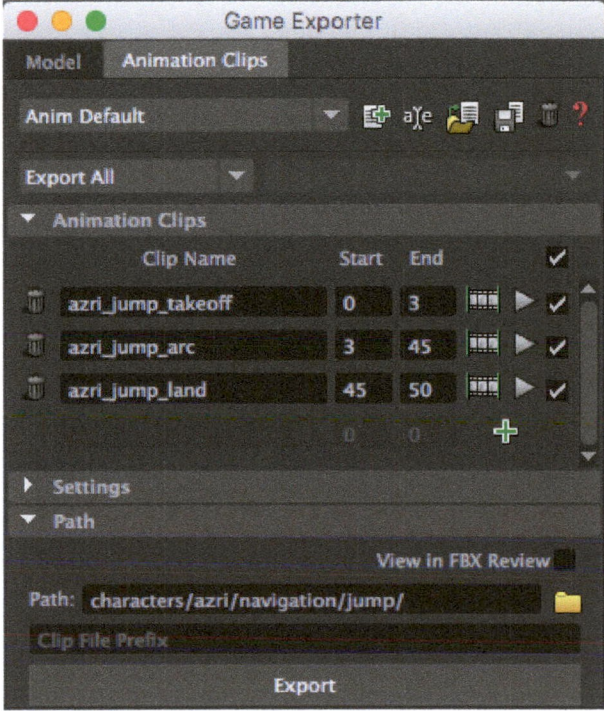

Unreal exporter within Maya.

Export Data Format

Exporting video game animations has changed little since the advent of 3D, essentially resulting in creating exported files that, when seen in their component parts (viewed through a text editor), contain lists of the bone rotation and/or position values for the entire skeleton for every frame exported. The only major change has been the size of these files as memory (and percentage allocation of the game's overall memory budget) for animation has increased with bone-count.

Exported animation file formats are often unique to the game engine of a particular studio, though a degree of standardization has come into place with the industry's widespread adoption of the .FBX file format, synonymous with popular engines like Unreal and Unity. While all exporters share a common collection of bone data, each will have its own quirks and rules to collect that data that must be learned by the animator.

Engine Export Rules

It is important for game animators to learn from technical animators what the expected rules governing successful exporting are and to adhere to them. A good series of questions for animators to ask whenever new to a project, studio, or engine is:

- How do you set the time range?
- How are characters specified when a scene contains more than one?
- What can and cannot break the rig?
- How are cameras and props exported?
- Is bone scaling considered? (Position and rotation are generally a given, though sometimes position keys are ignored unless specified.)
- What additional data can be exported/read by the engine, such as blend shapes?
- Are there additional/missing scene elements that can cause an export to fail?

Most of these questions are generally only asked when exporting doesn't work, so it's a good idea to know up front for debugging purposes. Sometimes an export is successful but the animation does not look like it does in the DCC. That's when it's important to understand why the data may be read incorrectly by the engine. This is almost always user error and not the fault or limitation of the export process. As such, it is preferable for the technical animators and engine programmers to render exporting as potentially error free as possible so as to unburden the animators.

Animation Memory & Compression

At some point in the pipeline, either during exporting or when the engine builds assets into the game, a process known as compression will be run on the animation values found in the export files to reduce their memory footprint, which will in turn unfortunately reduce the fidelity of the animation in game.

It is worth understanding how to modify these settings on a per-animation basis during production if possible rather than waiting until the project close, when time will be precious. Maintaining an eye on memory budgets throughout the project will reduce the likelihood of having to lower the overall quality of the game's animation via a blanket compression across all assets as time runs out.

Animation Slicing

Sometimes referred to as "cutting up" on export, exporting multiple animations from one scene is commonplace and allows for easier management of several actions required for a single move or system. It is also an essential technique for creating seamless transitions between two bespoke states or cycles by keeping all the relevant animations in one scene so the curves can be manipulated leading into one another. Exporting multiple animations from one scene should be as simple as setting export time ranges to follow one another contiguously as long as all are exported from the same scene.

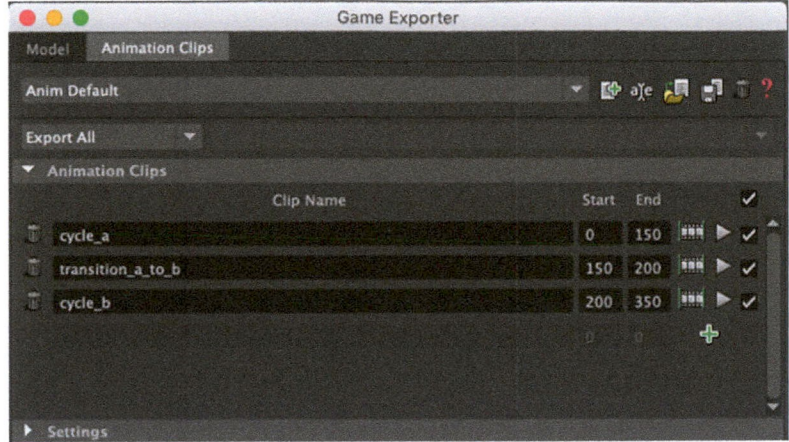

One animation sliced into multiple on export.

In the above example, while *transition_a_to_b* can likely interrupt *cycle_a* at any point in the loop, importantly, we know that *cycle_b* begins at the end of *transition_a_to_b*, so we can perfectly match the ending velocity of the transition animation into the start of *cycle_b*.

In-Engine Work

Once the animation is exported, the animator's work is not done. While it is possible to be a purely artistic game animator who doesn't touch anything once the animation is exported to the engine, that role is rare these days. A game animator is expected to follow up with all the technical requirements for each animation created, be it maintaining the organization of the animation system he or she is working on, controlling all the blend times between animations, or going so far as to implement the animations to a playable state via state machines or high-level scripting.

At the very least, the game animator should be in close contact with any other discipline that will work on the animation in the engine so as to share information on variables such as timing, interruptibility (animation canceling), required effects, and so on. Designers or programmers often implement the most technical aspects beyond the scope of the animator's knowledge, but this flows best when the animator is proactive in sharing ideas and desires to take the animation to a finished, shippable state.

Event Tags

Gameplay animators may be expected to add tags to the animation in order to trigger certain events on a frame. These can include any event that may be desirable to be under animator control, especially when the animation timing is expected to be changed often, and can include:

Animation event editor in engine.

- *Interruption*: The animation cannot be interrupted with another until this frame. This ensures animations don't need to play in their entirety before another is allowed, affording longer settles at the end if uninterrupted.
- *Facial poses*: When multiple characters share body animations despite having different faces, their unique expressions during gameplay may be triggered by tags.
- *Props*: Attaching or detaching, swapping between hands, moving to holsters, and so on. Anything that may be desired over one frame.
- *Hit-frame*: The frame (or range of frames) when a combat attack animation is desired to detect contact.
- *Visual effects*: Usually added by the visual effects artists, but animators may shift the timing should they edit the animation length.
- *Sound effects*: Same as above, but via the audio engineer or designer; again, useful to be editable by animators should they modify the animation timing.

Tags such as these can be added in the DCC itself via script or separate tool, or even inside the state machine. The former is often preferable so frames can be visually selected, but changes generally require a re-export and therefore exacerbate iteration times. Whatever the method, it is important for the animator to review by playing the game, especially when adjusting timing that affects gameplay.

Blend Timing

Engines now commonly offer some kind of visual editing tool to handle all the various states and abilities a game character can perform and move between. The positive side of this is that ultimate control over blending and similar often falls to the animator, with the downside being that it takes time away that the animator would otherwise be animating. But the difference between a 5- or 7-frame blend between key animations can strike the balance between animation fluidity and gameplay response and so must be carefully finessed.

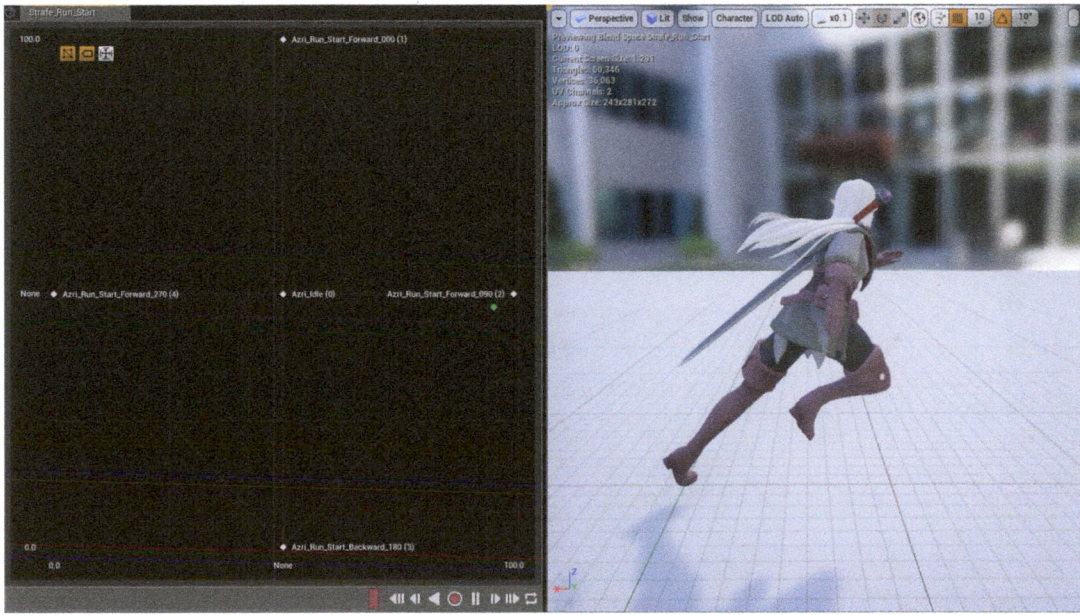

An in-engine blend tree.

Even without a visual editor, it is crucial that as many variables as possible related to game animation be exposed either through code or scripting and never hard-coded by the programmer, as these values are guaranteed to require tuning throughout development. Whatever the method, the animator should either have access to or be in close contact with the designer or programmer who owns these values to maximize fluidity between animations.

Scripting

Like state machines, visual editors for basic scripting functions are now found in many game engines, further opening the doorway for animators to manage all aspects of how their animations play. Even relying on classic text-based input, an understanding of how scripts function in the game engine will open up opportunities for the technically minded animator to go further in creating his or her own systems and test scenarios.

At the very least, this knowledge will aid in discussions with designers or programmers tasked with the final implementation and/or debugging of a given system when everyone is using the same vocabulary. Animators who can perform even basic scripting functions are a valuable asset to a team, as, just as with previz, they can go one step further in prototyping their own ideas. The simple ability to trigger animations when desired (such as on a button press or entering a region/volume in a level) can work wonders for illustrating a concept so others get on board with the idea.

Test Levels

Rather than waiting for the full game to be built before the animator can test animations, it is essential to create a series of test levels containing elements that trigger the animations you are working on so as to see them in game. For example, a parkour navigation system would greatly benefit from an obstacle course containing every possible size and kind of obstacle to be navigated across so as to display each and every animation making up the system in actual gameplay context.

Test level with obstacle-course example.

While test levels are essential for triggering and fine-tuning a variety of animations, they are only a stopgap and should never be fully substituted for testing in the proper game levels. Often there is a discrepancy between the kinds of elements present in the "ideal scenario" of a test level when compared to the more organic and design-oriented final game environments. Many a system that worked perfectly in the clinical test environment falls apart when used in actual gameplay levels, not least because the real context highlights just how often a system (such as feet IK on slopes, for example) will occur in the game so as to illustrate the requisite bang-for-the-buck value.

Asset Housekeeping

While network folders containing asset files can afford to contain temporary work or old and defunct animations, the engine side of asset management must be kept clean of unwanted animations to avoid unnecessary memory usage.

Similarly, naming conventions must be adhered to in order to allow anyone tasked with finding an asset the ability to easily search through potentially lengthy lists of exported animations. Maintaining consistency between exported assets and the DCC animation scene files they were exported from only strengthens this. Ensuring the house is in order inside the engine will greatly speed up the workflow when it's time to revisit polish tasks or fix bugs in the closing stages of a project.

Digital Content Creation Animation Tools

Like engines, tools inside the DCC involved in the creation of game animation also vary studio by studio. Some come as standard, but many are custom-built by either the studio or are plug-ins found online. Below is a list of the handiest tools to speed up your workflow that will be useful on a daily basis and so should be created or sourced online. Find a list of relevant animation tools at the related book website: www.gameanim.com/book

- *Save/load/copy/paste pose tool*: The ability to paste poses from other scenes is not only useful to match common poses like idles throughout the project, but essential for pasting difference/delta poses on layers when working with mocap.
- *Save/load/copy/paste animation tool*: Same as above, but for animation (usually found in the same tool). Essential when moving animations between scenes.
- *Pose/animation library*: Essential for storing a database of preset poses that are otherwise costly to repeatedly make, such as hand or facial poses, and aids style consistency across animators. Having all previous animation or mocap accessible in a visual library will be a valuable budget saver the more the library grows to avoid duplication of work.
- *Trajectory tool*: The ability to visualize trajectories is essential for debugging unsightly pops in the trajectories and arcs of your animations. Advanced tools even enable animating via repositioning the points on the trajectory themselves.
- *Snap-over-time tool*: Often an animator will need to transfer motion from one object to another in world space, independent of hierarchies (so copying/pasting the animation won't work). Snapping an object to another over a series of keys will prove invaluable.
- *Time-warp tool*: The ability to retime complex motions like motion-capture in a nonuniversal manner (different speeds at different parts— not simply scaling the whole animation) is incredibly useful to get a good feel and pacing in game animations, particularly mocap.

Interview: Masanobu Tanaka
Animation Director—The Last Guardian

(Courtesy of Sony Interactive Entertainment.)

The Last Guardian relied heavily on procedural animation to bring Trico to life. Of all the technologies developed for the character, what was the single most important or successful in terms of making the creature appear alive and believable?

The animation control for the fixed "look-at" was among the most important technologies we built. Initially we used rotation from the neck and then the head; however, the problem with this method was that it made Trico look robotic, almost like a toy snake. With guidance from our creative director, Fumito Ueda, we decided upon a method that first fixed the head position and rotation followed by the neck. Real animals have the ability to fix their head position while the body is moving, which was a source of inspiration. We believe that switching to this method allowed us to add more realism to Trico. We named this method *shishimai* or "lion-dance control" after traditional Japanese lion dancing.

What, if any, were the unique challenges of a giant quadruped character in terms of navigation around the environment, and what animal references did you use most of all for the many subtle animalistic details on display?

Controlling a quadruped animal is no easy task, which we made even more challenging with our desire to build a controller that allowed a huge creature like Trico to squeeze into tight spaces and walk around freely. Major development obstacles included slopes, stairs, corners, and jumping into an abyss. We took great pains to make the movement natural by combining hand-key and procedural animations. In creating Trico's movements, we referenced cats and dogs, and incorporated adorable animal gestures that were familiar to us.

Often it feels like The Last Guardian is the culmination of the studio's previous projects. What was learned from animating the many colossi in Shadow of The Colossus in terms of bringing weight to Trico?

Yes, the experience with Shadow of The Colossus helped us a lot in the creation of The Last Guardian's animations. However, the colossi were not alive, as it were; thus their movement was stiff compared to our desire to make Trico's more fluid and lovable. With Trico, we definitely incorporated our learning about expressing the colossi's weight while adding a degree of softness and elegance.

Trico generated strong responses from players in terms of invoking both empathy and frustration (the latter because he wouldn't simply obey orders), as real animals are wont to do. How important do you believe "disagreeable" AI is to rendering a convincing character?

While I was not in charge of Trico's AI, my personal opinion is that it's important to express the AI's will, not to be disagreeable. However, I think Trico's AI was not as technically elaborate as to allow for it to have its own will. Instead, we expressed its will with animations, staging, and so forth. With Trico, we emphasized simplicity of AI to allow for easier controls by artists.

The Last Guardian creative director, Fumito Ueda, notably has an animation background. Is there a shared animation philosophy that has developed over the course of the studio's games, and if so, what might it boil down to?

We have so many philosophies that it is hard to express them all. Regarding The Last Guardian, we took great reference from Fumito Ueda's pet cat. Personally, I used to have a dog but never a cat, so I frequently referenced the animations of his cat. Also, we were told to emphasize the expression of weight and eliminate popping between animation transitions, as those errors would spoil all the good parts of the game that we worked so hard to bring to life.

CHAPTER 9

Our Project: Gameplay Animation

Gameplay animation is the quintessential area of game animation, as it is the most unique to the medium, always involving game design and technical considerations in concert with the visuals. It is also often the single largest area of the game animation workload as modern gameplay systems necessitate ever-increasing numbers of individual animations be created to remain competitive. This has forced modern game animation teams to swell in ranks as the medium's progress, (and player expectations) necessitate quality gameplay animations the player will be viewing repeatedly for the majority of a game's full runtime.

Thankfully, gameplay animation is perhaps the most fun and experimental aspect of a medium that is continually forging the next "cutting edge" with every new technological advance. A great gameplay animator will not only produce visually appealing work but be involved in clever tricks to reduce or automate some of the less glamorous and repetitive aspects of data creation, leaving more time to focus on the animations that count. Ultimately, however, it doesn't matter *how* animations are created, as the scheduling and underlying systems are all but invisible to players—all that matters is the end result as they enjoy the game with controller in hand. An established way to evaluate how players experience the gameplay animations are what have become known as "The Three Cs".

The Three Cs

1. *Camera*: The players' window into the game world should never behave undesirably and always afford them the best view of what they need to play. The most successful gameplay cameras match the feel of the player character in terms of response (rotation speed) while never being adversely affected by the character or environment. Variables such as speed, lag, field of view, and offset from the character all determine the perspective from which the player experiences the game, so much so that entire game genres are defined by their chosen cameras.
2. *Character*: The character's movements and performance should reflect his or her personality and backstory, enabling the player's roleplaying in the game world. Memorable characters are a cornerstone of the most successful games series ever, from not just a visual but also an ability and

story standpoint. Quite how much the character's persona is predefined vs a blank canvas on which the player projects his or her own self depends on the project, as both approaches suit different ends.

3. *Control*: Control of the character must be effortless and minimally conflict with the desires of the player, with the right balance of response and complexity (or lack thereof) affording the player access to all the character's abilities. The most successful control schemes allow players to enter a flow state such that the player's own self-awareness melts away as he or she directly commands his or her in-game avatar, transporting the player directly into the game world for hours.

Essentially, improving each of these three core pillars of gameplay animation will only enhance the first and most important game animation fundamental—how the game "feels." While every game will contain different combinations of (and sometimes entirely unique) gameplay mechanics, we're going to look at some of the most common animation systems found in most third-person action games for our hypothetical project. This should provide a framework to start thinking like a gameplay animator and hopefully extrapolate toward creating entirely new and unique gameplay animation systems.

Gameplay Cameras

The control of the character by way of the animation systems, combined with how the camera behaves, are the player's conduit to the game world. Just a few decades ago with the advent of 3D games came the necessity for a camera control method, first using mouse-look on PC and later via a second thumb-stick on consoles.

Cameras are often the domain of design, and for good reason. A badly handled gameplay camera can greatly detract from the player's experience of any game. However, it is important for the animator to at least be involved in the relationship between player character animations and the camera. After all, this is the way the player will view the movement, and both camera and character should "feel" fairly matched in terms of response.

Often, design's desire for situational awareness by pulling the camera out to see more around the player will conflict with the experience of actually embodying the avatar, so a conversation must be had to decide upon the view that best matches the goals of the project. Is the game a cinematic experience with character-heavy narrative, or a more competitive one where gameplay advantage overrides everything? The more a camera moves with the character, the more it will offer a subjective viewpoint, like the player is embodying the character, while a camera that is more disembodied will feel increasingly objective, like the player is observing.

Settings & Variables

With so many different kinds of 3D game cameras (and many games have different cameras for different situations), here are the settings for a third-person orbiting camera for our hypothetical project. This is perhaps the most complex camera setup, with at least some of the variables shared by all games. As with the gameplay animations themselves, these values should be tweaked throughout development for the best experience:

- *Distance/offset*: Places the character onscreen, either at the center or to one side, defining how much of the screen real estate is occupied by the player character and how much the character obscures the player's view. Along with field of view (zoom value), this variable dictates how large or small the character appears on screen. In addition, the further away a camera sits, the more likely it will intersect with the environment as the character explores it. Typically, the camera features collision to overcome this, pushing into the character when backed against a wall, for example.
- *Field of view*: Not to be confused with distance, instead how zoomed in/out the camera lens is set. Wider angles (usually maxed out at 90°) allow more peripheral vision but warp characters and environments (especially at the screen edge) and render distant objects much smaller than otherwise. Narrower angles look more cinematic, with the narrowest reserved for cutscenes and other storytelling elements where gameplay awareness is less required. Wider FOVs convince players they are moving through the environment faster than narrower ones due to passing objects and environments changing size at a much faster rate than in the "flattened" look produced with narrower angles.
- *Arc*: Essentially, the distance and FOV settings that vary as the vertical angle changes from being centered behind the character. Often, the arc will be adjusted such that the camera moves in closer to the character as the player looks upward so as to reduce the likelihood of intersection with the floor, and vertically offset when looking downward so the player can view more of the ground beneath the character as he or she walks—important for navigating difficult terrain.

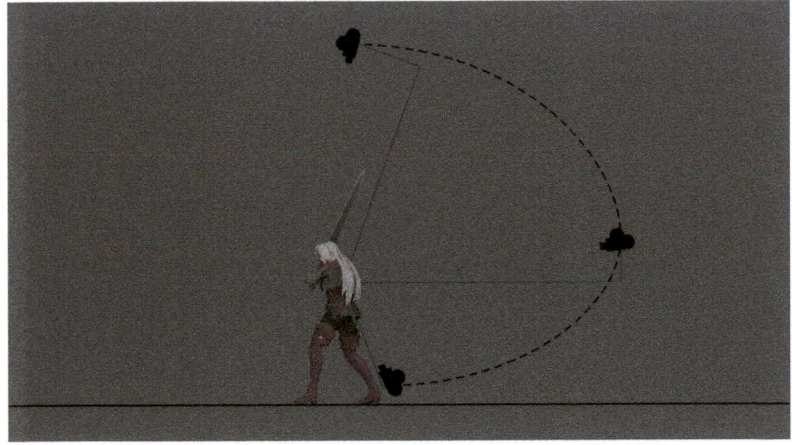

The gameplay camera arc.

- *Pivot*: The pivot is often the point on the character around which the camera rotates. Usually offset from the character's root/collision position with a degree of lag for smoother translation, it should never be attached directly to a joint on the character; otherwise, that region of the body will always remain static onscreen regardless of the animation. Pivoting around the character promotes a sense of the viewpoint being from that character as he or she remains in relatively the same position onscreen.
- *Rotation speed*: Almost always customizable by the player, the default should be set so that it works well with the pacing of general character movement. Too fast and the camera will feel flighty and hard to control, too slow and it leaves players at a disadvantage as they struggle to see enemies or potential hazards in time.
- *Rotational acceleration/deceleration*: Some degree of momentum given to the camera's rotation so that it doesn't start or stop rotating at full speed the instant control input is given, giving a softer look and feel and behaving in a less jerky and unwieldy fashion. Too much rotational inertia can leave the camera moving sluggishly, but completely removing acceleration/deceleration can feel cheap and unpolished. These values should be tweaked considering the necessity for precise aiming vs more broad-stroke reorientation to allow the player smooth navigation of the game world.
- *Positional dampening*: The lag or delay of the camera as it follows a character so that it is not stuck rigidly to the character's movement, giving the character some play from the default position on the screen. Increasing this gives more of an ethereal follow-camera feel, as if the player is merely a viewer along for the ride, while reducing it too much will leave camera motion jerky as it jumps with every controller input.

Camera-Shake

A general camera-shake can work wonders for breathing life into otherwise static cameras, especially when increasing the movement relative to the character's speed, as it removes the occurrence of dead (static) pixels on screen at any point in the game. Too much, however, and it can induce motion sickness in certain players, so it should ideally come with the option to be reduced in the game's settings.

Importantly, all but the noisiest camera-shakes should be animated primarily using rotation rather than position. Imagine a camera held on the shoulder of a camera operator who is breathing rather than weirdly bending his or her knees up and down (which would necessitate positional animation). Motions like running should add a little camera bob up and down as the camera operator runs to catch up, but should still be mostly sold with camera rotation.

Be aware of the difference between moving and rotating a follow-cam for shake purposes. Rotating will move the entire view, whereas moving the camera will only affect the nearby (foreground) objects in the view. The latter is more prone to causing motion sickness and should be minimized if used at all. In order to avoid camera-shake adversely affecting camera aiming, roll may be utilized more than pitch or yaw, as it doesn't affect the aim point at the center of the screen.

An essential addition for action animations (either triggered through events or animated by hand) is to use camera-shake to increase the effect of impacts. As a general rule, the camera should again rotate (not move) to increase the motion being shown across the screen axis upon which the motion is occurring. For example, a character landing hard from a fall will be travelling vertically onscreen downward from top to bottom. When the character hits the ground, the camera should initially rotate upward before settling back down so that the character continues to move down on screen, only now the entire world moves down with him or her to enhance the impact.

Utilize directional camera-shake to enhance the action on-screen.

Ground Movement

For most games, the first system (and therefore animations) to be created for a production will be ground movement—essentially allowing the player's avatar to move around the world. This is essential, as it allows all other disciplines, from design to art to audio, to begin testing and experiencing their own areas inside the game world as they move around inside it.

The All-Important Idle Animation

Cycles are employed heavily at the beginning stage of production, and the initial cycle for any project the second the animator obtains a character to play with should be the "idle," where the character stands awaiting player input. There's nothing more of a wasted opportunity than a lazy bouncing or breathing idle—this is an opportunity to imbue as much of the character's personality as possible, so much so that players can make assumptions about their character simply by seeing the character standing doing nothing.

Equally important is that many other animations and transitions will start and/ or end in this pose, so it's important to think a lot about how it'll look early on— changing an idle late in production will likely have a knock-on effect for many other animations. A first pass of this animation exported into the game should be a single-frame pose to test out how other animations move to and from it.

Asymmetry looks much more appealing than a character facing straight on, so choose a dominant leg to go forward. If the character is right-handed (usually denoted by a weapon hand), then it makes more sense to have the left foot forward so the dominant hand is already pulled back somewhat, ready to punch, draw a gun, or swing a sword. Note that every related animation will have to return to this foot forward, which may prove difficult to match when stopping from a walk or run but is still preferable to bland symmetry. (A solution is to mirror the idle and related animations at runtime depending on the stopping foot if possible.)

> Be wary of too wide a stance for your chosen idle. Legs akimbo makes it difficult to transition from idle to motion and back again without overly drawing attention to the feet sliding or repositioning. It looks even more unsightly when relying on straight blends between animations, too. A strong stance that doesn't invite issues needn't place feet much farther than shoulder width apart.

There may be multiple idle animations, one for each state, such as ambient, combat, crouching, and so on. Each idle should satisfy similar conditions (e.g., same foot forward) to easily blend or transition between one other. Different characters that share most animations can still display unique idles if we blend across from a base idle to the unique stance whenever the character stops, though only if the feet match, to prevent foot-sliding during the blend.

Later in the production, the character idle can be further improved with the insertion of "cycle breakers"—one-off incidental animations, played at random intervals, that break up the loop and are further opportunities for displaying the character's persona. Cycle breakers can't be too complex, however, as the player must be able to exit at any time, so they mustn't stray too far from the idle's silhouette lest they blend out awkwardly.

> Testing randomly playing animations like cycle breakers in game is time consuming as you wait around to see the one you want to review. When editing a randomized animation, temporarily set its likelihood of playing to 100% as well as upping the frequency.

Seamlessly Looping Walk/Run Cycles

From the idle naturally come the first movement animations—usually the walk and/or run. Again, this is an opportunity to give players more information about the character they are playing, so try to convey a mood with the main navigation cycles that supports the character's idle. It is highly likely that the player run cycle will be the animation viewed most in the entire game by a wide margin, so it needs to look flawless by the end of the project.

There's nothing saying that a run cycle must only be two steps—making it four, six, or eight enhances the uniqueness of any cycle but makes maintaining and polishing it more time consuming. Be careful, however: if it is handled incorrectly and the cycle has individual elements that are too noticeable, then the player will become aware of the repeating rhythm. It is necessary to create overall interesting cycle motions with no one part standing out more than the others.

> It is recommended to export a walk/run cycle starting from the passing pose (one foot up, one foot down under the character's center of gravity) with the idle's back foot up. This aids any blending or transitions that will take the foot from idle to motion as it moves the foot forward during the blend. Blending to a contact pose (both legs extended) is undesirable, as the feet will noticeably slide when starting to move.

Feet contact pose (left) vs passing pose (right).

A cardinal sin of movement cycles (or any cycling motion, for that matter) is when the player can tell the start or end of a loop because either the motion hitches (pops) or all body parts arrive at a noticeable pose simultaneously. This must be avoided at all costs, with a good habit being to ensure all curves in a cycle start and end with the same tangents. A worse offender is when the start and end keys don't even match and so pop horrendously, which is unacceptable.

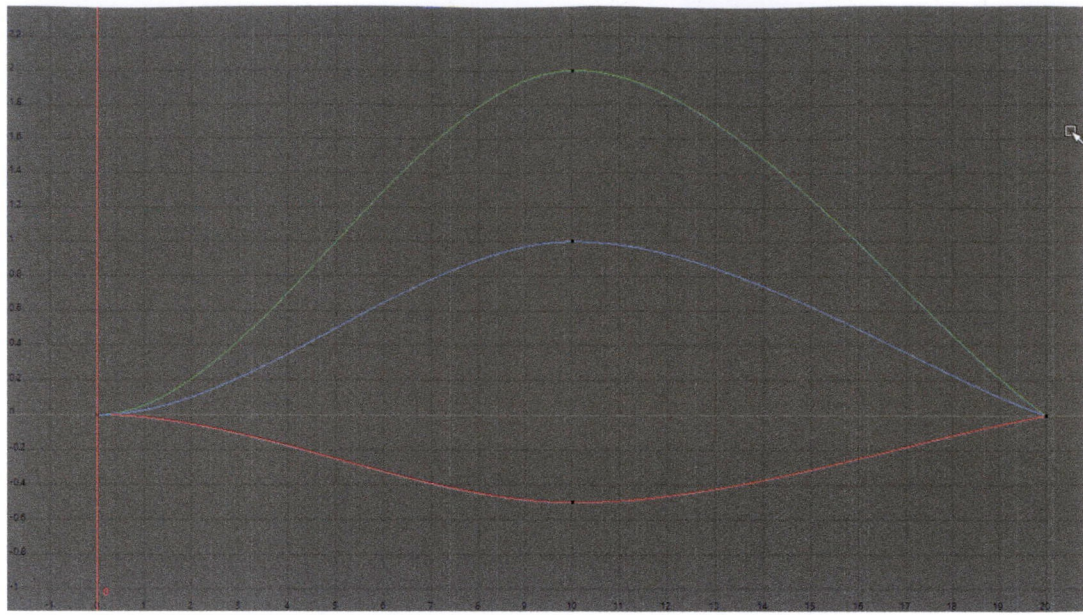

Even start/end tangents not matching will cause a cycle to pop.

The best way to remove the likelihood of a noticeable pose with all limbs arriving at a key simultaneously is to offset the keys to some but not all body parts. Group-selecting and manipulating the start and end keys of a motion on the desired limbs such as the arm swing or foot movement will alleviate this. An alternative is to adjust tangents so the same effect is provided by the tangents overshooting the keys.

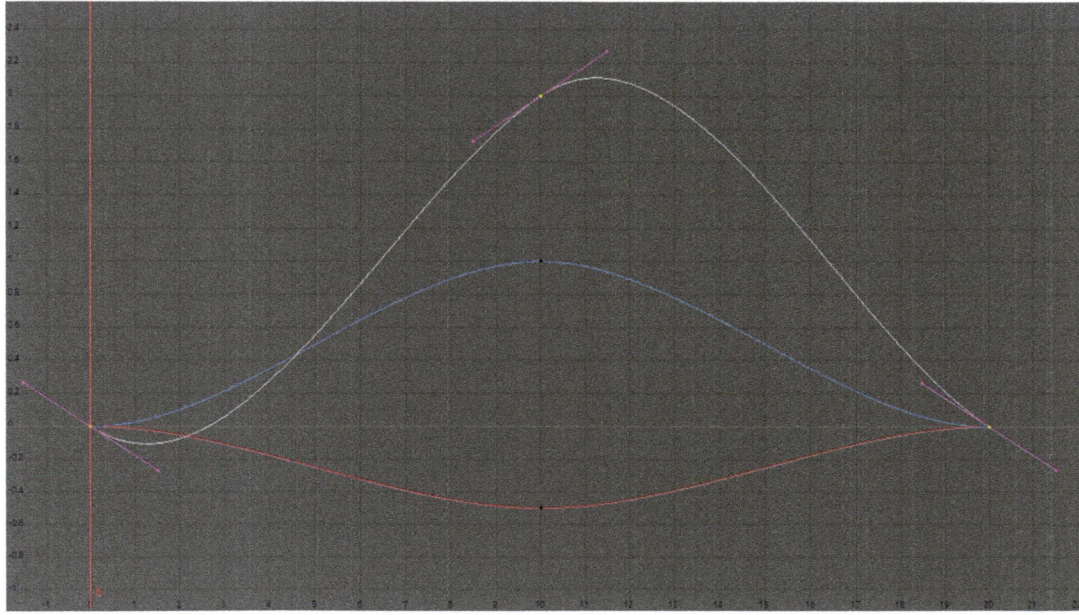

Tangents set to overshoot to provide overlap.

An invaluable aid for removing unsightly cycle pops is to visualize the curves before and after your keys. This can be enabled in Maya's Graph Editor by first checking *View* > *Infinity*, then *Curves* > *Pre Infinity* > *Cycle* and *Curves* > *Post Infinity* > *Cycle* from the menu.

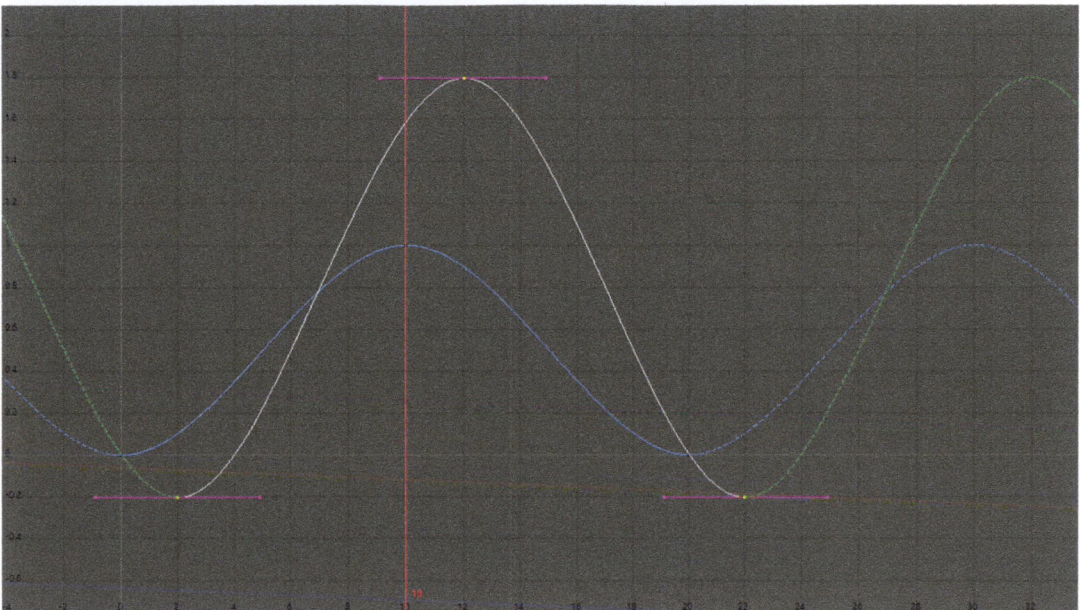

Curves set to show infinity, with key positions offset.

Animating Forward vs In Place

There are two approaches to animating navigation cycles, depending on export requirements. One is that the cycle is moving forward in the scene, such that the feet are static on the ground as the body shifts its weight forward. The other sees the character instead static at the origin, with the feet sliding underneath the character in an oscillating looping motion. Whichever approach the team chooses is usually dependent on whether the animation system for their chosen engine uses animation-driven or physics-driven movement, where the in-game translation is taken from the animation or controlled by code, respectively.

Quality-wise, however, the best results are usually found by moving the character forward, as it is better to establish the speed of the character and work within the limits of feet position and leg length to prevent foot-sliding than to use guesswork. The negative side of this is that it's difficult to match start and end poses, as well as to preview player character animations as the player will see it because the camera won't move with the character to easily show the cycle loop.

The best of both worlds is to have a top-level parent node such as a master control that is simply linearly animated backward so as to view the character cycling in place. This can easily be switched on and off by adding that simple animation to a layer that can be deactivated when desired.

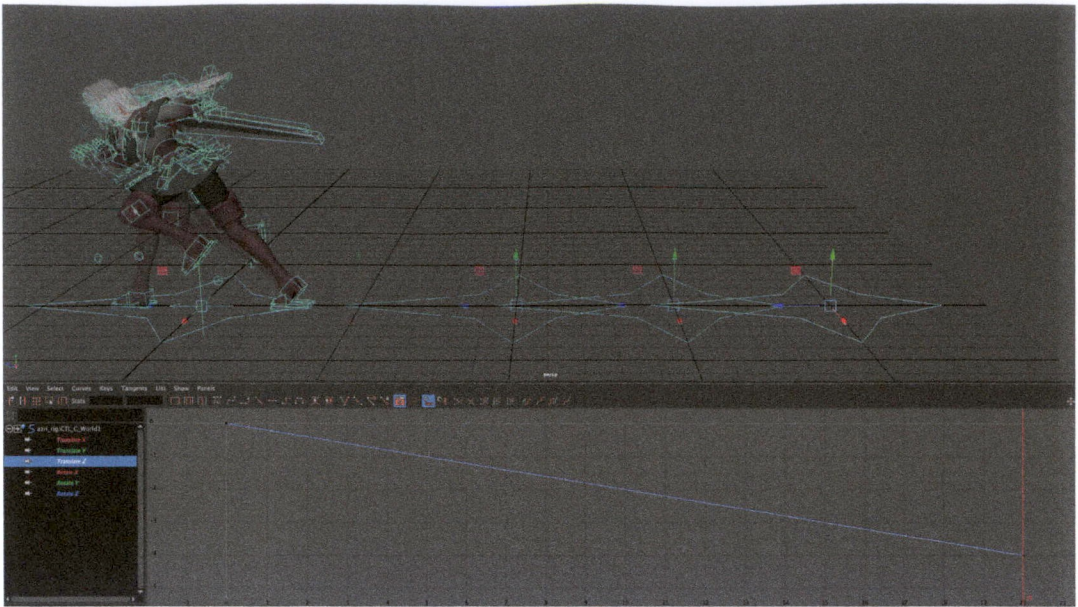

Top-level control moving backward to counter character moving forward.

The bane of many game animators, foot-sliding is most often the result of a mismatch between an animation being created for a particular speed, but the character moving at a different (usually faster) speed in the game. Sometimes it's just unavoidable, as the game demands speeds that would make a character look ridiculous running that fast.

Other times, however, it simply takes communication between the animator and designer tasked with balancing character speeds. As ever, expect things to change, so aim to polish as late as possible so you can revisit animations where speeds have been modified for gameplay purposes.

Inclines, Turning, & Exponential Growth

Implementing alternative versions of the core movement animations to account for inclines will go a long way toward further grounding your character in the world. Having the character use more effort, leaning forward and pumping his or her arms as the character runs uphill or leaning back so as not to trip and fall when going downhill is as simple as checking for the normal (the polygon's facing angle) of the ground beneath the character's feet and blending out the regular run for these alternative incline–appropriate versions depending on the angle.

Similarly, replacing the run with a left or right turning version that leads with the head and leans into the turn is an equally simple blend if you can detect the turning radius of the player character. Beware of where the lean pivots from in this case, as often games simply rotate from the base of the feet, which causes the character to appear to almost topple over like a bowling pin. For best results, swing the legs outward in a turn animation so the character pivots from the center of gravity nearer the pelvis.

Even better, why not blend into the new alternative animations on a body-part basis? Doing so first with the head, then the body down gives an even better impression of the character leading with the head and the rest following. There are many other opportunities for blending between different animations with different blend times per body part that break up the obviousness of a full-body blend and ultimately look more natural.

The flipside of increasing fidelity by creating entire alternative animations to play under certain circumstances is, as you might have already guessed, the number of animations grows exponentially. You'll be doing alternatives not just for run but for all the walk animations, too. And what about crouch variants? The same goes for transitions—each new addition for walk generally means the same is required for run, crouch, and even strafe. The point at which we stop is dictated only by the scope or fidelity of animation required for the project.

Strafing

Strafe systems, common in shooting games that require the character to move in multiple directions while facing forward, differ from regular ground movement in that, rather than rotating the character to face their heading, they continuously blend between different directional walk and run cycles depending on the angle of the player's movement relative to the camera direction. Beyond matching foot-fall timing, the biggest hurdle to overcome is always when the body must twist at some point as the leg motion changes from a forward action to backward.

Directional strafe animations for every 45°, featuring both forward and backward moving cycles.

Cycling animations can only successfully blend between similar synchronized motions. The forward run can blend with a "forward" run at 90°, and the backward run can only do so with a "backward" version of the same angle. Because a forward and backward motion cannot blend (essentially canceling each other out), at some point there must be a switch.

While there have been a variety of solutions over the years with varying degrees of success and complexity, games typically overcome this issue by covering more than just the eight directions at every 45°. Instead, they use additional animations to provide overlapping coverage for the problem areas to afford time to blend.

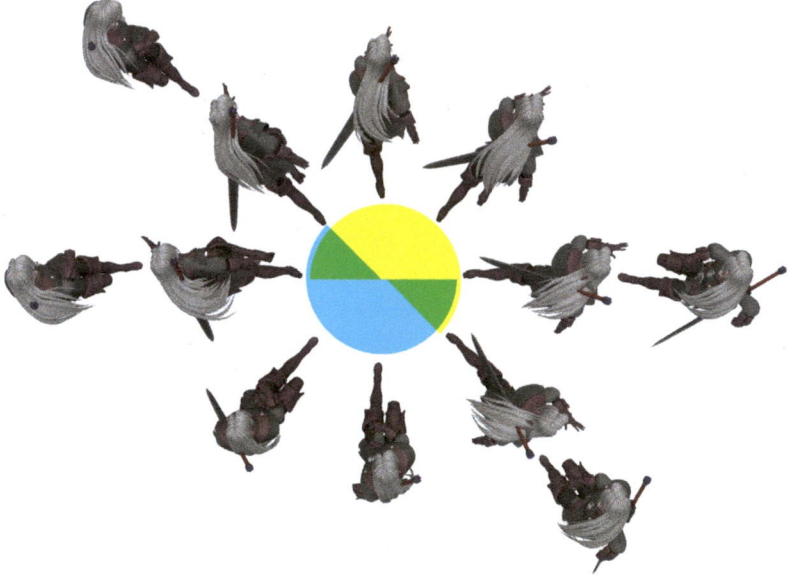

Overlapping strafe coverage with both forward & backward motions beyond the 90 degree angles.

The point at which the hips must switch will vary depending on the actual twist of the character when running forward. Games featuring two-handed guns, for example, may have the character already twisted to hold the weapon, so the problem area will be offset slightly from the image above.

Starts, Stops, & Other Transitions

Directional starts, stops, and 180-degree turns will add an extra layer of polish to a ground movement system beyond creating the basic walk and run cycles. Simply blending from an idle to a run can look cheap without the expected lean forward and push off to show effort and acceleration.

For even better results, instead of blending directly to a run, instead first go to a looping acceleration animation (hunkered down, arms pumping—giving the appearance of constantly accelerating, but must loop at run speed), then blend across from that into the regular run. That will give the character an extra level of believability, as we need the character to hit top speed in a matter of frames for gameplay purposes but can't put the full acceleration in the start animation due to its brevity. Just giving the visual impression the character is still ramping up to full speed despite already being there is just one example of how we achieve both gameplay response and fluidity.

Starts also improve greatly when displaying a variety of versions to cover pushing off in all directions, with blends between them. Similar to strafing, two separate 180-degrees of coverage will be required to blend seamlessly, as pushing right will start with the right leg and vice versa.

Coverage radius of directional starts.

To solve the overlapping angles, as with strafing crossovers, it is important to still rotate the character underneath the animation based on updated player input to avoid locking the start animation into an angle for its duration—something that would otherwise adversely affect the feel. Rotating the character underneath any directional coverage animations is a great way to cover all angles without the player noticing.

Starts and stops in particular go a long way to giving characters a feeling of inertia as they lean into the start and back from the stop. Making these animations overlong, however, can really encumber the feel of the character, and worse, become infuriating if the player is required to quickly avoid obstacles or may fall to his or her death off a cliff without precise stops. As such, starts should almost immediately get to full speed, only giving the visual impression of acceleration. Stops must similarly involve the visual reaction of stopping, albeit stopping almost on a dime. Ultimately, the distance allowed by start and stop animations will be dictated by the needs of your project and must be balanced between that and the visual results.

> Regardless of the feel or method of your game's starts and stops (or really any motion through the world), one thing that is never up for question is that the results must always be consistent so the player can make assumptions on how the character will control and handle the character appropriately.
>
> It is bad form to have different start or stop lengths based on actions beyond the player's control, like which foot the character is currently on or similar deciding factors. Controlling characters should always be consistent in feel with modifiers (such as icy floors), equally consistent and clearly visible and understandable by the player.

While characters can be made to simply rotate, 180°-turn transitions are another visual nicety to show the shift of weight as a character plants his or her feet to turn backward when the player changes direction. Here again, overlong animations or those that cannot be rotated underneath will punish the player and cause him or her to choose to instead carve out an arc rather than trigger a punitive animation.

A common problem with starts and stops is when the player nudges the stick briefly to reposition the character. If the movement system requires these transitions to play in full, then a simple nudge can take the character several meters. This is especially an issue when turning 180° on the spot back and forth quickly. The solution is to make starts, stops, and 180° turns easily interruptible by one another, by way of event tags or cutting the animations into even smaller transitions—the smaller the better for more response.

> A simple test to see how any game handles its start, stop, and 180° transitions is to waggle the controller's thumb-stick rapidly and see how the character handles it. The worst examples will leave the character uncontrollable, while better ones allow for precise repositioning.

Ten Common Walk/Run Cycle Mistakes

Convincing cycles are some of the hardest animations to create, not least because they will be seen over and over again by the player. Here are 10 common issues to watch out for when creating cycles, with some helpful tips on how to avoid them:

1. *IK arms*: Use FK for arms that are just swinging and not touching anything static; otherwise, you'll be counteranimating them every time you adjust joints further up the chain, such as the root or spine.
2. *Foot sliding*: The feet must match the rate of forward movement, or they will slide along underneath the character.
3. *Feet not moving continuously*: Feet move backwards at a constant rate when touching the ground during a cycle. Any time they deviate from this will cause foot-sliding. (Only an issue for cycles animated in place.)
4. *Overly asymmetrical*: Unless the character is limping, limbs should move similarly and with a constant 1–2 rhythm. Speed up your process by animating one leg, then copying to the other and offsetting by half a cycle.
5. *Animated in one axis only*: Be sure to check your animation by orbiting around rather than viewing solely in a front or side view. Junior animators often forget to have the character move side to side as the character's weight shifts from foot to foot.
6. *Root gliding forward linearly*: Every time we push off with a foot, we gain a little momentum until the next push. This should be reflected in forward/backward oscillating motion of the root.
7. *Not leaning into momentum*: We walk/run forward by pushing and falling forward before catching ourselves for the next push. Leaning too far back (or not leaning at all) will look unnatural, especially at speed.
8. *Leg hyperextension*: Using IK can sometimes cause the legs to stretch at the extremes of a cycle. Ensure the foot rolls enough such that it can still move constantly on the ground while reaching the pelvis without overstretching.
9. *Feet back motion underanimated*: Feet really roll back and up after kicking off, especially in a run. Underanimating this motion is a common mistake, so err on the side of exaggeration.
10. *Arms swinging backwards*: Floppy arms rolling in a backward cycling motion are another common issue. Ensure arms are tight during runs and are offset no more than a frame or two from the leg motion, as the two drive each other almost in sync.

Jumping

Games that place importance on exploration often do not merely exist on a flat plane, so players commonly expect to be able to jump over obstacles or up to higher ledges, even going so far as to be fully climbable in some instances as the game design permits. As such, jumping and climbing are a common system to be developed in part by the game animator, and there are a variety of challenges to overcome in the quest to make the interactive world more vertical.

As with ground movement in the game, the actual motion of a jump can be done either through physics calculations or precreated animations.

While the former is more easily tweakable by design, the latter allows the animation to best match the action and is usually created as if the character jumps off a high ledge, continuing to fall endlessly until interrupted with a landing. The best solution is usually a combination of both, where the animator can animate with a jump arc in mind, but the arc is eventually handled in game by code.

Jump animation sequences typically involve a jump to fall loop.

Arcs

The arc of a jump is usually a simple parabolic curve, as with the classic bouncing-ball animation exercise; however, it can be given more character and a better "feel" if manipulated by an animator. Such an arc can have more hang time or a harder descent toward the end if desired. Any modification of a straight parabola will improve the uniqueness of the game's feel under player control.

Regardless of the chosen arc, the key factor is to ensure the character's actions match the related point in the jump arc: stretching out on the upward motion, pinching (or flipping/somersaulting as desired) at the apex, then descending with legs stretched out preparing to land toward the end (the expected ground plane).

Take-Off

In a traditional animation, there would be an expected anticipation of crouching before the jump, but any anticipation before something as commonly performed as a jump will feel sluggish under player control.

Here it's possible to further use blending to our advantage by squashing the first frame of the jump takeoff so low as to compress the character enough that he or she would look broken if players ever saw that frame on its own, but they won't because it's being quickly blended *into* from the current action. This will cause the character to crouch down even as he or she is blending across to the start of the jump, all the while still blending out the previous animation. Creating unseen but exaggerated "broken" poses and animations to be used as part of a blending solution is yet another tool in the game animator's toolkit to achieve visual fidelity without sacrificing feel or fluidity.

In addition, the jump animation itself can somewhat compensate for lacking anticipation by featuring dragging elements like arms, legs, and any secondary objects at the very start, causing them to blend into this most extreme pose rather than be animated backward, giving the impression of dragging from wherever the jump was triggered.

Use an unseen "broken" frame to push poses further when blending.

Landing

Landing is almost always a separate animation that intersects the jump when the ground is detected, and more often than not shows different variations of impact depending on how far the character fell (often with a death after a certain height).

Unlike take-offs that show a character's effort before jumping, the landing is required to show the weight of the character, and its absence breaks the believability in the physics of the world. A tricky issue, then, is the potential loss of control when a character lands, especially when the player desires to continue moving forward. To solve this we can create additional landing animations for movement, such as walking and running lands, and potentially even directional changes during the landing impact for highest fidelity without sacrificing response.

A common issue with landing animations losing their impact is a delay of a frame or two as the character hits the ground, then detects it, then blends from the fall animation into the landing. While blends should always be minimal, you can again push the character lower than realistically possible during the blend to achieve the desired result. Importantly, be sure to work with the programmer implementing the landing animation to minimize delays in ground detection for maximum impact.

While at the programmer's desk, ray checks ahead of or below the character when falling can further anticipate the ground and be used to cause the character to extend his or her legs out as someone would in reality. Anticipating impacts can be used elsewhere, such as when running into a wall, so this technique quickly becomes a great way to increase animation fidelity across the board.

> With the ability to anticipate comes the ability to transition seamlessly into a variety of poses or gameplay states in advance, like jumping to a wall or a swing bar, or even simply detecting how high on a ledge the player might land and bracing for an appropriate knee, stomach, or hang landing. If the game is more realistic and features no air control, jumps can essentially be predetermined actions, so detection can take place at the point of take-off. This way, entirely different types of jumps, such as different height and length variants, can be played to perfectly match the desired jump and further promote the illusion of the character's awareness of the world around him or her.

Climbing & Mantling

Climbing differs from jumping in that we can almost always know the height of the object to be climbed over/onto. As such, the most typical way of handling climbing in games is to create a suite of preset animations for all heights deemed climbable by design. Here is perhaps the strongest argument for standardizing the height and size of environmental elements in a game, not just so that animations work but also so the player can read an area and know which elements can be climbed over and which are too high.

Height Variations & Metrics

Just as with blending cycles, similar animations here can be parametrically blended with one another to cover every height between the authored heights as long as the animations match each other well enough. Fifty percent of a 1-m climb and 50% of a similar 3-m climb should produce a decent 2-m climb animation, though the finer the granularity in animation coverage, the better. Just remember that if the 1-m and the 3-m animations are significantly different, then we require two 2-m animations, one matching the 1 m and the other matching the 3 m to cover all heights between 1 and 3 m.

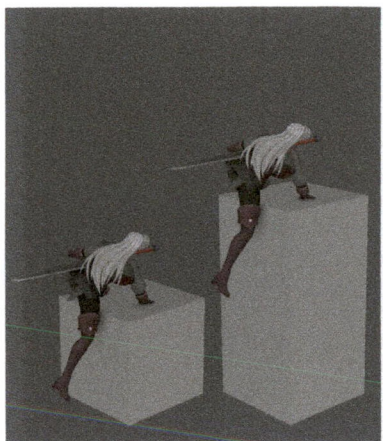 

1–2-m and 2–3-m parametrically blended climb heights.

Collision Considerations

While collision is useful to detect the ground during jumps, it becomes a burden during climb animations, as it often cannot intersect with the environment being climbed up and over. Typically, animations touching the environment will move the character so close as to necessitate leaving the collision cylinder, with the collision needing to be animated independently of the character so as to not get stuck. Turning collision off, then on, during an action is possible, but not always recommended should the action be interrupted and the character end up stuck inside the environment geometry when collision returns.

Cut Points & Key Poses

The workload can be lessened by cutting the animations into component parts such that the end of every climb height passes through a similar pose, such as one knee up, from which a variety of endings or transitions can play out. Landing on a knee, for example, can also work for jump landings that fall short of a ledge and must be climbed afterward. Conforming to poses through different systems such as this reduces the amount of work overall as well as maintaining a stylistic consistency.

Alignment

A key feature of climbing vs other looser navigation animation systems is that certain frames usually display exact contact points with the environment. If a character's hands do not *exactly* grasp the rungs of a ladder, it will not look good at all, just as if characters intersect with the environment because they aren't correctly facing a wall to climb over. To solve this, the animations must be authored not only with standard environment metrics, but there must also be alignment performed at runtime to move/rotate the character into the object to be interacted with.

The exact position and orientation of the ladder or other obstacle (or more likely an offset from it) must be assumed by the character's collision as he or she enters the climb system so that contact points will match. For nondistinct obstacles such as long walls that can be vaulted at any point or the top of a cliff the character is hanging from, these environmental features are generally marked up as "climbable" by design along their length.

Marking up the world in such a way improves the character's ability to detect opportunities for custom distinct animations like climbing, but can also be used for any bespoke action, such as opening a door, to provide more interactivity with the world.

Attack Animations

It is a basic truism that most games, in requiring a challenge to be overcome in order to progress, default to a binary kill-or-be-killed interaction with NPCs. Until the medium matures and finds equally satisfying (yet more meaningful) interactions with the characters we create, there is nothing more visceral in game animation than the visual spectacle of combat, and nothing yet that makes players feel they're impacting the game world as much as causing enemies to take hits, then fall around them.

While all animations contain the traditional elements of anticipation, action, and follow-through, nowhere in game animation are these elements so intrinsically linked to game design than in combat attack animations. Each of these three stages strongly contributes not only to the feel and fluidity of the character's actions, but also the gameplay balance—especially in competitive multiplayer games.

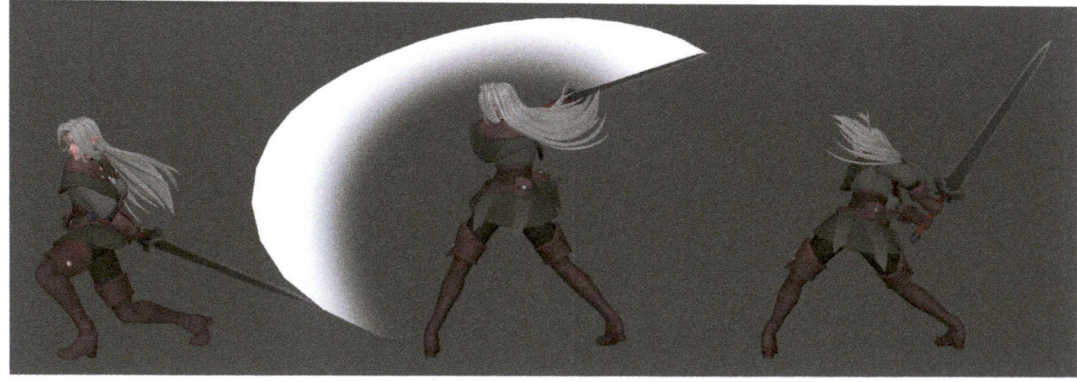

Anticipation, attack, and recovery phases.

Anticipation vs Response

Anticipation, by rote design logic, is always to be minimized such that the action players desire to perform is as instantaneous as if they did it themselves. While it is important to make the connection between player and avatar as seamless as possible so as to maximize the feeling of inhabiting the character, the gap between player input and result is where much of the opportunity for gameplay "feel" exists—not to mention that actions with zero anticipation forfeit a large degree of weight.

This, too, exists in an action that cannot instantly be executed due to visually supported situations or previous decisions such as your avatar being immobilized after being knocked down to the floor or still swinging the previous punch. Therein lies a large degree of the strategy and essential challenge of character control gameplay.

Despite a standard push toward response, there is an empirical understanding by both developers and players that the stronger/heavier an action, the longer we can play with the anticipation. When wielding a heavier weapon like a club or giant axe, or simply when bare-knuckling with a larger character, the player understands that attacks may land with less frequency but should expect them to hit with more damage commensurate with the visuals.

The reverse is true for faster, more rapid attacks or those thrown by a character with smaller stature. This promotes a player-understood gameplay balance of fast (weak, small, or light) vs slow (strong, large, or heavy). Character designs, and therefore the animations supporting their visual representation and these adjectives, generally fall somewhere along a scale where these two groups of traits are at the extremes.

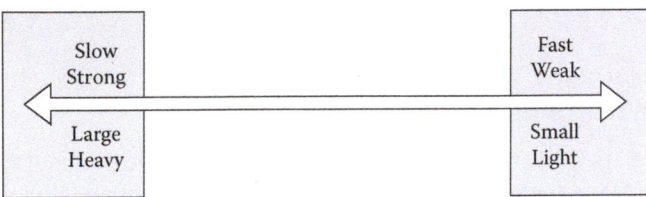

Fast, weak, small, or light vs slow, strong, large, or heavy.

And yet, with anticipation, we're often still only talking about the difference between a 1 or 2-frame anticipation and a slightly longer animation (beyond outlier games that build their whole core mechanics on reading lengthy anticipation). As with jumping, relying on blends to first get to an anticipation pose then follow through with the attack can quickly feel unresponsive. Blend times into attacks should therefore be kept to an absolute minimum of only a couple of frames if at all, with an aim to provide just an impression of an anticipation pose and then taking the action to a contact frame as quickly as possible.

Visual Feedback

When we talk about the time it takes to respond in combat, what we really mean is the time to the contact frame where the player sees the result of the input, scoring a hit on the enemy. It is important to understand the difference between a visual response and the time it takes to get to the desired result or contact frame. A car turning at speed may take some time to take the corner, but the steering wheel is visibly turned instantly. The player still gets immediate feedback on actions taken while visually understanding the reason for a noninstant response. As such, a character immediately pulling back a giant axe then holding that pose to wind up for a powerful move feels far different from one that casually does so over the same number of frames before contact.

Telegraphing

Telegraphing, a sports term widely adopted as the NPC equivalent of anticipation, is used by design to alert the player that an action such as an attack is coming and the player must block, evade, counter, or similar. When telegraphing an attack in combat, we exaggerate not only the length of time required to wind up the attack, but also the posing to ensure the player can see it coming, as well as any visual-effects bells and whistles to ram the message home.

Unlike in competitive player-vs-player (PVP) combat, we generally favor the player in player vs environment (PVE) situations so as to promote the fantasy of overcoming great odds, when in reality the player has many advantages, not the least of which is the ability to outsmart the AI. PVP telegraphing, while present, is generally on a much smaller scale, with less generous windows of anticipation and interruptability to match real player response times.

Follow-Through & Overlapping Limbs

Most of the selling of weight and power in a gameplay attack, without the benefit of long anticipation, is usually done instead in the follow-through by holding strong poses where the player can continue to read the action just performed. A follow-through action that never really displays a distinct pose for a number of frames after impact can feel weak and weightless, so reaching a pose that's the result of the previous action and holding there for long enough to be read is desirable. This can literally be a still held frame if the animation style allows it, but usually is a pose with some slight continued motion as the major force-driving body parts come to rest and overlapping actions catch up. This is often called the "recovery" section of a gameplay action because the length of time the player is unable to perform another attack following the initial action is a large part of the risk in a risk-vs-reward design.

A common mistake that beginners make in animating attacks is to have the entire body perform the action (such as a sword swing) simultaneously—all arriving at the recovery pose (and every pose throughout), at the same time. Here the concept of "drag" is essential, with more applied depending the power of action or weight of the weapon. Throughout the "action" portion of a sword swing, the head should lead, with the shoulders and body next, and last the arm carrying the sword, powerfully swinging only at the end over very few frames.

Because anticipation frames are at a premium, this is often only a 1-frame delay between body parts, but it is important to enhance the power of an attack that will look weak otherwise. No person punches with the arm first and then the body catching up afterward; we instead shoulder the force of a punch, moving our body first, with the arm snapping forward at the end. For maximum impact, there should be minimal frames (if any) between the arm's drawn-back pose and its outstretched contact pose, as too many poses in between will slow and weaken the punch.

Strong punch wind-up poses in a punch's recovery phase pre-anticipate the next action in a combo sequence.

While we generally start any combination of moves with a near-instantaneous action, subsequent follow-up moves can afford more anticipation, as the player already understands the second attack cannot always interrupt the first until a given time (via an event tag). As such, a valuable trick is to ensure a combo attack animation recovers in a pose that builds anticipation for the next hit, such as a right hook ending in the left arm already drawn back, ready for the next punch to explode when the player inputs. This works even for repeating the same action (such as throwing knives), where the throw animation ends with a follow-up knife drawn and held back ready to throw as part of its follow-through.

Cutting Up Combos

Combinations of moves in sequence, common in even the most basic of melee attack systems, pose a challenge in that after each attack, they branch to two different possibilities—either the next attack in the sequence or back to the combat idle. There are two approaches to creating branching sequences of animations like this:

1. Create each move as its own complete animation (albeit likely within a single file), with each individual attack returning to idle but the second attack onward starting from an appropriate recovery pose of the previous animation.
2. Create an entire sequence of attacks, exported as separate animations, and then only afterward animate the returns to the combat idle to be played when the player doesn't continue the combo.

While both workflows have pros and cons, for the most versatile results, the former approach is recommended because the exact frame at which follow-up attacks can be triggered will likely change with design iteration, meaning the latter complete sequence approach quickly becomes too rigid to work with, as it requires constant updates.

The latter approach arguably creates a smoother and more fluid overall sequence if played to completion, however, and also fits best for mocap that is likely captured all in one sequence. If using motion-capture, the best results will come from capturing both a complete combo sequence *and* individual actions in order to cover and edit all possible parts of the sequence.

Regardless of approach, it is important that subsequent actions in any such sequence begin with a start pose chosen from nearer the end of any window of time marked for triggering the next animation so as to avoid reaching the end of the time range and jumping to an earlier pose for the proceeding action's start frame. Whenever blending into the next in a sequence of actions, combat or otherwise, it is important to visualize your character still progressing the animation forward during the blend to avoid unsightly hitches should they blend into a pose that is essentially "behind" where they should be once blended.

In this example, subsequent combo anims should start with the sword further back in the recovery phase.

Readability of Swipes over Stabs

When considering the actions for your characters, remember the fundamental of readability. As we often cannot guarantee the camera angle from which an attack will be viewed, actions done in only one axis, such as jab punches or sword stabs, will often be either hard to read or completely obscured by the character's body, especially when viewed from the common angle of behind the character. As such, it is preferable to use swiping motions over pointed stabs, ideally at an angle other than exactly horizontal or vertical, again maximizing their readability.

This is also relevant for visual effects, where often a trail from the weapon or body part can greatly enhance the readability of an attack. Trails from stabbing attacks are virtually nonexistent, as the weapon or arm will overlap the effect, while swipes will leave large arcs across the screen. It is always best to consider the most common camera angle and play to that, ensuring that any gameplay motion can be read in two or more axes so it is never lost to view.

Damage Animations

As with attacks, there are different considerations between player and NPC animations. Damage animations usually scale in severity commensurate with the attack meted out and can have different attributes such as knocking the character into a downed state and therefore further animation considerations. Regardless of the type of attack/damage combination or the overall animation style, it is always better to err on the side of exaggeration over realism so as to make attacks read well for the player—especially when the camera is further from the action due to game type or when attacking enemies from a distance.

Directional & Body Part Damage

Directional attacks that connect with a single unidirectional or, worse, wrong-directional damage action are unsatisfying at best and unsightly at worst. As such, it is always a good idea to at least include a variety of directional/body-part damage animations that can be played to match the direction the attack comes from or body part being hit.

Beyond melee, projectile weapon damages are often played back based on the part of the body targeted; such is the more precise nature of projectiles. For such games requiring precision damage, characters tend to still use a standard cylinder/pill-shaped collision for navigating the environment while employing a more complex collision for damage detection to better match the character's shape and silhouette when animated.

The number of damage animations can quickly scale up if there must be considerations for body part, direction, and severity. The realism or precision of your game will ultimately determine the granularity of different damage animations, not least because these will also likely be required by all skeleton/character types. The same will be true of death animations.

Contact Standardization

Depending on the game's fidelity, all high sword swipes, for example, should connect at roughly the same height on the enemy so that the same damage animation can be used for multiple high attacks that hit at that same point. In this case, it is advisable to use visual references like locators or other scene geometry to indicate chosen damage points. To ensure consistency once a damage point has been decided upon, it needs to be brought into each different damage animation requiring it. This is a perfect opportunity for referencing so damage locations can be updated globally if and when the values change.

Metrics standardized for any purpose should be referenced into scenes so they can be modified from one central location. Other commonly used examples are those to do with speed and direction. An eight-pointed wireframe circle on the floor can illustrate distances in different directions to be used for directional strafe animations such as cycles and starts/stops, or to standardize directional damages that are required to move the character a consistent distance. Climb heights, cover objects, ladders, and other standardized environmental props are also good candidates to be referenced in a library of sorts. Doing so also ensures multiple animators working on the same system are obeying the same standards.

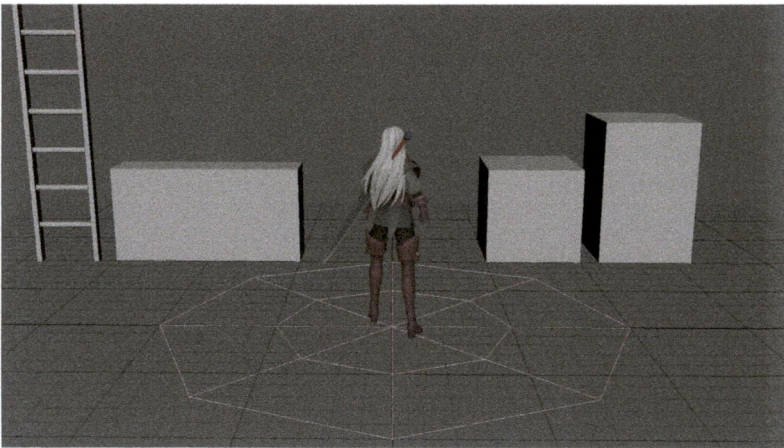

An eight-way directional guide and other metric props.

Synced Damages

For melee combat when a perfect match of action and reaction is desired, attacks that trigger a unique damage animation on the recipient synced with the attacker are the best option. This is a rigid approach that, on detecting that an attack is or will be successful, the recipient is matched to the position and orientation of the attacker (or vice versa, or a balance thereof), and the damage animation plays in sync from the point of contact. This gives a lot of control to the animator, as both characters will be animated in the same scene rather than potentially separated into standardized damages, and can afford a greater degree of precision.

While more predictable and visually impressive, the downsides of this approach are that it increases the workload immensely due to the 1:1 ratio of attacks to damages, and moreover disallows the type of gameplay that promotes attacking multiple enemies simultaneously or via glancing blows that might be possible by more granular methods of detecting and triggering damage animations.

This approach, however, is essential for actions that require sustained contact between two characters such as throws or holds. When contact is required between characters, use of IK is essential. Use locators or similar dummy objects parented to one character at the grabbed body part that can constrain the position and orientation of the grabbing character's hand IK. Parenting a locator rather than directly constraining hand IK allows the locator to be animated relative to the grabbed body part, with the constraint animated on/off to allow for grabbing and relinquishing the hold.

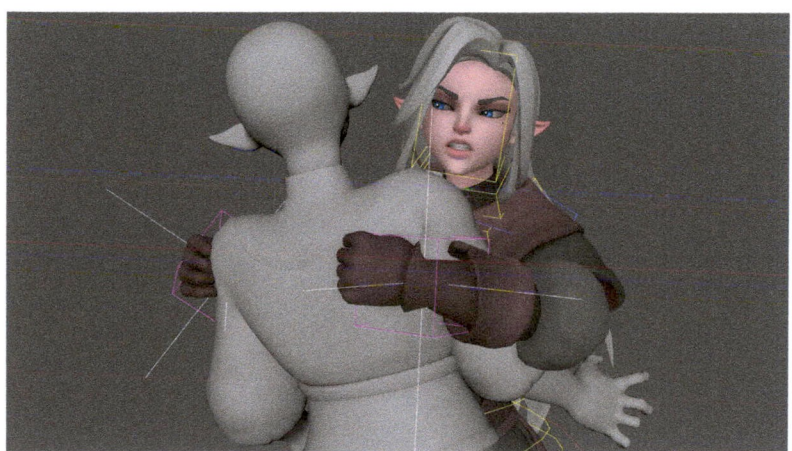

Simple two-person IK connection setup.

Recovery Timing & Distances

Small damages often do not interrupt the character's current action so as to avoid the frustration a player might experience, for example, of being rooted to the spot while attempting to evade enemy fire. Conversely, large attacks might knock the character down, leaving him or her vulnerable to follow-ups. While the latter is often a simple full-body animation, the former requires some degree of systems support to overlay or combine the damage animation with the current action the character is playing. The most natural candidates for this are additive actions that "flinch" on top of the current animation, but body-part animations can also be used in their absence.

For hits to the player, large damage animations are usually only interruptible by other damage animations, as they are essentially a punishment for being unsuccessful. Smaller damage animations should be either short enough or lower on the priority scale such that they can be interrupted by actions that might reduce the chance of being hit again such as dodges, rolls, or other evasive maneuvers. The timing of damage animations, at least until the frame at which the player regains control again, is often key to gameplay balancing, especially in fighting games where balancing damage frame counts is as vital as attacking ones.

The interruption priority of all actions is something to be discussed with design, and blend times between different animation combinations should be balanced such that bad examples (midway through a somersault that leaves the character upside-down and would flip 180° if blended) may be better with either no blend at all or require custom transitions.

The travel distance on damage animations can be equally crucial to how a game plays, especially in games that might knock the player off a ledge. Typically, a short stumble that moves both feet is all that's required to prevent a character from appearing rooted to the spot. Distances must be standardized such that being hit left has the same distance and timing as being hit right even if the actions are themselves different to avoid any disadvantage from taking damage from a particular direction.

Impact Beyond Animation

The visceral impact of damage animations, combined with other methods such as impact sounds, visual effects such as blood, or the ever-useful camera-shake, is essential to make up for any shortfall in an attack's perceived power due to the limitations on anticipation. Working with other departments closely to ensure correct timing to match the desired frame will greatly benefit the final look of the attack and damage animations.

"Hit-stop" causes the movement of both the player and NPC to freeze for a few frames on successfully landing an attack to further enhance the feeling of connection. This is usually done programmatically, but the illusion can be baked into the attack animation somewhat by enhancing and hanging on the attack pose longer—the downside here being the attack still appears to connect even when it misses. In this instance, attacks may branch into different outcomes whether they hit or miss.

Interview: Mariel Cartwright
Animation Lead—Skullgirls

(Courtesy of Autumn Games.)

2D animation in games since the advent of 3D was becoming rarer and rarer but has seen a resurgence with the indie scene. How did you get started and where do you tend to hire most of your animators?

I went to CalArts to major in character animation and built my foundations in both 2D and 3D there. I knew then that I wanted to work in games but assumed that any game animation job would have me animating in 3D so that's what I focused on (indie games as a scene was still in its infancy). However, the game animation jobs I started getting out of school just happened to be 2D—both pixel and HD—and before long I was full time on Skullgirls, which was all 2D HD animation.

At Lab Zero, we typically find our animators on Twitter and Facebook, actually! We have three full-time animators (including myself), and everything else is handled by contractors online. Our pipeline is organized in such a way that we're able to do the animation/design heavy lifting in-house and use contractors we find online to finish the animation we've started.

Fighting games have gameplay response timed to the individual keyframe. What is your process for animation creation knowing that every frame counts?

We get our animations in game to test as early as we can. Often, this meant testing out barely legible scribbles. Once it's in the hands of our designer, though, he sees how it feels and tells the animator how he wants it timed, so the animator can go back and make those adjustments. It helps in our case that our designer has a decent sense of animation timing—he'll remove or hold frames to get the timing he wants—and then the animator can take that info and just finish the animation up.

What are the advantages of using Photoshop for your workflow instead of a dedicated 2D animation software?

I always preface any dialogue about Photoshop as an animation tool with a disclaimer—Photoshop is not the easiest tool to animate in. However, there are definitely reasons we use it. One is that for each frame of line art, we need to have a separate flat color layer underneath it that's the silhouette of the frame—this makes it so you don't just see through the line art into the background. Photoshop actions make generating these frames a largely automatic process, which is super helpful. We also have Photoshop scripts to help us export frames in the format we need. For contracting, Photoshop is the safest bet as far as a tool most any artist will be familiar with. And finally, at this point, it's just what we know. It can be tricky teaching it to animators who are familiar with better tools, but in house, using it is second nature to our animators.

How did you settle on your established anime drawing style and why do you believe that Japanese aesthetic is so popular in the west?

For me, it's just what I grew up around and had been into. I actually tried a few times to draw more western, if you can call it that, but it never felt natural to me and I fell back into my anime-styled stuff. I think for most people that consider themselves anime fans, it becomes a big part of our lives because of the diverse stories, themes, and styles that we don't often see in western animation. There's still the perception in the west that most animation is for kids, with a few outliers—but there are no such rules or limits in anime. While to me, the anime aesthetic is definitely appealing on a surface level, there's so much more that it can be about beyond the visuals, and I think that's part of the draw.

2D animation frees the animators from rigging limitations, though must be harder to stay "on model." Are there any other benefits and trade-offs that you can share?

There are a lot! I love the ease of quickly scribbling my keys, drawing an exaggerated smear or just creating new things without the worry of designing, modeling, or rigging. It's also great to be able to animate transforming or shapeshifting, or inject personality into facial expressions easily, with your primarily limitation being what you're able to draw. However, there are definitely drawbacks. Designs have to be made with ease of creating drawn animation in mind; things can't be too complex, difficult, or time consuming to draw. Keeping things on model is definitely an issue, and fixing model issues can add up to take quite a while. It's also incredibly difficult to do things like skins or different outfits—anything of the sort requires almost complete reanimating, since every frame is uniquely drawn (though we have done it!). While sometimes we'd love some of the luxuries that a rig could provide, to our team, the trade-off is worth it for the fun and charm we get into our animations.

CHAPTER 10

Our Project: Cinematics & Facial

Story, once an afterthought in the majority of game releases, is now the central hook that drives many players through game experiences as they desire more depth and meaning from their chosen pastime. While a great story can be conveyed in games via something as simple as text on screen, the animator's role will only aid in creating memorable moments for the player, often with dialogue delivered by the characters.

This is the only time we consistently bring cameras close to show off faces, and there is an arms race in the industry to have the most "believable" (not just "realistic") characters to tell these stories. Each time the bar is raised, the effort to match it across the industry increases, and so too does the importance of animation being taken seriously at any game studio with storytelling ambitions.

Quality cinematic cutscenes are perhaps the single most expensive animation element that can be added to a game. With mocap, voiceover, and high-resolution characters, not to mention the writing and all the technical expertise required to pull all this together into a cinematic pipeline, it is a project in itself.

Conversely, there are no other elements of a game production that players expect to be able to skip with a button press, such is the divisive nature of linear noninteractive storytelling when juxtaposed with the dynamic interactivity of the rest of the medium. So when telling stories, why do we use cutscenes at all? The answer is twofold.

1. Unlike practically every other element of the game development process, they are quantifiable. Once a pipeline has been created and a few cutscenes made, it is entirely possible to schedule, sometimes to the day, how long it will take to complete these sections of the game.
2. As a storytelling method, the team can focus the player's attention on what the story is conveying in a fully authored manner with none of the randomness and emergence expected in the rest of the game resulting from the unpredicatabilty of players interacting with gameplay systems.

These two certainties are valuable commodities in a medium where every other production element is in such flux. Plus, with over a century of techniques already figured out in film, there's a wealth of knowledge out there to maximize the quality of these noninteractive parts of game development.

The more complex and honest answer is that we still haven't found a compelling alternative that will work in a universal manner across all game stories. There have been individual successes at alternative storytelling methods, all bringing with them risk and uncertainties that cutscenes avoid, but no one-size-fits all solution like cutscenes.

Cinematic Cameras

Before discussing the uses of cameras within cinematic language, it is important to understand how cameras work and how they can be manipulated to get the required shots. Three-dimensional cameras in DCCs, and now in freely available game engines, too, do their best to imitate their real-world counterparts down to the last detail.

Field-of-View

Field-of-view (FOV) describes the size of the viewing angle we render to the camera; imitating lenses of real-world cameras allows it to move between narrow and wide angles for zooming purposes. Measured in millimeters , high values (~85 mm) correspond with zoomed-in shots due to the narrow viewing angle, while low values (~28 mm) instead represent wide shots (note that lens values in the DCC and/or game engine may be represented instead by angle-of-view, so translation is sometimes required because high/low numbers run in reverse).

Narrow vs wide camera shots.

While the complete range of angles is available to be exploited by the game animator for the purposes of storytelling, it is important to consider that wide angles are already the domain of gameplay due to the desire to see more on screen and therefore maximize situational awareness for the player. This and a history of cutscenes in early 3D games simply using the gameplay camera for cutscenes without adjusting the FOV means that games with a desire to appear more filmlike should tend toward narrower cameras for cutscenes unless absolutely necessary, not to mention that 3D characters and objects simply look more solid when viewed from narrow angles than wide ones with increased perspective warping.

A camera pushed further back but zoomed in can display a subject as the same size on-screen as a camera placed close but zoomed out, thought the latter will render the subject far more warped toward the edges of the screen. Understanding this should avoid some of the worst cases of game cinematography that mistakenly shove cameras in characters' faces, showing them under less-than-flattering circumstances.

How field-of-view affects characters, with a "cinematic" narrow field-of-view (left) and a warped ultra-wide angle (right).

It is recommended for a cinematic lead to create a list of pre-approved lens angles for stylistic consistency across animators. While animators are free to move between angles while zooming in or out it is undesirable to stay on an arbitrary angle value for visual consistency.

Depth-of-Field

Essentially a flaw in real-world camera lenses, their ability to draw focus on only a slice of the complete depth field has been reintroduced to virtual cinematography to emulate the desirably stylistic blurring of nonessential elements in a shot. This can be used to draw a player's focus to your subject by blurring out the foreground and background elements, not to mention looking more pleasing by emulating film.

Ryse: Son of Rome utilized depth-of-field to dramatic effect. (Copyright 2012 Crytek GmbH. All Right Reserved.)

Depth-of-field (DOF) is typically driven by setting a focal-point distance from the camera and then associated values to set the distance before and after that point to determine the field of focus, often with values for fall-off and blur strength.

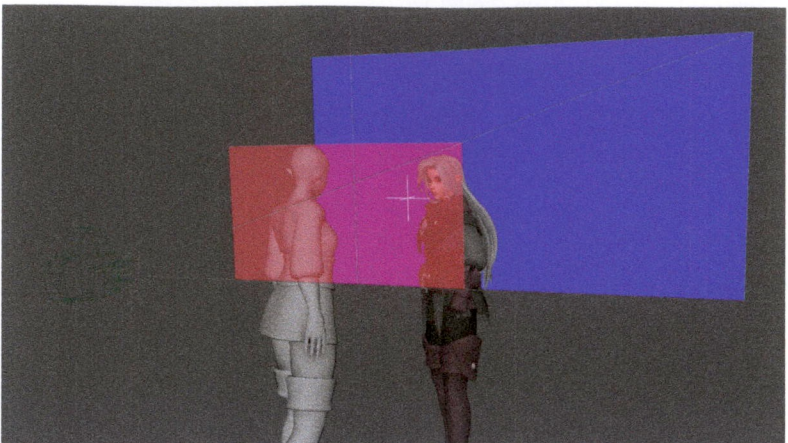

Placing characters within the bounds of visual focal planes causes just the background image to blur.

Use of "rack-focus," the process of animating the focal distance values within a shot, can be used to great effect to change the player's focus between different elements without cutting. The shallower the focus, the more noticeable the effect. This is often used to move between two characters at different distances from the camera to highlight the one talking.

Because focus is dependent on fixed values relative to the human eye, it is important to never simply add blur to a shot that would not trigger one in real life, such as in a wide angle, as the player will detect something is off with the scale of the shot—producing something akin to macro-camera "tilt-shift" photography simulating a miniature scene.

The Virtual Cameraman

With the ability in CG to create pretty much any shot possible by placing cameras anywhere, it is all too easy to stray very far from shots that a real camera operator in live action can achieve. This can quickly lead to nonsensical camera movements that, while once in a while may be exciting, when used en masse will take audiences too far from the constraints established by over a century of cinema and appear amateurish.

As with game camera-shake, visualizing an actual cameraperson when creating shots is a great limitation that gives a real sense of presence in scenes that crazy flying and spinning camera shots will not. This also includes mechanical shots such as dollies and cranes that are standard tools in cinema. Even going so far as to imagine your cameraperson in a chase car following an intense driving sequence will work wonders for preserving a grounded viewpoint from the perspective of a real person.

The Five Cs of Cinematography

The Five Cs of Cinematography, by Joseph Mascelli, are a great starting point for anyone unfamiliar with basic cinematic camera language, with rules established over his entire career of film, television, and teaching. Put simply, they cover:

1. *Camera Angles*: The camera is the perspective from which the viewer sees the point of interest or subject of the shot. Wisely choosing the angle can go a long way in supporting the mood or perception of the shot's subject by changing the camera's view of the subject or a given scene. This is generally the only time we fully author cameras, wresting control away from the player to enhance the narrative.
2. *Continuity*: Describes the importance of consistency between shots, as errors can be introduced in a live-action scenario due to actor breaks and other pauses between shooting. This can be likened to bugs in a cinematic cutscene where noticeable issues occur between different shots, such as teleportation of characters to different locations inadvertently causing lighting and physics pops.
3. *Cutting*: The editing of different shots such that they flow naturally with no jarring issues that might lead to viewer confusion. Games feature the additional challenge of moving in and out of gameplay cameras, sometimes bookending cutscenes with jarring transitions that can be avoided with careful consideration.
4. *Close-Ups*: Intimate shots highlight details rather than an entire scene, enabling subtlety in a manner that standard gameplay cameras struggle with. Focusing in on our game characters' faces enables the display of emotion and internal thought—more powerful storytelling devices than exposition alone.
5. *Composition*: The framing of visual elements only further supports storytelling. Subject positioning, lighting, and other elements become vital storytelling elements in the frame. Only possible when cameras and all moving elements are authored, artfully composing shots only aids the presentation of gameplay information and goals to the player.

Cutscene Dos & Don'ts

The more that can be learned about cinematography, the more tools animators will have at their disposal when tasked with telling a story in as efficient a manner as possible. There are so many possible camera choices for every situation that a larger cinematic vocabulary will only aid the efficacy of imparting story or gameplay information to the player.

That unplayable cutscenes run opposed to the strengths of the interactive medium demands they last no longer than the minimum time required to impart their message before getting the player back into gameplay. Here are some tips to make cutscenes work for the story.

The 180 Rule

This defines that subjects should generally remain on a consistent left/right side of the screen regardless of cut. Breaking this rule is referred to as "crossing the line" and can most often be avoided by authoring all cameras on a single side of a two-person conversation or similar directional scene, always leaving subjects on a consistent screen side.

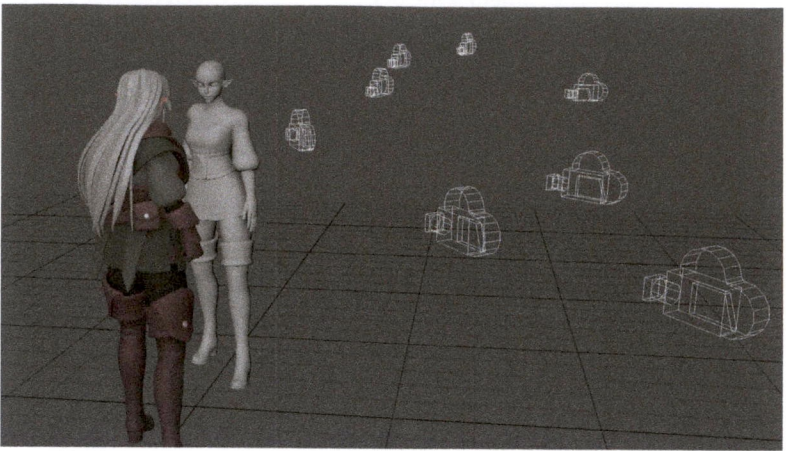

Cameras should be placed on one side to obey the 180 rule on basic setups.

Cut on an Action

This describes cutting, for example, mid-stand as a character stands up rather than after the standing action. This creates a better flow, as the action leads through to the next shot and gives the player's eyes something to follow. Importantly, ensure the composition is such that the action continues in roughly the same place on-screen in both shots straddling the cut to avoid the viewer having to re-find the action.

Straddle Cuts with Camera Motion

Cutting between two shots can be softened further by matching a slight camera motion tracking the subject at the end of the first and start of the second shot. For example, again with our midstanding cut, adding a slight upward motion to the end of the former shot, then beginning with this same upward tilt at the start of the latter shot as the camera comes to a rest in its new position will help lead the eye as the motion flows from one scene to the next.

Trigger Cutscenes on a Player Action

When entering cutscenes, especially from gameplay, triggering the cinematic when the player reaches an unmarked destination is far more jarring than cutting into the cinematic when the player triggers a gameplay action, such as a vault or door opening, with the action continuing after the cut at the cutscene's beginning. Funnel the player into such actions in collaboration with level design.

Avoid Player in Opening Shot

On the occasion we cannot guarantee the manner in which the player might enter a cutscene, do not start the first shot with the player in frame. Instead have them enter into it, perhaps beginning by looking at something/someone else as the character arrives in shot. A player running into a cutscene that immediately shows him or her walking or vice versa is an undesirable intro easily avoided by this technique.

Use Cuts to Teleport

While jarring cuts can disorient the player, smart use of them can be taken advantage of to cheat the player character to a new location in the world. Utilize cuts on actions where we cannot control the player's location in order to move him or her to the desired location post-cut.

End Cutscenes Facing the Next Goal

Finish cutscenes with cameras oriented toward the player's next goal whenever possible, giving him or her a helping hand as to where to go or what to do next. In the event your game does not support transitions out of cinematics, orient the player in gameplay afterward, ideally with the character ending the cutscene facing that direction.

Avoid Overlapping Game-Critical Information

The classic animation principle of staging aims to make an intention as clear as possible to viewer. This is really where animators must use every trick at their disposal to ensure players get the information they need to know from every scene, shot, and action within them with no excess baggage or confusion. A good rule to remember when developing a scene is to use separate beats to allow each element the player sees time to breathe and be taken in by the viewer rather than overlapping them for expediency.

For example, in a car chase cutscene, if the player character's vehicle is to swerve to avoid crashing *and* the player needs to be shown the car up ahead he or she is chasing, ensure it's not the swerving that reveals the target but instead that they happen sequentially: swerve first, then reveal the goal. This reduces the likelihood of the player missing the goal behind the dynamic action happening during the swerve. Missing key information can be disastrous when it leaves the player unsure what to do next when he or she returns to gameplay.

Acting vs Exposition

The actions and expressions of your characters can say much more than their words, and often a simple nod when animated convincingly will express as much as several lines of dialogue. Over-writing has been a failing of many a video game story, though to be fair, until the last few generations, video game writers could not rely on the nuanced acting players now enjoy. Film's mantra has long been "show, don't tell" for this purpose.

Nowadays there is no excuse for game writing to represent anything other than natural dialogue between real people when we use physical and facial acting to convey the true intention of characters. The degree of subtlety available to the animator will depend on the fidelity of the character and the emotions he or she can express, as well as the closeness of the camera to displaying the acting.

A standard over-the-shoulder shot during Mass Effect's conversations. (Courtesy of Electronic Arts.)

Allow Interaction Whenever Possible

A particularly egregious mistake in video game cutscenes is when the player's avatar performs an action that the player can do in gameplay. When this occurs, players instead wish they were the one to pull off the exciting move or trigger the event that drives the story forward. Whenever this occurs in your project's story, ask why at least this element can't be done by the player in gameplay before returning to the cutscene as necessary. Where film's mantra is "show, don't tell", games are instead "do, don't show".

Avoid Full-Shot Ease-Ins/Outs

A sin among game camera moves is the single-shot camera pan with ease-in and -outs on either end. This is particularly jarring because the player can sense in advance when the shot will cut. A live-action shot would be clipped on either end as part of the editing process and would therefore already be in motion at the start and likely not have come fully to a rest at the end.

To recreate this more natural look, ensure your panning shots have a slight movement from the beginning by adjusting the tangent of the initial camera frame of the shot and the same for the ending, if required. Like all in this list, this is not a hard rule, and often the camera move reaches the final position long before the end of the shot, but if so, ensure that the camera does not come to a complete stop and instead let it breathe (move) a little, lest it create dead pixels on-screen as they noticeably stop moving.

Track Subjects Naturally

When tracking a subject moving in frame, take care not to lead the action with the camera. Always imagine the cameraperson responding to the subject's movements as an observer might and not the other way around. In the case of a character jumping, the character would initiate the jump, then the camera would move to follow and reframe a few frames afterward, causing the jumper to get closer to the top of the screen, perhaps even leaving it slightly, and the camera only catching up and coming to rest some time after the character has landed again. The degree of following depends on the predictability of the motion, so a character walking from left to right can display more camera leading, as the subject motion is linear.

A more dramatic example would be the fast fly-by, where a fast-moving object such as a spaceship approaches and passes the camera before receding into the distance. While the camera can attempt to track the spaceship and even lose it briefly as it passes by, sometimes a camera cut in such an extreme motion will work even better.

Consider Action Pacing

Something for the game animator always to be aware of is the pacing of the cutscene in relation to the gameplay action before and after. For example, a cutscene inserted in a high-energy moment in the middle of a boss battle will appear jarring and kill the sequence's momentum if shots linger too long on any element. As such, maintain the consistency of rapidity of camera motions and frequency of cuts that match the intensity of not just the visuals on screen but also the gameplay bookending the cutscene.

Place Save Points after Cutscenes

More a technical concern on the design side but something an animator should be aware of nonetheless—the player should never watch a cutscene twice. Some don't even watch once! As such, cutscenes should never be placed right after a save point, especially if it is right before a notoriously hard section such as a boss fight where player death results in restarting and rewatching the boss intro cutscene.

Whenever possible, automatic save points should occur after cutscenes, provided they don't drop the player into a hazardous situation. In the event this is unavoidable, the cutscene should either be shortened as much as possible or split such that only the ending plays on repeated playing to offer a lead-in to gameplay.

Planning Cutscenes

Due to their complexity, cutscenes require a degree more planning than most other elements of game animation, ensuring rework and changes are minimized after any time is sunk into their creation due to their cost-prohibitive nature.

Cutscene Storyboarding

Because of their linear nature, it is tempting to borrow the traditional method of storyboarding cutscenes as one would a film or animated feature. This is worthwhile early in a game's development before any asset has been created, so it can give an idea of the scope of the first scenes to be created with no requirements beyond pen and paper.

While still useful for fully keyframe cinematics, storyboards can however become obsolete more quickly than they can be maintained and updated when motion-capture comes into play. Cinematics change and develop organically at the mocap stage as writing, directing, and performance-captured acting all play a part in shaping the final performance, so any rigid direction dictated by a storyboard becomes more a hindrance than a help, not to mention final camera shots are often best implemented only after the performance has been acquired.

> The recommended name prefix for cutscene assets begins numerically with *010_*, *020_*, *030_*, and so on to list them in order (as some of the few game animation files that can be ordered) while leaving room for additional scenes inserted via intermediary numbered prefixes like 025_.

Cutscene Previsualization

Instead of rigid storyboards, previz in a rough 3D layout is often faster and, importantly, easier to update and maintain, not to mention the scene will already exist in some form to be immediately implemented in game in a rough state, allowing story sections of a game to flow and give an early sense of pacing.

Like gameplay previz, cinematic previz helps answer questions ahead of cutscene creation or mocap shoots and allows the camera to scout the 3D location of the scene (if already created), looking for the best shots and points of interest. This all helps the actors or animators create the scene in visualizing the performance ahead of time.

No more than camera positions and moving T-posed characters are required for loose composition, all with the understanding that on the shoot day, actors are still free to come up with the best performance and the previz cameras, layout, and editing are simply adjusted to accommodate. Performance is key, so actors should be constrained as little as possible.

Fallout 3 concept boards by Adam Adamowicz. (Fallout® 3, copyright 2008 Bethesda Softworks LLC, a ZeniMax Media company. All Rights Reserved.)

Cutscene Workload

The standard way to calculate the amount of animation work required to create a cutscene is scene length measured in seconds, with that number divided by how many seconds the animator/team is expected to produce in a week. This number will vary depending on animator output, driven by not just skill but tools and workflow, but most variably by the scene complexity. Complexity is affected most by how many characters it features (two characters naturally take around twice the time as one), but also the nature of the shot (character actions and interactions, facial performance, prop manipulation, or distance to camera).

> Be aware that real-time cutscenes (as opposed to pre-rendered), require additional maintenance and so require buffered scheduling toward the end even after completion to ensure they don't acquire bugs as part of shipping the game. This is not the case for prerendered cutscenes that must be finished some time toward the project end before rendering/recording and going to postprocess, existing in the game only as video data.

Scene Prioritization

While workload can be calculated granularly, cutscenes should generally be grouped into types based on tiered quality, such as gold, silver, and bronze, with the most time and attention being spent on gold scenes, less on silver, and even less on bronze. This ensures that the most effort is spent polishing cinematics that are essential to the experience and less is spent on scenes that are tertiary or can be avoided altogether by the player.

###	Scene	Length (s)	Characters	Complexity	Polish
000	Cutscene_Intro	240	5	High	Gold
010	Cutscene_Story	180	2	High	Gold
020	Cutscene_Sidequest	25	2	Low	Bronze
030	Cutscene_Story	150	3	Medium	Silver
040	Cutscene_Sidequest	30	2	Medium	Bronze
050	Cutscene_Story	130	4	High	Gold
060	Cutscene_Story	165	2	Medium	Silver
070	Cutscene_Sidequest	45	3	Medium	Bronze
080	Cutscene_Story	100	2	Medium	Silver
090	Cutscene_Story	135	3	High	Gold
100	Cutscene_Ending	220	4	High	Gold

Scenes will take different priority depending on a variety of factors.

This approach to game animation in general allows for more sensible scheduling so equal effort is not spent on non-critical-path elements (aspects of the game that are less important or optional to the player) in order to focus on what is front and center and important to the overall game experience.

Cutscene Creation Stages

Cutscenes, while still prone to nonlinear editing and changes as with other areas of game development, are still the most linear element of game creation. As such, they can be scheduled with hard deadlines (or gates) that mark each step of the cutscene's finalization. While every studio is different depending on team structure and budget, a fairly standardized approach to locking down a cutscene is as follows:

- *Previz*: The initial exploratory and planning phase shows character placement and movement through the scene with appropriate camera angles. Can be entered into the game for continuity purposes.
- *Mocap/animation pass*: Shot mocap replaces previz animation, or keyframe animation is blocked in and the overall scene is adjusted and retimed. Camera is re-edited to match the mocap. A pass on eyelines illustrates who is looking at whom/what in the scene.
- *Polish*: Facial mocap or keyframe is taken to "final". Contact points between characters and the environment and each other are finalized now that character models should be complete.
- *Post*: Primarily bug-fixing/maintenance on the animators' part. Once timing is locked, it allows audio, visual effects (VFX), and lighting to begin working.

As with all areas of game development, there is still expected overlap between these distinct phases. For example, animation can be timing-locked at any point during polish so other disciplines can work simultaneously. Importantly, they should be convened to give input and perhaps early rough passes of lighting and VFX earlier in the process to aid the animator in providing opportunities for raising the scene's final quality.

The Eyes Have It

With cinematic cutscene cameras drawing us close in to the game's characters comes the opportunity to imbue an extra layer of life and character with facial acting. Just a few console generations ago, cutscenes aiming to give this level of detail to characters' performances needed to prerender higher-quality characters offline (playing the cutscenes back as movies).

Detroit: Become Human recorded facial performances on a massive scale to give the player choice as to how the story plays out. (Courtesy of Sony Interactive Entertainment.)

Nowadays, in-game and cinematic characters can be one and the same so as to only require the creation and maintenance of one character asset, with the biggest difference in the visual quality of cinematics falling solely in the fidelity of cinematic lighting.

Contrary to popular belief, the single most important aspect to get right in facial animation is not lip-sync, because while still important, players will focus primarily on the life or lack thereof in a character's eyes during close-ups—making them essential to place as a top priority.

Eyelines

In a cinematic shot, especially when more than one character in a conversation is visible on screen, it is essential for the eyes to be looking where the viewer would expect them to be in order to make the connection between characters. Failing to do so will leave characters gazing off into space or even confuse the player as to who is looking at what, especially when cutting between multiple subjects.

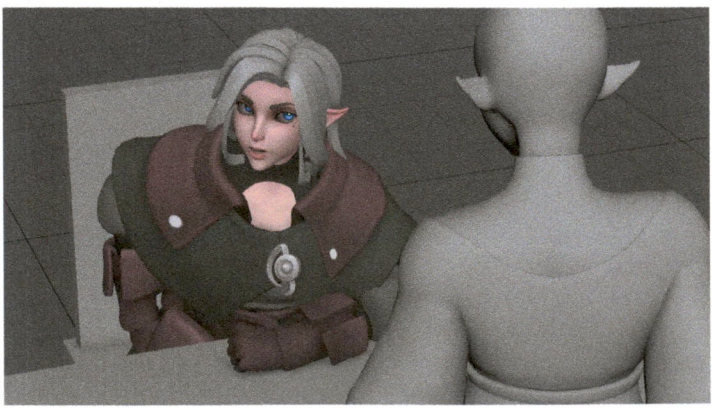

Eyelines are essential to show characters looking at one another.

As with the 180 rule, characters looking to screen-left should cut to a responding character looking to screen-right, even if their head position doesn't necessarily match. The same goes for eyes looking up or down in shot.

> Due to the high polygon density around game characters' eyes, eyelines can be adversely affected by lighting in this incredibly detailed area such that eyes that appear correct in the DCC may appear to look at a different angle when lighting is applied in engine due to shadows. As with all game animation, be sure to check the final result in the game before signoff.

IK vs FK Eyes

The surest way to make a character's face appear dead and lifeless is to not animate the eyes at all. The next surest way is to animate the eyes in FK, counteranimating against the head's movements in order to have them maintain a direction. Known as the "vestibulo-ocular reflex," real eyes automatically rotate in relation to the head in order to stabilize their view.

Glazed eyes in FK vs focused eyes in IK.

If, even if for a fraction of a second, your animated eyes "swim" inside the head, they will lose focus and appear lifeless. Constantly moving in and out of phase is incredibly distracting for the player when the eyes should be the centerpiece of a beautifully composed shot, not to mention counteranimating against the head means much more work for the animator, especially if the head animation is still being worked on.

To make things easier, using an IK aim target (or world vs local rotation) look-at solution is the absolute best way to go, not only because the eyes need only be animated (at least as a first pass) when they change focus to look at something else, but because it allows polish and iteration of the underlying body animation without having to constantly rework the eye direction. In order to keep the eyes "alive" regardless of the method you use, you must always consider saccades.

Saccades

Saccades, the jerky rotation of eyes to acquire new targets, impressively rotate at 900 degrees per second for humans, which means there's absolutely no excuse for short saccades taking any more than a frame or two depending on style. Even a character simply looking forward at someone he or she is talking with displays saccades as his or her gaze moves from eye to eye, to the hairline and mouth of the person he or she is talking with.

When the eyes are turning over a large angle to look in an entirely different direction, in real life, the eyes involuntarily do so in steps as they always lock onto something. While this is the most realistic way to animate eyes, it's not always necessary when animating such large movements; just ensure the eyes take no more than 2–3 frames to reach their destination (often the left/right limit as the head turns slower), lest they appear lazy and tired.

Jumping a large angle will often be accompanied by a blink, not to avoid having to animate saccades but to punctuate a change in thought as the character acquires a new subject in his or her vision. Just make sure not to do it on every single large turn so as not to appear formulaic and unnatural.

Eye Vergence

Convergence, when the eyes draw in together as the subject of their focus is closer, is an essential element to include when animating eyelines, especially when the character is looking anywhere other than far off in the distance (in which case the eyes diverge to look straight ahead—the default in a character's T-pose).

Eyes converge as objects looked at become closer.

A simple way to always account for this is not only to use an IK look-at to animate the eyes, but also to have both eyes focus on the same point in space rather than on a point each, which good facial animation rigs also support. This means that moving the look-at target to the correct distance away will automatically provide the correct convergence and ensure your character appears to be focusing at the correct distance. Not doing so will contribute to the 1000-yard stare sometimes seen on game characters even when eyes are animated.

Do not be afraid to converge the eyes greatly when characters are focusing on something really close, as that's exactly what happens in real life, though when animating to a cinematic camera, it may be necessary to make minor adjustments to increase or decrease on top if need be.

"Pseudo" (*Pseudostrabismus*) is the false appearance of cross-eyes, mostly in infants, due to the space between their eyes growing temporarily out of proportion—something often occurring in 3D characters when the eyeballs are incorrectly placed in the head. This is something that absolutely must be ironed out with the character team when rigging the face in order to avoid having to compensate with animation throughout the project.

Thought Directions

It's important that the eyes reflect the inner thoughts of the character you're animating, especially during dialogue. Even with slight saccades, a character talking while constantly looking forward is not only uninteresting but unnatural.

Animate eyes looking away at times from the character their owner is conversing with to highlight changes in thought or pauses between speaking for punctuation. Looking up and to the side might support a character remembering something or searching for an answer, shifting the gaze left and right can illustrate nervousness, and eyes downward will help convey sadness or shyness.

The eyes should be the most interesting thing on screen during close-ups, and every time they change their gaze, it only aids this. After eyes, though, the next most important element during dialogue facial animation is the mouth.

Lip-Sync

Lip-sync is easily one of the hardest elements of facial animation to get right, not least because it's one of the hardest character elements to rig correctly. Just understand that when it does work, it should go unnoticed, with the player's attention ideally instead drawn to the eyes.

Phonemes

In its most basic application, dialogue animation is determined by a series of preset shapes named "phonemes" that when grouped together cover every noise required to produce dialogue. For example, the same shape that produces the "A" sound also does so for "I." The complete series of pose groups are:

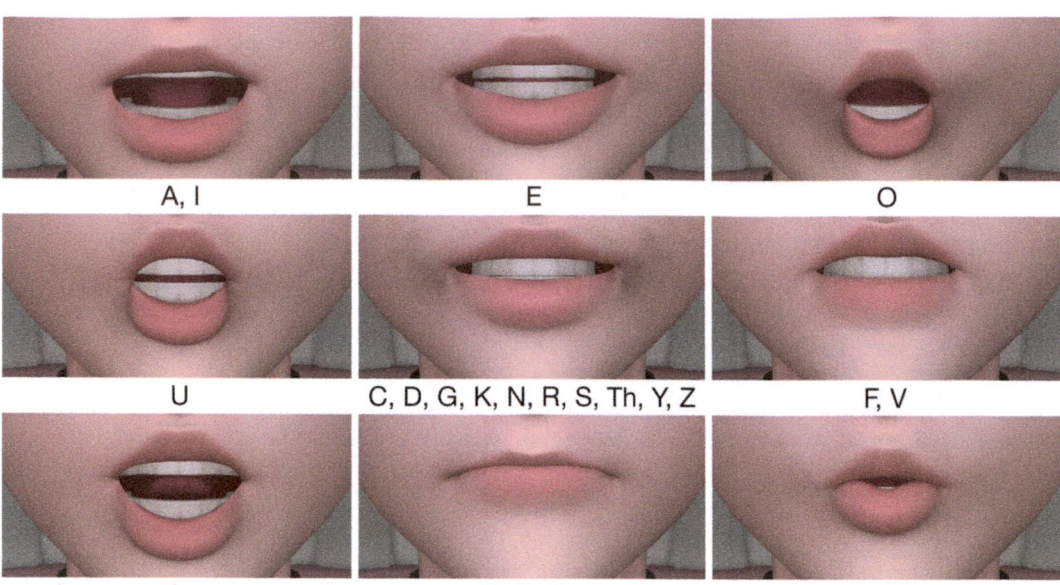

The basic phoneme mouth shapes.

Shape Transitions

It's not as simple as lining up these shapes with their timing in the dialogue (although that is a great first start to ensure correct timing). The mark of a good lip-sync animation is how it transitions between the shapes, as well as which shapes may not hit 100% or be skipped over entirely so as to avoid rapid lip-flapping during fast speech or complex words.

Ultimately, the best aid to achieve natural lip-sync is a low-tech solution. A shaving mirror on your desk will allow you to rehearse and reference over and over again as you work through the sequence of lip shapes. Just be sure to talk as naturally or as exaggeratedly as your animation style requires. Unlike most animation, it's best to err on the side of caution when moving the mouth so as to not animate overt lip-flapping.

Facial Action Coding System

When keyframing lip-sync, the standard working method is the animator has access to poses easily accessible (in a library or accessible via DCC slider controls) and begins by pasting them in time to match the dialogue audio.

Importantly however, unless the project does not require it due to simplicity or budget, the preset poses should not only be those listed above. Instead, those poses should be created from more granular shapes determined by smaller muscle movements that when combined can reproduce phoneme shapes. In addition, controls are required for every other fine detail required to bring a face to life, such as subtle skin movement around the eyes, nose, forehead, cheeks, and neck, as well as the mouth and jaw.

The highest-resolution characters in games often feature hundreds of individual shapes, driven by sliders rather than posed manually, that are derived from the facial action coding system (FACS). The FACS comprises microexpressions forming the large variety of muscle movements possible in the face, originally categorized by Paul Ekman and Wallace Friesen in the late 1970s. The granularity required, and therefore the number of shapes, will be different for each project depending on fidelity and importance of facial animation.

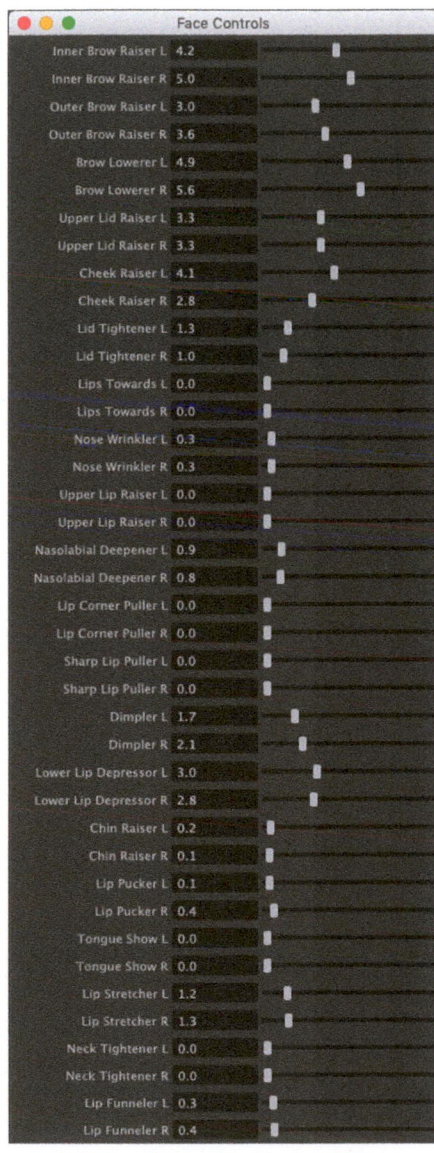

DCC sliders driving the many FACS poses.

Sharing Facial Animation

Unlike standardized body skeletons, it's likely that different characters in your game will have unique faces, which typically means the one-size-fits-all approach, while perhaps still sharing bone counts and names, will not be available for faces. As such, to create animations that work on multiple characters with different faces, the facial animation must be exported as a series of values corresponding to each character variation's unique poses.

Exporting simple values between 0 and 1 not only allows this animation to save memory (when each pose would otherwise require the position and rotation for each bone in the pose), but allows the simple binary value to play on characters that are set up with entirely different facial rigs, bone counts, and pose shapes entirely. For example, an eyebrow-raise pose on a dragon could also play on a mouse despite the disparities in visuals. As such, an animation comprising poses that match in name if not visuals will play across multiple character types.

Sharing facial animation across characters in Fortnite. (Copyright 2018 Epic Games, Inc.)

Creating Quantities of Facial Animation

With facial animation being the most difficult and time consuming kind of animation to create from scratch, games that are dialogue-heavy such as RPGs or any lengthy story-based adventure often require a solution to help animators save time.

Thankfully, there are several software solutions available to generate lip-sync procedurally from a combination of audio files and text input, creating a low-quality solution when quantity is desired over quality. The resulting animation can also be a great base for animators to then work on top of for the most important scenes.

Video-based facial capture is now becoming affordable enough for even the tightest game development budget, with software combined with simple hardware like webcams or cell phones producing decent enough results for a first pass (or facial far from the camera) while again providing a better-than-nothing place for the animators to start.

Troubleshooting Lip-Sync

We know when it's wrong, but it's often hard to find the exact reason why something is "off" with lip-sync. Try these simple troubleshooting items for the most common lip-sync issues to quickly eliminate these common causes.

- *Timing*: The most common issue with lip-sync not looking right is the timing being off. Try grabbing the keyframes around the area in question and shifting them forward or backward. Be sure to playblast/render a video each adjustment to ensure low frame rates in the DCC are not affecting your judgment. When editing performance-captured facial mocap, sometimes the whole animation is simply out of sync and must be adjusted.
- *Mouth Shapes*: Sometimes one or more shapes just aren't hitting enough to be seen, or are wrong entirely. If the shape is not noticeable enough, try holding it for a frame or two longer if timing allows, then adjust from there.
- *Lip-flapping*: Often the mouth movement is just too noticeable because you are posing out every shape to match the audio. As always, check yourself reading the whole line in the mirror to see if each shape needs to be seen or can be skipped over (or passed through more quickly) when talking just gets too fast.
- *Transitions*: The mouth doesn't simply move from pose to pose, but transitions through intermediary shapes to hit poses, especially when enunciating clearly or speaking slowly. In fact, many phonetic "shapes" require multiple poses, such as the "B" sound, with the mouth starting closed then opening to release the sound. Again, check your mirror or video reference to find when the lips purse, open, or close between phonemes for best results.

Interview: Marie Celaya
Facial Animation Supervisor—Detroit: Become Human

(Courtesy of Sony Interactive Entertainment.)

Can you please explain the process of producing facial animation on Detroit: Become Human and your role on the project?

Facial animation at Quantic Dream is a highly particular process, as our ambition is to truly recreate our actors' appearance and performance, exactly as it occurred on set. We are storytellers first and foremost and our aim is to immerse the player and draw them fully "into" the experience. We animators have a saying here—"The best animation is the one you don't notice." Animations must be credible, believable, and so elegant as to fully render the real thing.

Detroit is a production-heavy title with its branching storyline necessitating vast numbers of facial performances. Did you arrive at any formulas that you would apply to all performances as a starting pass in order to quickly raise the quality of the performance capture before improving further?

We make use of a specialized tool that identifies a gallery of key poses and expressions. Having identified such an expression (by registering an offset of markers between a neutral and smiling lip/eye differential), the refinements I made to the actor's initial FACS recordings are automatically applied. This smooths out any anomalies in data capture and provides a first phase of refinement before I finalize the details by hand. This saves us a considerable amount of time, though there is an art to having the tool identify the right expressions and apply the right weight of correction.

What is your attitude toward technology vs art in your approach to facial performance? How much should studios be focusing on pipelines that capture high-quality facial performance vs one that instead frees up time for animators to polish more once they receive the motion capture?

Art and technology are the mother and father of our work. Given the volume of data we handle, small improvements in efficiency scale up to enormous effect. That's why we've perfected the data capture process as much as possible, minimizing the time needed to refine by making improvements at the head of the work stream. Some refinement is and always will be necessary, but that's the price you pay if you want true verisimilitude.

The studio understands and reflects this focus on technology as a means of freeing up animators' time. But the company also understands that no tool will ever be totally perfect; even the cleanest possible data will require an artistic touch that must be human because it is truly a subjective enhancement. We often add REM (rapid eye movements entailing tiny darts of look or attention) or other microexpressions that are essential to make a performance feel real, even if most people wouldn't consciously notice them. Whether to add such expressions and how many is a question of camera angle and proximity, et cetera, but we are always looking for ways to make such humanizing enhancements.

Some of the best performances have no words spoken. What do you find most helps sell a character's internal thought process when a performance features no dialogue?

The eyes are the key. Truly miniscule details can make the difference between a disconcerting performance and an entirely absorbing one. I mentioned that we add darting eyes: other examples include half-blinks, flickers of attention, the direction of a look, the length and frequency of blinking, even whether and when a character's gaze moves to an interlocutor or not. All contribute to an expression of realness and emotional depth. Most players are not conscious of these miniscule details, but the presence and quality of such details is what separates a moving performance from a distracting or uncanny one.

What in your experience is the single most important element to focus on when polishing a captured facial performance or animating one from scratch, and where might others misplace this effort?

It is essential that characters look at each other during dialogues. Not all the time and not continuously (at least, not in all cases) but when and where the performance dictates it. Again, this is partly a subjective finesse, which is where the artistic consideration comes fully into play.

Eyes carry the weight of a performance. They are the window to the soul and actors use them to indicate the interior life of a character. Darting looks are critical not only for realism but to convey emotional depth. As with any animation, they must render the performance faithfully and be created efficiently.

For realism, "less is more." Adding too many emotive details and quirks will result in something cartoony. By the same token, an almost-faithful rendition of a performance will drop you into the "uncanny valley," which is why an excellent rig is required for treating performance data. This is where I must provide controllers and constraints to the animators and personally review every detail.

Consistency in animation approach is a huge plus. Wherever possible, I used the same animator for a character's repertoire of scenes. Production constraints meant this wasn't always the most effective way of working, but wherever a particular animator had a certain passion for Kara, Connor, or Markus

I would assign them the character's signature shots. This meant their work was a labor of love but also that they intuitively understood the refinements needed for the best results.

Everybody must be given a chance to shine. I take the view that every animator has the potential to contribute something truly artistic and meaningful to the project. That means whether they are a senior, a junior, long-serving or a newcomer, everybody must have a high-value sequence (e.g., a close-up dialogue) as an opportunity to show what they can bring to the table. This is the best thing for the individual, for team cohesion, and for the project as a whole.

CHAPTER 11

Our Project: Motion Capture

Arguably, the single largest innovation in game animation in the last few decades has been the widespread adoption of motion-capture (mocap for short)—the process of capturing motion from live actors.

Gameplay mocap actors must often be very physical. (Courtesy of Jay Britton & Audiomotion.)

Much was said about mocap in the early days along the lines of "It's cheating," "It's not real animation," and "It'll replace animators and we'll lose our jobs," but one must only look a decade earlier to see the same fears vocalized by animators regarding the shift from 2D traditional animation to 3D computer animation. The idea then that a computer character could have the same life as a series of artfully hand-drawn images was incomprehensible to many at the time, but later proved possible when handled by talented animators, and the same is true now of mocap.

The simple fact is that as video games have matured and their subject matter moves from simple cartoonlike characters and actions to more realistic renderings of human characters and worlds, the old approach of keyframing humans simply wasn't cutting it visually, not to mention the sheer volume of animation required for a fluidly moving character with all its cycles, blends, and transitions would simply be impossible to create any other way.

That's not to say that mocap can't be a crutch, and when wielded incorrectly, the results are far from satisfying. There are some in production still who incorrectly believe that we shoot mocap then implement in the game and the job is done. A search for a "silver-bullet," one-stop solution to capturing the subtleties of acting is ongoing, though this technology is merely yet another tool for animators to wield in their quest to bring characters to life. Mocap is but another method to get you where you want more quickly, and the real magic comes when a talented animator reworks and improves the movement afterward.

Do You Even Need Mocap?

For our hypothetical project, long before getting into the nitty-gritty of motion-capture production, a very important question to be asked should be whether to even use motion-capture or stick with a traditional keyframing approach. Here are some considerations to help answer this question.

1. *What is the visual style of the game?* A more realistic style benefits greatly from mocap, whereas mocap on highly stylized characters can look incorrect. Cartoony and exaggerated motion will help sell characters that are otherwise lacking in detail and visual fidelity, including those seen from afar. Mocap makes it easier to achieve realistic character motion.
2. *Are our characters even humanoid?* While some games have been known to mocap animals, the approach is typically used only for humans. If our main characters are nonhuman creatures or nonanthropomorphic objects, then mocap often isn't even an option.
3. *What kinds of motions will feature most in the game?* If the characters are performing semirealistic motions such as running, jumping, climbing, and so on, then mocap will suit, whereas if every move is expected to be outlandish or something that no human could perform, then keyframing might suit better. The balance of these actions should determine the project's adoption of mocap.
4. *What is the scope of the game?* Mocap gives the best value for the money when used on large projects with lots of motion, at which point the production cost of setting up a mocap shoot and the required pipeline is offset against the speed at which large quantities of character motion can be created. That said, cheaper yet lower-quality solutions are also becoming more readily accessible for smaller projects.
5. *Would the budget even cover it?* While affording an unparalleled level of realism, motion-capture shoots can be expensive. When compared to the cost of hiring additional animators to achieve the same quantity of motions via keyframe (depending on volume), the cost sometimes becomes more comparable, however.
6. *What is the experience of the team?* An animation team built over the years to create stylized cartoony games may take issue with having to relearn their craft, and attempts to adopt mocap may meet resistance. That said, motion capture does become a great way to maintain a consistent style and standard across animators.

How Mocap Works

While not absolutely necessary for great results, an understanding of the mocap process will only aid the game animator in finding ways to speed up the pipeline and get motion capture in the game faster and to a higher quality in as little time as possible.

Different Mocap Methods

Optical Marker–Based

While there are several alternative motion-capture methods, the traditional and most commonly used is via the triangulation of optical markers on a performer's suit, captured by arrays of cameras arranged around a stage so that they create a "volume" within which the performance can be recorded. This provides the highest quality of motion-capture but is also the most expensive.

Optical camera-based mocap is the standard for AAA development.

These arrays of cameras can number anywhere between 4 to upward of 36, and highly reflective markers are tracked at higher frame rates than required by the game project (typically 120 frames per second). As long as no fewer than three cameras can simultaneously follow a marker, the software simulation model will not lose or confuse the markers for one another. When this does happen, the cleanup team (usually provided by the stage) will manually sort them again.

Accelerometer Suits

The performer dons a suit with accelerometers attached, which, when combined with a simulated model of human physics and behavior, provide data without the need for a volume of cameras. However, unless the animation team is prepared to work longer with the data, the results are far from the professional quality provided by marker capture. Accelerometer mocap is therefore useful for lower-budget projects or previz before real captures for larger ones.

Depth Cameras

A third and experimental approach is to use depth-sensing cameras with no markers, applying body motion only to a physical model. This provides the cheapest option of all, and has created interesting results for art installations that deal with more abstract representations of the body. Depth cameras may provide some decent reference-gathering and previz but are ultimately less than ideal for an actual videogame project due to the amount of work still required to make it visually appealing post-shoot. That said, the quality of all options is increasing at an encouraging rate.

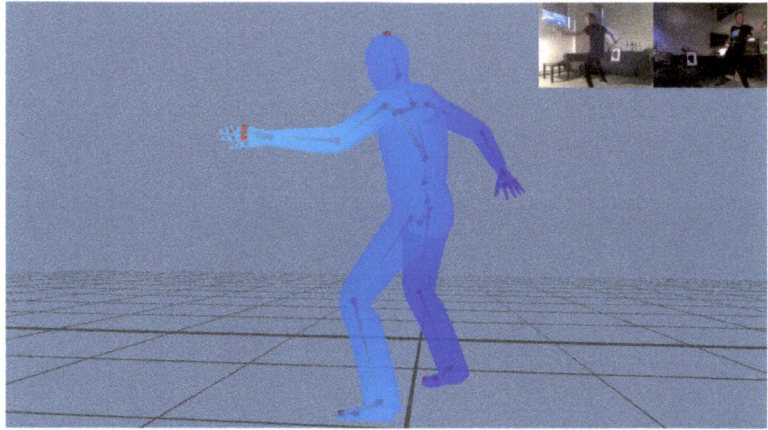

Microsoft's Kinect has made basic mocap available to the masses.
(Courtesy of Richard Boylan.)

Performance Capture

Perhaps the biggest breakthrough in increasing acting quality in recent years has been the introduction of performance capture. While motion capture refers to the recording of only the body, performance capture records the body, face, and voice all at once by using head-mounted cameras (HMCs) and microphones. Doing so adds a level of continuity in subtle facial acting that was simply impossible in the previous method of recording everything separately and recombining in a DCC.

Real-time face capture in Unreal Engine 4 via head-mounted camera.
(Copyright 2018 Epic Games, Inc.)

While this method has become ubiquitous with cinematic cutscene shoots and head-cams are becoming more affordable, care must be taken to ensure all three tracks (body, face, and audio) remain in sync. As such, the mocap stage will generally provide time codes for each take, which must be maintained during the assembly and editing phase.

While it used to be a requirement for real and virtual actors' faces to match as much as possible in order to best retarget the motion to the facial muscle structure, current methods employ retargeting to digital doubles first, then translate to the desired face of your chosen video game protagonist, though the extra step naturally makes this process more costly at the benefit of freeing you up to cast the best actors regardless of how they look.

Due to the extra overhead of camera setup and calibration, cinematic shoots typically go much slower than the often rapid-fire process of in-game shoots, not to mention the reliance on scripts and rehearsals and multiple takes to get the action just right. While rehearsals can certainly benefit in-game shoots (most notably when requiring choreography such as during combat), they are less of an absolute necessity as is the case with cinematic cutscenes. The secret to successful cinematics isn't a technology question, but ensuring the performance (and writing) are as good as possible. There's only so much an animator can polish a flatly delivered line of awkward dialogue from a wrongly cast actor.

For the remainder of this chapter, we'll be focusing on the first approach, (optical marker-based), as this is the most commonly used method at video game studios and therefore the most likely one an animator will consistently encounter in his or her career.

The Typical Mocap Pipeline

The typical workflow for optical marker–based mocap involves:

1. The actor arrives and, once suited up, is calibrated into the system matching his or her height and size (and therefore unique marker positions) with a character in the capture software.
2. The actor is directed on a stage to capture the desired motion. Either then, or later via a viewing software, the director decides upon which takes (and sometimes frame ranges) he or she wishes to purchase from the stage. See the "Directing Actors" section later in this chapter for some best practices when directing actors.
3. The stage crew then clean up the motion by fixing lost markers and smoothing out extraneous jerky motion due to marker loss or interference. This process can take anywhere from a few hours to a few weeks. The cleaned-up motion is delivered to the game studio as "takes."
4. A technical animator at the game studio retargets the delivered data onto their in-game character, checking the quality of the delivered mocap and requesting redeliveries if the quality is off.

5. The animators then begin working on the mocap that is now driving their game characters. This usually consists of a mocap rig and control rig both driving the export skeleton, allowing the animator to trace motion back and forth and work in a nondestructive manner, adding exaggeration and appeal without destroying the underlying motion that has been bought and paid for. For details on this stage, the most involving step for the animator, see the section "Working with Mocap" at the end of this chapter.

Mocap Retargeting

Because actors rarely match the dimensions of the video game characters they are portraying, the studio must incorporate retargeting of the motion from the delivered actor-sized motion to the game character. There are a variety of settings to get the best possible translation between characters without issues that are difficult to fix at a later stage.

This process is generally performed in MotionBuilder, and the single biggest potential issue to be wary of is the use of "reach" to match limbs' captured positions regardless of the difference between the source actor and game character.

Used generally for the feet to ensure they match the ground and prevent foot-sliding, reach can also be used for hands when it is essential they match the source position, such as when interacting with the environment like grabbing onto a ladder. However, leaving reach on for arms in general can be disastrous, as the hands will always match, causing the arms to bend or hyperextend unnaturally to maintain the source position.

At this stage the person tasked with retargeting should also keep an eye out for individual bad retargets or jerky motion where lost mocap markers weren't correctly cleanup up, systemic issues that plague every delivered motion such as bent clavicles or spines, or loss of fine detail due to smoothing applied as default to all motions by the mocap studio.

Mocap Shoot Planning

The absolute worst thing an animator can do is arrive at the stage on the day unprepared. Here are several essential practices that will ensure as smooth and productive a shoot as possible.

Shot-List

A shot list is invaluable both on the day of shooting and in the run-up to the shoot, as it's the single best way to evaluate everything you'll need to capture, so it helps plan out the shoot. While the mocap stage will often provide their own formatting as they require a copy before the shoot day for their own preparation purposes, you can make a start yourself within Excel or Google Docs. Any shot list should contain these following columns:

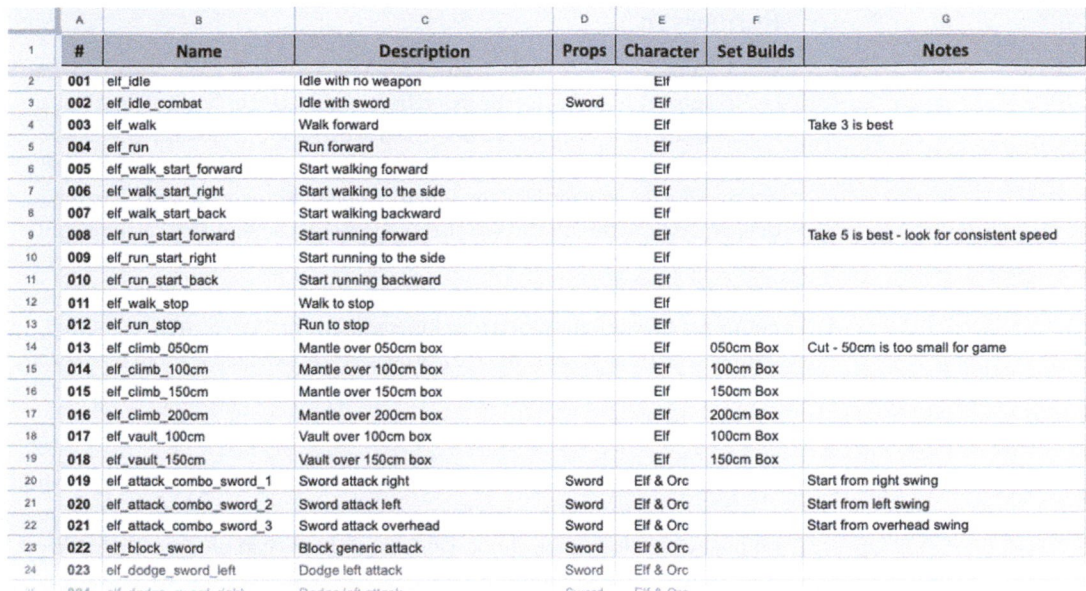

#	Name	Description	Props	Character	Set Builds	Notes
001	elf_idle	Idle with no weapon		Elf		
002	elf_idle_combat	Idle with sword	Sword	Elf		
003	elf_walk	Walk forward		Elf		Take 3 is best
004	elf_run	Run forward		Elf		
005	elf_walk_start_forward	Start walking forward		Elf		
006	elf_walk_start_right	Start walking to the side		Elf		
007	elf_walk_start_back	Start walking backward		Elf		
008	elf_run_start_forward	Start running forward		Elf		Take 5 is best - look for consistent speed
009	elf_run_start_right	Start running to the side		Elf		
010	elf_run_start_back	Start running backward		Elf		
011	elf_walk_stop	Walk to stop		Elf		
012	elf_run_stop	Run to stop		Elf		
013	elf_climb_050cm	Mantle over 050cm box		Elf	050cm Box	Cut - 50cm is too small for game
014	elf_climb_100cm	Mantle over 100cm box		Elf	100cm Box	
015	elf_climb_150cm	Mantle over 150cm box		Elf	150cm Box	
016	elf_climb_200cm	Mantle over 200cm box		Elf	200cm Box	
017	elf_vault_100cm	Vault over 100cm box		Elf	100cm Box	
018	elf_vault_150cm	Vault over 150cm box		Elf	150cm Box	
019	elf_attack_combo_sword_1	Sword attack right	Sword	Elf & Orc		Start from right swing
020	elf_attack_combo_sword_2	Sword attack left	Sword	Elf & Orc		Start from left swing
021	elf_attack_combo_sword_3	Sword attack overhead	Sword	Elf & Orc		Start from overhead swing
022	elf_block_sword	Block generic attack	Sword	Elf & Orc		
023	elf_dodge_sword_left	Dodge left attack	Sword	Elf & Orc		
024	elf_dodge_sword_right	Dodge left attack	Sword	Elf & Orc		

A typical shot list for planning a motion-capture shoot.

- *Number*: Helps to count the number of shots and therefore make a time estimate.
- *Name*: Shots should be named as per your file naming convention.
- *Description*: A brief explanation of the desired action lest you forget.
- *Props*: Which props will be required by the actors—even if not captured.
- *Character*: Essential for multicharacter shots for retargeting purposes.
- *Set builds*: Similar to props but rather walls, doors, and so on actors will be interacting with.
- *Notes*: Added on the day as required, describing directing notes such as preferred takes.

Ordering/Grouping Your Shots

There are a variety of factors that will determine the ordering of mocap shots, not least being the priority in which they're needed for the game schedule to ensure work isn't delayed should you fail to capture everything, which happens often. In addition, grouping multiple actions requiring the same set builds and props (especially if the props are captured) will ensure a good flow onstage.

Perhaps the largest time sink on any shoot day is the building of sets, so great consideration must be taken to try to capture everything required on one set build before it's dismantled. It is wise to avoid capturing high-energy actions at the end of the day (or even right after lunch), as the actors will naturally be more tired then. Conversely, start the day with something fun like fast and easy rapid-fire actions that will build momentum and set you up for a great day of shooting.

Rehearsals

The most proven way of having an efficient mocap shoot while obtaining the highest quality of acting is rehearsing beforehand. Not only is it a great way to build a relationship with the actors, it also allows them to go deeper into any performance. While not needed for many in-game actions that can be quickly done on the day, rehearsing is essential for cinematic or story shoots that require deeper characterization and will likely have closer cameras that can highlight detail, especially for full facial performance capture. Something as subtle as a thoughtful pause or a tilt of the head can make the world of difference to a performance when an actor is fully invested. Giving them time to know and understand the characters they're portraying is impossible without rehearsing.

Mocap Previz

Another excellent way to avoid costly wasted time on set (or afterward when you find the actions just won't fit the scene) is to previsualize the actions before even going to the shoot. This way, not only can progress be made on the various gameplay and story scenarios without having to wait for shoot day to roll around, you'll already have figured out many of the technical issues from within simple cost-effective scenes, such as how much of the set you'll actually need to build based on touch points.

Importantly, understand that the actors will likely improvise and suggest much better actions than your previz on the day of shooting, so it should be used as a guide and initial inspiration only, giving the director a better evaluation of what will and will not cause technical issues when new suggestions arise.

Previz of a mocap shoot reduces guess-work regarding staging and sets.

Working with Actors

While it can be physically exhausting to shoot mocap, sometimes over a series of days, working directly with actors can be one of the most rewarding aspects of video game animation as you work together to bring your characters and scenes to life. The improvisational collaboration, sometimes to an intimate level as you work together to create the perfect performance, can be a refreshing break from working at a computer screen.

Casting

Before starting shooting, the correct casting can make or break the quality of your game, especially in a narrative-heavy project. Unless the studio has an in-house mocap facility, game animators often travel for mocap, so booking nonlocal talent (actors) makes the logistics difficult. Requiring regular access affects any decision in casting local vs distant talent, often resulting in many game studios adopting a hybrid approach where performance actors are used only for cinematic shoots and voiceover, with the majority of gameplay actions being performed by other more easily available actors and stunt performers.

Watch_Dogs built their character to the exact measurements of the stuntman for better retargeting. (Copyright 2014 Ubisoft Entertainment. All Rights Reserved. Watch Dogs, Ubisoft, and the Ubisoft logo are registered or unregistered trademarks of Ubisoft Entertainment in the U.S. and/or other countries.)

While every cinematic game character will require different traits depending on the story, much more uniform are the requirements for in-game motions. As such, it is possible to break down the things you should be looking for when casting and auditioning (if the budget allows).

- *How well do they take direction?* A key interaction between the director and the actor is massaging the action toward the desired result. While it is as much down to the director to communicate effectively, if the actor requires too many takes to get it, doesn't listen, or gets easily distracted, then shoots will run much less efficiently than otherwise.

Like much of the team-oriented nature of game development, motion-capture is very much about human relationships, so a good rapport with the actor is essential.

- *How imaginative are they?* An actor is expected to bring much of the performance to the table themselves, only improving what the director had in mind. If their acting choices are always pedestrian and expected, then it may as well be the director in the mocap suit. Does the actor delight and surprise with how he or she reads the lines, attacks the monster, or climbs over the obstacle? Actors should ideally be making suggestions for alternate takes, even more so as they grow to know the project and roles they're playing.
- *How do they carry themselves?* Entirely a question of physicality. It's very difficult to change an actor's natural walk or keep up with mistakes if they tend to always favor the wrong foot forward when returning to idle. Do they walk heavily when the character is supposed to be light of foot? Are they able to retain the game character's idle pose without being reminded?
- *What are their measurements?* Height will affect retargeting of the motions, and weight comes across in every movement. While it is possible to replay motion from a 5-foot actor onto your 20-foot ogre, the closer you get to the required height and weight, the less time spent completely reworking the motion later. This is especially important when casting your lead character, as having them match their virtual character's size as much as possible will reduce retargeting issues and touch points throughout the project.
- *Do they have the required skills?* Martial arts, weapon-handling, or dancing cannot just be learned on the spot. If your character requires a specific skill, then you must ensure that the actor already has the required training. Similarly, if they are also to play non–martial arts trained characters, can they "unlearn" it enough to fight regularly?
- *How physically able are they?* If your game character is expected to be acrobatic and able to perform flips and somersaults, ensure that the actor is physically able to do that, at least at the beginning of the day before he or she is exhausted. If the character is supposed to be awkward and clumsy, can they recreate that kind of motion well?

Directing Actors

So the day has been set and the shot list has been delivered to the mocap studio, but how do you get the best performance on the day and ensure you get through as much of the shot list as required with minimal takes? One common mistake many animators make when first directing actors is to mold their movements as one might a 3D animation, literally describing the actions in anatomical terms such as raising arms higher, crouching lower, moving faster, and so on. That is, however, the surest way to capture unnatural, mechanical movements as the actor struggles to remember and incorporate these modifications in each successive take.

Direct by storytelling: Give as much for actors to work with as possible, such as who/when/where they currently are. Provide what just happened and where they're going next. After the initial explanation of what the shot involves, actions must be improved by using visuals that keep the actor in the fantasy that was created. If you set up a run cycle as the character being chased by a dog and want them to run faster, then tell them they're being gained on, or that it's a pack of wolves. If you need them to crouch lower when moving, tell them they're being shot at or ducking under a laser trip-wire. If a tired jog simply isn't tired enough, then suggest they're in the last mile of a marathon.

Using scenarios over simple verbs is essential for directing any creative mind because not only does it avoid simply doling out the aforementioned technical instructions, most importantly, it leaves ownership of the final result with the actors. They are providing a better performance by getting even more in character and you are getting the desired result in as natural a manner as possible. It's even better if you can ask the actor how he or she thinks the character would react. While as director you always have the final say, it works so much better when you come up with something out of a conversation rather than one-sided instruction. (This goes for any collaboration on the game team as well.)

Never criticize: One golden rule is that acting is a very personal art form and actors are putting themselves in a position of vulnerability to deliver you their performance. Never use negativity when describing why a take isn't what you want—instead, always move in a positive direction such as, "That was great. Let's do another take and incorporate this…," or ideally, "If the situation were to change, how would [your character] react?." Don't feel the need to always have all the answers immediately. Again, it is a collaboration and keeping the actor in a state of always giving and bringing more to the performance is the key to avoiding dry, unimaginative performances.

Single point of contact: Another sure-fire way to confuse an actor is to give multiple different directions. If you are discussing the take with another team member, make sure only one is giving the final decisions to the actor. It's okay not to know what you want initially, but direction must be clear when it's finally decided upon. Such discussions should take place away from the actor rather than becoming a three-way street, and usually involve one animator handling the performance while another ensures the technical or design considerations are catered to.

Props & Sets

Props are an essential part of any game mocap shoot, usually taking the form of weapons or other gameplay-related items. Importantly, props give actors some tangible "business" (something to play with in their hands or touch in the environment) to work with in cinematic story scenes and make the scene more natural.

A typical weapon prop armory required for games. (Courtesy of Audiomotion.)

Characters interacting with the sets they are in, such as leaning on tables or stepping up onto platforms, grounds the character in the video game environment much more than a performance taking place on an infinite flat plane. Sets require that communication and planning must take place between the animators, level artists, and level designers to ensure at least important elements of the background are relatively locked down and do not change after the shoot.

Prop Recording

Prop manipulation in cinematic scenes is an excellent way to give more visual interest to a scene and gives the actor something to play with, be it a cigarette to smoke, a keyboard to type on, or simply an inanimate object like a ball to pick up and handle while delivering lines. However, it does make an order of magnitude more work for the animators to deal with later, as contact points must be maintained and cleaned, proving especially difficult if the object is picked up and placed down repeatedly in the take or passed through the fingers.

Some of this difficulty can be alleviated by recording the motion of the prop in the same manner as we record the actor by marking it up and entering it into the system, and this will require the prop to be retargeted on delivery of the mocap. As such, care should be taken to measure props for digital recreation so as to ensure the best retargeting on delivery of the mocap.

On the flip-side, however, giving an animator essentially two actors to manipulate can make a scene overly complex depending on what is required. For example if the prop (such as a rifle) stays in the hands throughout, then its exact position and orientation are not required, or if it's not shown in a cinematic close-up shot, fidelity is less important. In cases like these, it can be easier simply not to capture the prop and just use the provided video reference to place it back in the actor's hands and keyframe it when it comes to be animated.

Let's look at the example of a pistol. If you are capturing a set of movements to create the pistol strafing system, you will likely rapidly record shots of the actor walking and running in various directions while holding a pistol. As the pistol is always held in the right hand and does not move much in each of these actions, it is easier not to record the pistol and simply attach it to the character's hands (or rather, the weapon joint of the hand) on receiving the mocap. However, if you are capturing a complex reload, weapon switch, or other action that requires the prop to be moved around inside the hand or between hands, or be put back in a holster, then it is valuable to capture the pistol prop's motion and retarget it, giving the animator all the data required to get the best possible fidelity.

Set Building

Building sets is an essential part of any mocap shoot that requires the actor to interact with the environment. All motion capture facilities should have an inventory full of pipes, ladders, and boxes of all sizes that can be combined to create the required sets. Importantly, only the touch points that an actor will interact with are important to build, with the rest falling to the actor's imagination (aided by whatever direction and reference materials you provide).

Some mocap stages provide the ability to visualize a virtual set in a real-time view, allowing the actors to get a better sense of the environment they're currently in (provided your team has built it already, of course). This can be a distraction when recording, however, as the actor may be captured looking at a screen, so is best used only before a shoot for context. Relevant geographic locations such as distant mountains or buildings can just as easily be given to the actor as corners of the mocap stage or someone holding up a prop off-camera.

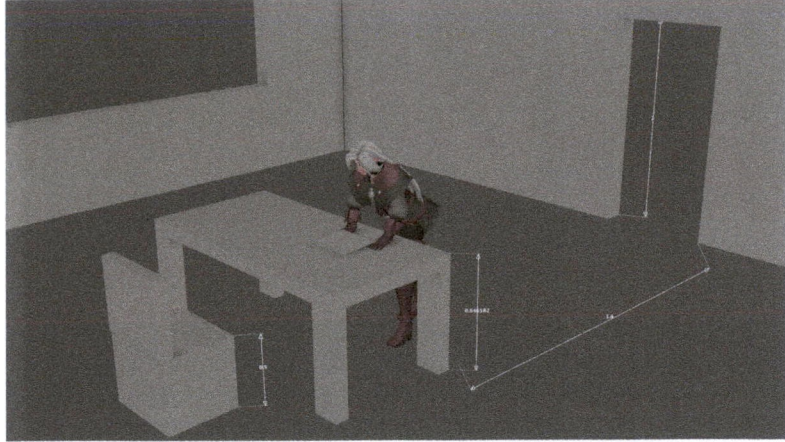

Building out sets to measure before a shoot.

When planning to build sets, care must be taken to ensure measurements are accurate for the best possible results, such as chair and desk heights, for example, and distances between objects. This is where previz again comes in much more handy than storyboarding, as you are planning out the set in 3D and can measure relationships there. All this assumes the game and characters are built to real-world scale, with correct sizes worked out in the DCC (a recommended practice for scale consistency even non-mocap games will benefit from).

Before attending the shoot, it is important to consider that large set pieces may occlude the cameras, so often walls and doors and so on must be built with mesh to allow as many cameras to triangulate the markers as possible. As such, the people best equipped and most experienced in set building will be the stage team. Make sure to communicate any complex sets with them as early as possible ahead of the shoot so they can plan accordingly, sometimes even building the set ahead of time. Set building is time consuming on the day of shooting, so consider set complexity and frequency when estimating how many shots you hope to capture.

Being smart about shared set builds allows the day to go as efficiently as possible. For example, if there are three separate scenes or actions that require an actor to jump off a wall, then capture them out of order in the shot list to get them all with the one set. While it may help, there's no need to arrange this in the shot list, as the stage crew will be used to jumping around the shot list for expediency, even adding new unplanned shots as long as all information is kept up to date. Entering the set build info into the shot list ahead of time will allow these shortcuts to be anticipated.

LA Noire's set matches only the important touch points of the in-game boat. (Courtesy of Rockstar Games.)

Mocap sets are built primarily from various-sized boxes for solid platforms to stand on, with piping used to create scaffold frames that represent walls and other parts the actors must touch without requiring full walls that might occlude the markers. It is the stage crew's responsibility to ensure the sets are built safely, so it is recommended to leave set-building to the professionals beyond helping to clear away any minor parts as sets are deconstructed. Unlike the rest of video game creation, motion capture is a very physical activity, so care must be taken to avoid injury even when simply picking up objects.

The more time you spend at a stage, the more familiar you'll be with their inventory of props and set parts, so you will be able to plan ahead of time by knowing what sets can be made from. The most important element of set building is that you get the motion you want, so don't be afraid to make requests of the stage crew if you feel the set isn't solid enough for the correct impact or not high enough for the best fall.

Virtual Cameras

Motion capture is always searching for ways to get the actors more invested in the scene or action they're currently performing for the best possible performance. Beyond showing background information to them via scripts, character profiles, concept art, and previz videos, one exciting way is to put the actor into the scene by way of the real-time connection between them and MotionBuilder, or, even better, the game engine.

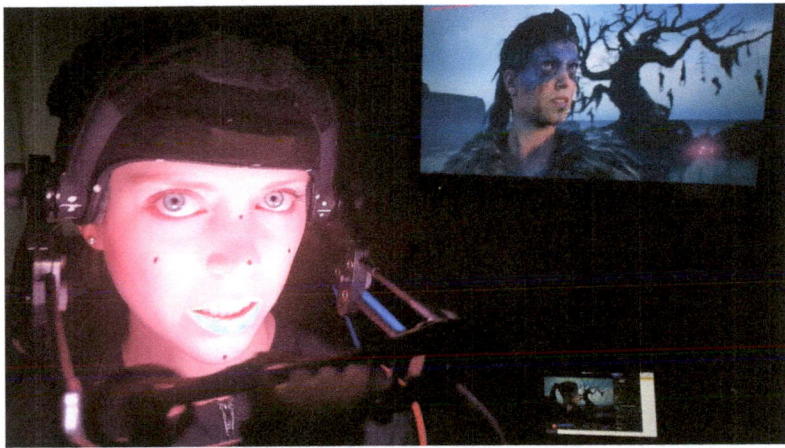

Real-time feedback of sets and facial acting on HellBlade. (Copyright 2015 Ninja Theory Limited.)

A step further allows screen-mounted virtual cameras to move through the volume (tracked via markers), with the real-time render displayed on its screen. This allows the animator to see the actors perform in a similar manner to a live-action shoot. This can even take place at a later stage without the actors, where just a replay of their motions is combined with the real-time capture of the camera.

Getting the Best Take

At the mocap stage, it can sometimes be difficult to decide which of several takes is the one you wish to work with back at the studio. Preparation can only go so far in protecting an animator from returning to the studio with an unworkable shot. Here are some points to keep in mind when shooting or deciding between multiple similar takes.

- *Remember key poses*: If your character's idle stands left foot forward, then always keep an eye on the footing. Changing this back at the studio is one of the biggest time-sinks that can be avoided by paying attention. If the actor is struggling to remember, or if you just want to be sure yourself, provide the stage with a file of your character's mesh exported in key poses to bring up on the real-time screen. For extra peace of mind, having the actor assume the pose and taping the ground where his or her feet lie helps (though ensure the actor doesn't look at the ground when returning to the pose—it should be for the director's reference only).
- *Mocap mirroring*: If an actor generally prefers to jump up a ledge with their stronger leg but it's the opposite of what you need, remember you can always mirror animations later. If the action is asymmetrical (e.g., gun must be in the right hand), consider carrying the gun in the left for this shot only and starting/ending in a mirror of the idle pose. Better actions will always be done by whatever the actor is most comfortable with so don't force something, especially a large action, in a way that the actor's body won't perform naturally.
- *Weigh the amount of rework*: When several takes all look equally good, go for the one that will require the smallest amount of work back at the studio. As a general rule, it is easier to remove motion than to add it. For example, choose a take where an actor walks a little longer than necessary rather than less. If an actor shuffles his or her feet at the end of an action to hit the mark, choose instead the take where they confidently hit near the correct pose. Changing the final pose is easier than removing the foot-stepping. With more practice, you'll eventually make decisions on the stage to move onto the next action without too many retakes, confident in the knowledge that you can work the action captured to make it perfect rather than waiting for that one perfect take.
- *If in doubt, get coverage*: In a similar manner to getting different line reads when recording voice, "coverage" is a tried and tested way to increase the chances you'll get what you want for a single action. That basically means trying a variety of different approaches to an action with variations of attitude and speed and so on. When you're unsure of exactly what will look best, keeping takes loose like this gives you more options later when deciding on the one you'll choose to work up. Sometimes you might even want the start of one take and the end of another—as long as it's not too difficult to make the join, this is an entirely valid approach when choosing takes.
- *Watch the actors, not a screen!*: A classic mistake when choosing takes, and when directing in general, is for the director to watch the performance on screen rather than live on stage. Screens are fine for rewatching, but the initial performance should be viewed live on the stage in order to see subtleties not caught by video or the mocap played back in 3D. Eventually, it'll come naturally what to look out for and where to focus your attention— just be sure to watch from the best angle so as not to miss anything.

Working with Mocap

In a reverse from keyframing that begins with key poses and then is timed out before working on the in-betweens that flow between them, "raw" mocap at the untouched stage can be likened to the animator having first created all their in-betweens and now needing to add in exaggerated key poses and timing.

There are two main methods to mocap editing, both with their pros and cons, but it is quite easy to choose the one you want depending on the action at hand.

1. *The "destructive" approach*: Manually removing keys so as to make the mocap more malleable for a human, lessening the key density allows animators to manipulate mocap as they would key-frames, shifting the timing of the now-reduced key poses as well as only having to worry about these poses when required to amplify and exaggerate them. This works for less-realistic styles that don't require the realism afforded by mocap to be as strictly adhered to and is generally employed on gameplay-centric animations such as melee combat, for example, where fast response times and strong, identifiable poses are desired. However, this approach isn't referred to as "destructive" for nothing, and in doing so we are destroying much of the detail that was sought and paid for in employing motion-capture in the first place. Once we've deleted those keys, they can't come back, so this approach is best used in combination with the following only when confident in manipulating mocap while retaining its essence.
2. *The "nondestructive" approach*: Very rarely deleting keys, instead adjusting them as a group and working on top of them. Retiming mocap by scaling sections of keys and employing animation layers to paste adjustment poses onto the mocap underneath retains all of the realism and detail unique to mocap while still allowing the animator to exaggerate poses in the same manner as above minus the risks. Maintaining many layers can become complex, especially when counteranimating adjustment layers to iron out issues, so it's best to stick to only one or two adjustment layers at most. This is the recommended method for mocap manipulation and the one most commonly used by video game studios, so we'll continue exploring this method in more detail.

Retiming

The first thing you'll want to do with your mocap is figure out the timing, which generally involves speeding it up. Sometimes a blanket increase is a good way to give actions more punch and start from there. Assuming a nondestructive method, this can quickly be achieved by scaling the motion universally in either the timeline or graph editor, though understand that keys will now no longer fall on full key intervals (not an issue if you plan to work on layers).

However, any game animator worth their salt knows that simply scaling an action to speed it up is something only a designer would do. As such, while that might be a good base, the way you really bring an action to life is by emphasizing the important elements like a punch to make it faster while leaving elements like the ensuing follow-through with a longer delay. As such, another method is to scale different elements of the action individually by way of a time-warp curve that allows for custom speed adjustment across different parts of the action rather than a one-size-fits-all linear scale. A cleaner method is to keep the motion in a clip editor such as MotionBuilder's Story Tool or Maya's Time Editor and cut the clip up so as to overlap and blend it back onto itself. This method eliminates any pause or hesitation on the part of the actor while affording a good visual representation of where the edits were made.

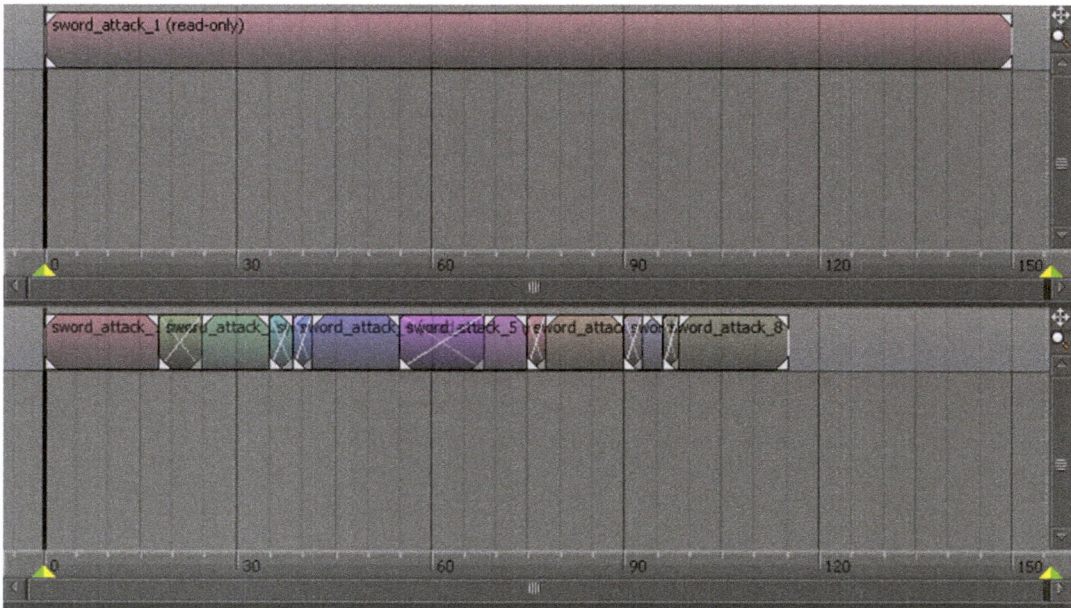

A mocap clip cut up for speed in MotionBuilder's story editor.

Should you opt for the destructive route, simply deleting keys and moving them on the timeline to increase or decrease spaces in between will allow for fine-tuned scaling of every part of an action. This is more desired for actions that will be heavily modified timingwise—just be careful not to remove too many frames, as some of that beautiful detail and overlap will be lost. As such, it's recommended to keep more than just the extremities of key poses, also maintaining poses that deliver overlap such as an extra forearm bend after the shoulder has settled into a punch.

Pose Exaggeration

Exaggeration comes by way of modifying the underlying pose at certain points. In using real actors for our motion, we push for realism, warts and all.

Before and after accentuating a motion capture performance via exaggeration, aiming for a clear line of action.

In real life, humans rarely hit appealing poses or dynamic silhouettes that work from all angles as required by video game animation. To overcome this, modifying key poses to amplify their readability and silhouette will greatly increase the motion's appeal as well as aid any timing changes made at that earlier stage.

If characters jump, make them jump higher and land harder. If they swing a sword, pull it further back before swinging and end in a strong posture. If the actor pulled their punches, make sure your character connects deep inside the target with an equivalently painful reaction as the head snaps back with full force. Real life just isn't real enough for a video game, so mocap should be treated as such.

Of course, the extent to which you exaggerate poses (or timing) depends on how stylized the project is and how willing the style is to move away from the pure realism afforded by mocap in the first place. But even "realistic" games go to pains to exaggerate poses for readability and appeal. Even something as non–action-oriented as an idle loop can be immeasurably improved by pasting a more appealing pose onto it.

Offset Poses

The process of modifying an action's pose generally begins with pasting an approved idle pose at the start and end of an action on an additive modification layer. However, the further the captured motion is from the standard pose, the more it will cause the entire action in between to veer wildly from the original capture. For example, if the established idle pose is more leaning backward, then the character will lean backward throughout the action.

Because of this, it is advisable to paste the new pose only just before the action begins, then paste a zero pose (where the offset value is zero so the motion reverts back to the original mocap) once the action begins. Then, once the action has played out, paste another zero pose just before the action returns to its ending idle position (where again we paste an offset pose). This is a good quick first pass, though it will likely cause side effects that can be overcomed below.

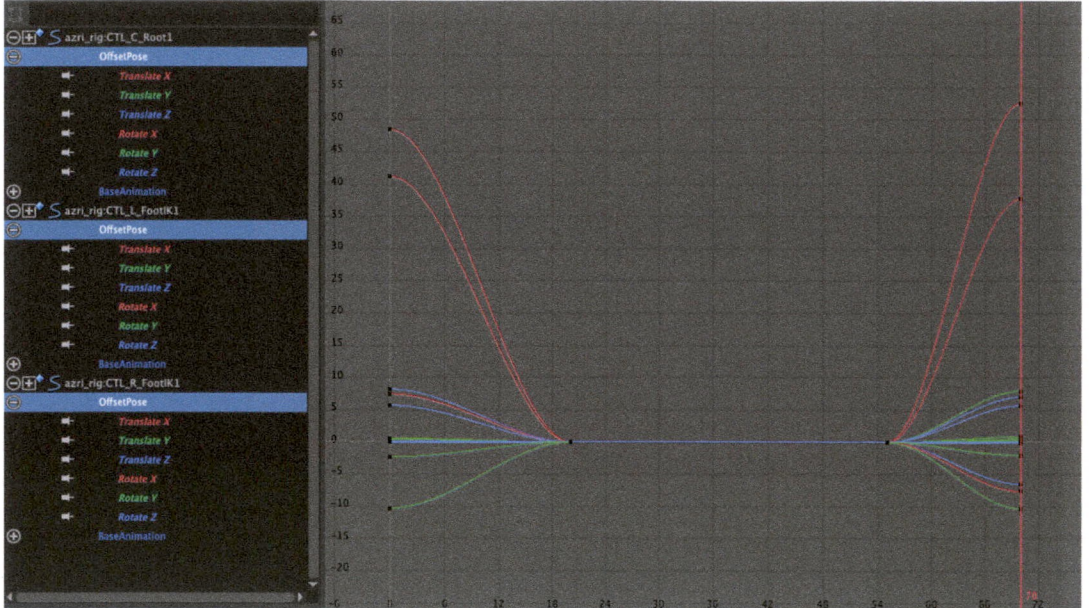

Offset vs zero poses when manipulating mocap via layers.

Hiding Offset Pose Deltas

Typically, once an offset pose is placed, it will be apparent to the viewer where the offset and zero poses occur as the character morphs between the new pose and the original, with foot-sliding and weight-shifting occurring across the delta between poses. A good trick to avoid foot-sliding here is to copy and paste the offset pose key from the start of the action to a point where the foot steps or performs another large action such as twisting on the ball of the foot.

Once the foot moves to a new position, paste a zero pose so the movement masks the transition from the original position. Retain that zero-pose position until the last time the foot moves in the action, this time by pasting the zero-pose before the final move, then copying and pasting the final offset pose from the end of the action to where the foot finally rests.

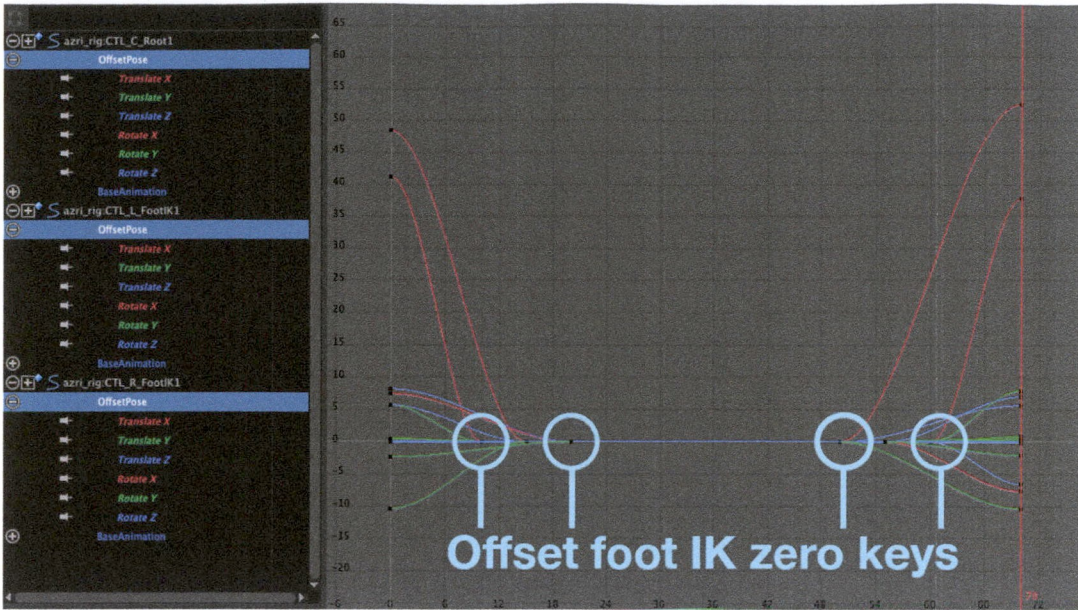

Offset foot IK poses relative to the main body movement so as to eliminate foot-sliding.

This method of pasting either offset or zero keys can be used for any part of the body (not just the feet) to better mask the blend between appealing offset poses and the original mocap. The trick is to have different body parts move between the zero pose and the offset pose at different times, ideally as the underlying animation moves also, so as to make the delta between them invisible.

While referred to above as the zero-pose, the adjustment pose used needn't have a value of zero (therefore reverting back to the original mocap), but can instead be any offset value that allows for natural movement in between the standard idle pose bookending the entire action. Should the idle be too far visually from the underlying mocap, you'll likely instead use a nonzero adjustment pose closer to the new modified pose while still allowing the mocap to play cleanly underneath.

Blending & Cycling

Working with nonlinear actions in mocap is made significantly easier by using a clip sequencing tool (such as Maya's Time Editor or MotionBuilder's Story Tool) because of their ability to overlap and blend between different actions. Rather than having to animate the joins between two takes that more than likely do not match exactly, as long as two elements of the action are similar enough, we can overlay both actions at that point and simply blend across them such that the end of a cycle blends back to its start.

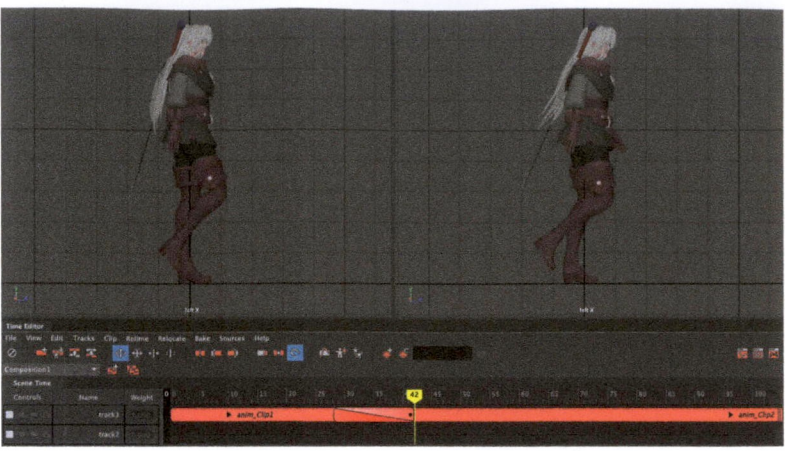

Two similar passing poses with a blend across clips in a sequencer.

Importantly, when blending, it is important not to look for two poses than match, but instead look for two matching motions (such as a crouch, a step, a turn, etc.). This allows the actions to be blended together across a moving action rather than a static one, further masking the transition with motion and making the clean-up work easier afterward. Blending across two actions at a relatively static portion (such as leaning against a wall), will leave visible artifacts as the actor shifts uniformly between the two different takes, as the poses are never identical.

While this method is commonly used for joining two takes together, it is even more powerful as a tool to create seamless cycling actions—something commonly used in video games. This is made especially easy because cycles by their very nature feature repeating actions required for seamless blending (a walk repeats itself every second step, for example). For a walk cycle to be blended, the motion must feature at least two matching steps, meaning at its very minimum, three steps (L-R-L or R-L-R) to allow a blend over the third step back across to the first.

The results of blending across a motion in something as important as a walk or run that will be seen by players repeatedly throughout the game are invaluable. This gives the best visual results, and starting with a seamlessly cycling action is a great first step before the long process of massaging the mocap into the looping cycle the player will eventually see. Attempting to create a similar walk cycle via a destructive approach by simply working into the join at the end will not only take much longer but likely require the deletion of keys from perhaps the last step of an entire run cycle, losing all that valuable motion and attitude in the process.

Interview: Bruno Velazquez
Animation Director—God of War

(Courtesy of Sony Interactive Entertainment.)

Revitalizing the style of such a well-known character as Kratos after working with him for over a decade must have been a fun and challenging experience. Were there any animation rules or dos-and-don'ts you built up for him over the years?

Over the course of seven games, we kept an internal document called "Kratos Rules" that the team adhered to for all aspects of realizing Kratos. Everything from the way he looked to the choices he would make and of course the way that he would move and be animated. These rules included such things as "Kratos always maintains eye contact with the enemy unless there is a major rotation; otherwise he is dialed in and focused on the enemy at hand." The hit frame should personify this idea so his hits feel deliberate and final.

For the new God of War, we looked over each rule and revised them accordingly to reflect an older, more measured Kratos now responsible for raising his son Atreus. For example, "Kratos never runs away or takes a step back from the enemy. He is always moving forward or making the player feel like he is about to move forward."

While this is still true in the new game, we added the following to the rule: "When forced to fight, Kratos will advance and maintain a smart dominance of the situation. However, he is older and wiser and attempting to turn away from violence as a solution. He wants to change to show his son there is a better way to resolve a problem."

This was the first entry to the series that heavily utilized motion-capture. What were some of the key challenges of shifting the team over from a keyframe approach, and how did you maintain consistent style between the humans and creatures?

At the beginning of the project I was concerned about getting a team primarily built for keyframe animation to transition to a motion capture–heavy project. The way that it ultimately worked out was to get the whole team to jump head-first into the process. We purchased a motion capture suit that did not require cameras or a complicated setup and encouraged the animation team members to try it themselves. We spent many hours taking turns at wearing the suit and recorded as much data as we could.

Once the animators got to apply their own motion to our various characters, they were able to quickly get past any misconceptions and concerns about the technology and became more comfortable with it. This process emphasized the use of motion capture as one more tool available to us and by experiencing the process themselves from beginning to end it helped them to accept its use. In the end, we did hire professional actors and stunt performers to capture the motion, but having the animators understand the process from beginning to end was a big step for us.

Once we got comfortable using more realistic animation data we were able to determine how much we could push our fully keyframed characters. We always used Kratos's and Atreus's motions as a barometer to keep us consistent.

You state that achieving the balance between fun and responsive gameplay and natural movement is one of your key goals. Do gameplay requirements ever conflict with animation and how do you typically resolve them?

Gameplay requirements always seem to affect and conflict with our inner animation desires. However, our team understands that gameplay is king. This is why we worked very closely with the combat designers who are responsible for building Kratos, Atreus, bosses, and all enemy AI characters. As we figure out the gameplay and identify the timing of motions that will serve the gameplay best, we identify data that includes hit-frame numbers and the total amount of frames a combat move needs to feel responsive. The animation team then finds creative solutions to maximize the use of keyframes available by focusing on the spacing of our poses.

A good example of this is the motion of the Blades of Chaos, which are keyframed frame-by-frame because the spacing and positions of each frame had to work for gameplay as well as being smooth enough so the trail effects wouldn't look linear. When working on the cinematic kills where Kratos dispatches his enemies, however, the animation team had much more freedom to let loose with the animation timing. This allowed for the animation team to reach a nice balance with the gameplay team.

A notable visual style choice in God of War was a complete omission of camera cuts in cinematics and action scenes. What was the reasoning behind this decision and what were the related challenges?

Early on in the project we decided that we wanted to make this God of War more grounded and unflinching. Our goal was for the player to feel like they are right there next to Kratos and Atreus, along for the entire duration of the adventure by only focusing on their perspective. Because of this we decided not to cut the camera to show a passage of time or a glimpse of what "the bad guy" was doing in his lair. This was all in aid of a more personal story, so not cutting helped us to make it feel more realistic and visceral than previous games.

We quickly discovered that it was going to be very challenging to shoot scenes, and planning was critical. The moment that things fell into place was when we changed our approach from shooting like a film to instead producing more of a stage play. Once the actors adapted to approaching scenes like this, it really made a big difference. We would spend at least one day rehearsing before shooting so the actors could do a table-read together, absorb all the previsualization we had prepared, and rehearse the staging and movement with the virtual camera. In the end, it all worked out as a well-coordinated dance between our actors and cinematographer.

CHAPTER 12

Our Project: Animation Team Management

Scheduling

With game projects often spanning multiple years and requiring hundreds if not thousands of animations to be created, not to mention a whole team working simultaneously together to bring the entire game together, it is imperative to have a good understanding of the creation of an effective game animation schedule. This chapter features a number of best practices and things to consider when building a schedule, with the ultimate goal being to deliver the best animation quality within the finite time of the development schedule.

Front-Loading

In an effort to avoid an overload of work at the end of the project, it is worthwhile to aim to produce as much as you can at the start. The obvious catch with this is that game development is such an unpredictable beast that it's hard to know what will stay and what will be cut. As such, teams may sometimes wait until certain elements are locked down before moving onto the next stage, not starting cutscenes, for example, until the entire script has been approved.

Front-loading eschews this for an approach that essentially accepts that things will be cut or changed, and it's easier to redo a certain percentage of work than it is to wait until everything is certain to not change (which never really exists) and only really start then, which is often too late. The traditional method of waiting forces all the work to be done toward the end of the project, which makes quality content almost impossible. As such, gameplay animations and cutscenes should be created as early as possible with the understanding that a percentage will be redone—but that is the nature of video game animation.

Prioritizing Quality

Prioritizing work is essential to ensure the animation team is working on what is required the most at any point in time, so prepare to be flexible on this throughout the project. A common pitfall working in a creative field is that creatives often want to work on the most enjoyable and satisfying work, but often that is not the most important work needing to be done first, with the groundwork for a game project often being laid by more mundane and standard tasks.

That said, the highest priority in animating great games is quality of both the assets and the overall experience. Leaving all the best parts such as "easter eggs" or polish to the end or, as is often the case, saying no to them when you've a mountain of work laid out until the end of the project will usually see these elements cut from the game at the end.

A Battlefield series easter egg. Nonessential but adds to the player's enjoyment and can result in another round of press when discovered. (Courtesy of Electronic Arts.)

Saying no to too many great ideas in order to fit in a schedule results in a dull game, so it's highly advisable to make sure to squeeze in little details and things players will notice and appreciate throughout the project even if it blows out the schedule (which usually just results in rescoping the quantity towards the end). That is where the magic of a great game really lies.

De-Risking

De-risking unknowns is the fastest way to get a real handle on your schedule by eliminating or succeeding in tasks or aspects of the design that are the furthest from the team's prior experience. This is more common in new IPs (intellectual properties) than sequels that already have an established way of working and general gameplay feature set.

Due to this, previz and prototyping should be focused on these areas as early as possible, with the aim being to either prove that these elements will make it into the game or at least to establish how long the creation of such assets may take so that a more accurate schedule can be drawn up. If the schedule is simply not workable, then either a new approach must be investigated or the importance of the the new gameplay scaled back so if it fails to materialize there is less chance of it adversely affecting the whole project.

Unknowns can also come in the form of new technologies or pipelines that must be developed in order for the animation team to work. Many a game project has been sunk because a vital piece of technology the team was waiting on became available too late in production. While it may not be possible to know whether this risky new tech or approach will work in the early stages of development, a go/no-go deadline must be established, with backup plans for alternative tech or pipelines accounted for.

In addition, at the start of the project, all the risk must be weighed and reduced if it adds up too much. For example, unknowns such a new IP + a newly formed team + a new game engine + an entirely new gameplay mechanic all compound the overall risk when at least one of them is guaranteed to become a major issue. While no ambitious game project is without its problems, too many problems can cause a project to fail, so they must be recognized and dealt with from the beginning.

> A conservative approach to scheduling and risk management can help avoid time sinks, but the flip side is it may also stifle creativity. No great animation system was ever created without some risk of the unknown. Knowing when to attack or hold off only comes from experience—just make sure your experience retains a good a dose of youthful naïveté and a cavalier approach to exciting new ideas.

Predicting Cuts & Changes

The single best approach to prioritization one can develop in order to minimize wasted effort is to look ahead and evaluate all the potential issues that might arise with each individual system, section of a game, or complex cinematic. While front-loading work assumes a degree of cuts and changes, and previz and prototyping are a great way to de-risk potential hazards, simply becoming aware of the incoming work that is most likely to be cut and lowering its priority so you attack it as late as possible means you often avoid having to even deal with many of these tasks, as they're often cut from the game before you spend any time on them.

As an example, if a raft of cinematic scenes is to be created for a level over the coming months, but there's an area of that level that is highly suspect—displaying "red-flag" warning signs that haven't worked in past projects—do not create the scenes for that part of the level until last rather than working sequentially. There's a high chance the other disciplines will either figure out the issues (saving you rework) or cut it entirely. Importantly, be sure to raise your concerns with the individuals working on that section to get conversations started to ideally fix the problem area before you reach it.

Adaptive Schedules

A schedule need only be stuck to until it no longer works. Reprioritizing to fit the ever-changing game means that the schedule must adapt. The point of a schedule in the first place is not, as is often mistakenly thought, to know exactly what things will be done on the game and when. Instead, the schedule should serve only as a constantly updating document to allow educated decisions to be made on the fly, as early as possible, as to how to deliver the best-quality game within the allotted time.

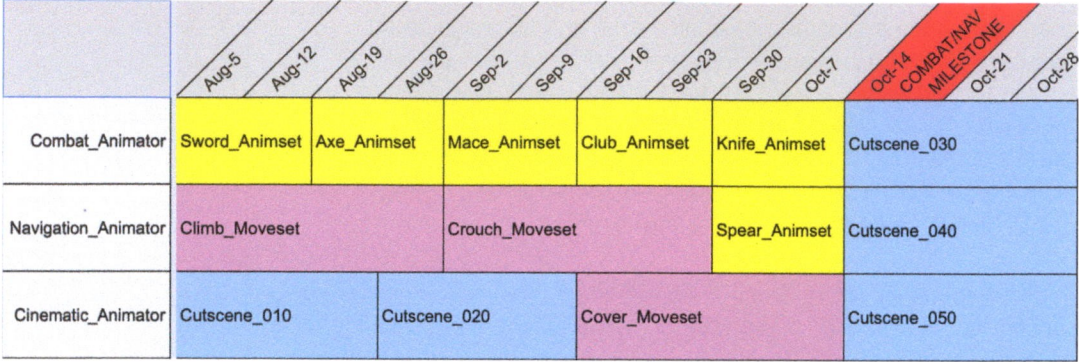

Moving asset quantities around to adapt to a living schedule.

For example, knowing that it takes 2 weeks to fully deliver a weapon set of animations, when there are only 10 weeks before the milestone with six weapons remaining serves as a tool to potentially drop one weapon, speed up the process while reducing quality, or shift animators around to free up additional help to achieve the milestone, depending on its importance. Knowing the incoming issues 10 weeks out offers a variety of options that simply don't exist when surprised by an incoming milestone with no time to adapt.

Conflicts & Dependencies

No game team discipline works on its own. Characters first need concept art. Rigging first needs a character. Animation needs the rigged character, and design needs it all put together to start making the character playable. If any one element of the chain fails to deliver their part on time, that can have a knock-on effect down the line.

Typical dependencies related to the animation team.

The animation schedule should take into account major dependencies they have with other disciplines and, importantly, communicate as quickly as possible when they become aware of impending issues with teams that are depending on them. It is also important to remain in continuous contact with teams upstream so as not to be too adversely affected should they slip up on their end.

It's better to overcommunicate than be caught unawares when that asset you were depending on hasn't even been started because another team's priorities shifted. In an ideal world this would never happen, but human nature means some things get missed, so best to protect your own team in this way.

Should an unforeseen conflict arise, it can be mitigated by always having other work the team can continue with in the interim until the asset is delivered, allowing them to bounce around and make progress elsewhere in the schedule.

This can be done on an individual basis, too, where a gameplay animator can often become stuck waiting for the animation's implementation or other adjustments from a programmer or designer co-worker. It's useful to have more than one DCC scene open at once, even, provided your computer can handle it, so you can immediately jump back and forth to avoid ever being stuck waiting.

Milestones

Milestones, the mini-deadlines often created for the purpose of appraising the current state of the game's schedule (often for an external publisher) can be a double-edged sword. Too far apart and they become meaningless, as it's hard for a team to visualize what they need to do today in order to hit a target several months out. Too close together and they also become meaningless because the game is always in a state of panic to hit the next target.

The best deadlines for an animation team are practical and measurable goals such as the initial pass of a new character's basic move set or implementing the raw mocap and camera pass for a certain section of the game's cinematics—something that can be viewed by anyone on the team and established as being achieved or not. Milestones that require assets to be finished or polished are subjective and unnecessary beyond finishing the game or preparing the game to be shown outside the studio, such as for a demo or the capturing of a promotional video—something that should ideally only occur very infrequently.

External demos for conferences or trailers are often cited as the biggest time sink in any game project, as unfinished elements rush to appear finished or better than they would otherwise at this stage of development. However, when properly scheduled, demos and similar visual milestones can be a great galvanizer for the team, allowing them to coalesce on a vision of the game that may otherwise meander, not to mention provide an example to the team of what finished animation looks like.

Teamwork

Games are rarely animated alone (the big games, at least), so it's likely that you'll be working as part of a team while animating. The trinity of gameplay animation is most often the combination of animator, programmer, and designer. Similarly, character setup requires an animator, character artist, and rigger/technical animator. Environmental animations benefit from a combination of animator, level artist, and level designer. Cinematics most often bring together animator, character artist, and level artist. Put simply, no one element of a game can be created by an animator alone, so a desire to collaborate and an empathy for others' requirements will allow the animator to be of maximum effectiveness in a team environment.

Collaboration

Collaboration is the act of working with others to create something, and in games, that something is often that which has never been created before. As such, there's no real wrong answer to any creative challenge, only an ever-improving result after much discussion and trial and error until the game ships. After an initial discussion of the task at hand involving all parties, each should return to his or her desk with an understanding of what is required to achieve a first stab at the goal.

For example, it may often only require an animation and the programmer to implement an attack action into the engine to get it working, from which point the designer can iterate on the "feel" of the action. Ideally, the programmer will have exposed variables (such as speed, hit-frame, damage etc.), to the designer such that the designer can make modifications without the others' involvement, so the others can each move onto the next task until another pass at the initial animation or change to the code is required.

This iterative, parallel workflow is essential to allow a team of collaborators to work in lockstep and make as many adjustments in as short a timeframe as possible. Moreover, they can be working simultaneously with one another such that the animator should create a quick animation for the programmer to implement so the animator can continue improving and updating the visuals at the same time as the programmer and designer are collaborating.

Being personable with those you work with will pay dividends over the course of a game's development. When someone asks a favor of you (such as requesting a quick animation for prototyping), always remember that at some point, you will likely have need of something from that person to realize your own ideas. An entire team going the extra mile for each other can create amazing things, especially toward the end of the project when operating at full steam.

Remember that everyone wants the game to be as good as possible, so on the rare occasion that another discipline's work is negatively affecting your own, such as environment art in your cinematic scene that keeps changing and breaking the shots, the best way to solve these issues is communicating how both teams are depending on that area both looking great and working.

Sometimes a slight camera adjustment to accommodate a better environment is worth it and doing so will increase the likelihood of requests being reciprocal.

The hands-down best way to get someone on your side with regards to fulfilling an idea is first to show it to them. As stated earlier, a game animator has the unique ability to mock up ideas via previz, so exciting teammates with something they can already see, improve, and embellish with their own ideas will almost always win them over to your side.

Leadership

Assuming a leadership role on the animation team, be it a lead or a technical or artistic director requires a varying skill-set depending on the studio, but all have the prerequisite that the team must look to you to enable them to work on a daily basis.

Many young animators wrongly believe the role of lead is somehow easier due to producing less work for the game overall, at least from their vantage point. Worse still, some animators' desire to attain the role can come from wanting to be "the boss," calling the shots on how every detail of the game's animation is created. This could not be further from the truth, with the most effective leads assuming a subservient role to the team and expending all their efforts to ensure the team is best supported to create the best animation possible.

Moreover, if the lead is the best animator on a team, then they are generally wasted in a lead role. An effective team makeup balances individuals proficient in animation, technical knowhow, experience, and youthful enthusiasm, and hires should ideally be stronger in at least one of these areas than the lead. A great lead must only have a general knowledge of all aspects of game animation creation, and, importantly, can view the project from a higher level than simply "does this individual asset look good?"—allowing the lead to see everything in context.

A team, naturally, is made of people. Being strong in soft skills can be one of a good lead's best assets, such as:

- The ability to clearly communicate direction and give feedback
- An awareness of potential issues before they arise, and how to avoid/ solve them
- Answers to questions or, just as importantly, knowing how to obtain the answer
- An empathy towards team members' issues and an eagerness to listen
- An innate ability to inspire and motivate the team by providing an example to follow

Once an animation team is operating efficiently, then and only then can leads find time to squeeze in some of their own animation tasks, though they must be careful not to take their eye off the team long enough such that problems can creep back in.

A lead role under time constraints towards the end of a project can often feel like protecting the team from an encroaching workload, where every new animation request adds to an already intimidating schedule. While any leadership position should provide a buffer between high-level (potentially chaotic) decision-making and a team member's day-to-day work, and animation schedules should ideally account for late additions, the desire to keep a team in the dark is never as fruitful as having them engaged.

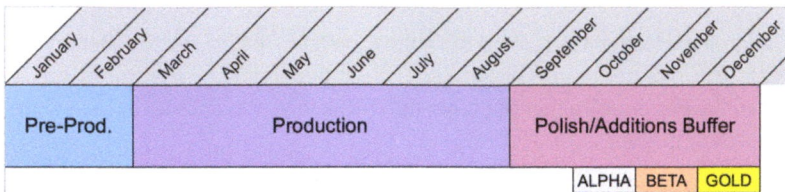

A realistic schedule, buffered for requests and unforeseen issues.

In situations like this, it is often tempting to fight against new additions, as the lead sees the planned polish time toward the end of the project dwindling, but ultimately, the lead's main role is to lead the team in creating the best game possible. When these requests come in, it is recommended to consult with the animators themselves on whether they wish to take on the work so they have some ownership of the decision themselves.

> Leads must caution against referring to the team as "my" team. It is not "your" team, it is "the" team—the one on which you serve. "My" team misconstrues a feeling of protectorship with that of ownership, which is true only insofar as when the team fails, the lead is responsible, but when the team succeeds, the team is responsible.

Mentorship

Mentoring mostly occurs informally by osmosis. Leading by example, and a corresponding animator emulating a lead, allows the mentor to pass on experience to the mentee, both good and bad. If ever there were an artform that would benefit from standardized apprenticeship training, it would be game development, with a junior animator so akin to an apprentice learning on the job.

Formalized apprenticeships such as paid internships are a great way for smaller studios to fill less-crucial or demanding positions while training up potential future hires, but the best mentorship comes by way of pairing off an experienced animator with one less so who looks to him or her as a role model. Ideally, working together on the same area of the project, discussing current problems, and asking for specific advice works much better than general advice on how to be better.

> Unfortunately, internships in game development are even rarer than entry-level jobs, most of which request a certain amount of experience, creating a Catch-22 for students. It is advisable to ignore the experience stipulation on job descriptions when first applying, as a good reel will count for more, and smart studios that weren't initially considering an entry-level position would do well to bite at the chance of mentoring a student already displaying raw talent.

As a young animator looking to learn, the hands-down best way to get a better awareness of the goings-on around you is to speak to other developers and ask them what they're working on. It may seem obvious, but game developers are often very happy to discuss their work with anyone willing to listen, especially if you are as enthusiastic as they are. It is highly recommended to engage with more than just animators. The best game animators cultivate a degree of understanding of all areas of game development so as to be most effective in any given situation.

Hiring

There are few single decisions in a multiyear project that, if chosen wisely, will make all the difference to a team's success from that day onward. Hiring the right person for a spot on the team is one of those, while hiring the wrong person can be the single most costly mistake for a game budget, as excess time is sunk into righting that wrong on a daily basis.

Hire for a combination of skill and attitude, not skill alone. New hires can and should learn on the job and improve their skills, but changing a negative or even lackluster attitude is next to impossible. In general, the best animation team hires, regardless of skill level, are self-motivated, autonomous actors who seek out opportunities to improve the game, displaying an appropriate balance of artistic and technical aptitude with a constant desire to improve.

Each studio (and team within it), has a distinct culture, and the ultimate decision of an interviewer always rests on the question "Would I work with this person?" However, it's crucial to be wary of simply hiring future colleagues similar to yourself lest the team become homogeneous in its creative output. Diverse hiring to round out a team so it excels in a variety of criteria always makes for a better game. A variety of life experience, not just animation skill, allows every creative discussion to become more fruitful as team members come from a variety of angles, which often results in out-of-the-box thinking. This can be the largest deciding factor between the most memorable games and those that fail to leave a mark and are consigned to the forgotten annals of gaming.

The Animation Critique

Growing a thick skin is something every animator needs to do to be effective on a team. The surest path to mediocre animation is to refuse all comments, feedback, and criticism of your work. Animation as a craft can be so all-consuming that you often can't see the forest for the trees and are unable to step back and see your work-in-progress with fresh eyes.

That's why a great initiative to implement on any team is a formal critique process, regularly showing and reviewing work in a group setting such that everyone can have input and learn from others' work. Not to be confused with design by committee, the final say still lies with the lead/director and the animator is free to choose which feedback to act upon. It is simply an invaluable resource to have the combined talent and experience of a team contributing to the overall quality, as well as learning from each critique as a group.

Held as regularly as desired (filmlike "dailies" would be overkill due to game development's tighter timelines), meeting in a room and volunteering work to be reviewed for feedback creates an incredible motivator in seeing your peers' work. Importantly, the lead should drive the meeting forward so as not to dwell on any one animation too long, with longer conversations taken "offline" for deeper discussion later. Animators who rarely participate (in either showing or vocalizing) should be encouraged to do so, with care taken to allow less-confident animators a voice so that no one participant dominates. Beyond improving the overall quality and promoting stylistic consistency, sharing feedback is a great team-building exercise, making every team member feel involved in the common goals of the team.

Outsourcing

External and/or contract work is becoming more and more a standard practice as higher budgets and the boom/bust nature of game development teams make it difficult to scale up or down a team appropriately during and after a project. Due to this, many areas of game development that are considered less tied to gameplay (requiring rapid iteration), such as concept work, cinematics, and tertiary art assets, can all be farmed out to other studios with varying degrees of success.

The biggest trade-off is cost/quality. Even if the external artists are competent, the distance just makes the iteration loop that much harder, at best causing misunderstandings due to communication errors or at worst causing problems because the external team didn't put their best artists on the task after an initial glowing art test.

In order to dramatically improve the quality of external work, beyond supercharging that communication loop via internal team members dedicated to receiving work and giving feedback, it is vital to make the external teams feel as much a part of the main team as possible. Real-life face-time with at least their leads is an essential way to maintain a human connection. While there are more high-tech solutions—regular contact via an old-fashioned phone call while both callers have the same video(s) up is the best way to give feedback and share project news that the external contact can then forward onto the team. Just as with the main animation team, sharing the latest videos, concepts, and other exciting visual developments is an incredible motivator as well as regularly reminding them of the quality standards they should be shooting for.

Interview: Yoshitaka Shimizu
NPC Animation Lead—Metal Gear Solid Series

(Courtesy of Konami.)

You've now been at large studios in both Japan and North America that have a focus on high-quality animation. I'm sure readers would be very interested in how you perceive any differences in work culture?

I think that game development in Japan is quite different from that of other countries. In Japan, we tend to have a generalist approach so each animator has several responsibilities at the same time. Japanese game animators need a variety of skills, such as handling tools, rigging, scripting, and so on. In fact, I have worked on planning the schedule, managing, animation supervising, operating capture sessions, mocap acting, creating animations, and so on as a lead animator. While this might sound extremely challenging, thanks to that we are able to acquire a holistic view of the game development process.

On the other hand, in other countries animators tend to become specialists. Animation direction and management are separated and there are more supervisors than in Japanese game companies. Individual members have fewer responsibilities and as a result, it's hard to have a clear overall view of the project. I believe that both developing styles have pros and cons. In a perfect world, it would be best for animators to try their hand at as many challenging and varied tasks as possible at the same time for a few years… That would allow them to become specialists with a global understanding of the game development process, and as such, able to contribute a lot more to the team.

You have an interesting combination of cinematics and NPCs on your resume. Why have you focused on those areas in particular?

I love MGS's story, so I focused on cinematic animations. When MGS3 was released on PS2, the animators still had separate responsibilities: gameplay animation and cutscenes. I realized that sometimes these two areas lacked consistency. In MGS4 on PS3, I created a new animation team composed of 10 animators that worked on both game and cutscene animations called the "keyframe animation team." We worked on the following elements (including rigging): bosses, robots, and animals. We didn't work on human characters (Mocap data) at the time. My responsibilities expanded as a team lead; however, I was still able to see the work produced by the whole team, so it was easy to find consistency issues between gameplay and cutscene animations.

Regarding MGS5 on PS4, it was difficult to work on both animations because everything had become a lot more technical than on PS3. I decided to solely focus on NPCs as I love the technical side, and because I believe NPCs are the characters who truly enable players to play the game by framing the context. They are a crucial element of creating a realistic world. AI characters are living on a virtual plane, and I would like to learn more about life structures and living things in general so as to be better able to create a new form of life in games.

Metal Gear Solid 4 in particular had many experiments in interactivity during cutscenes. Was this something the team was consciously pushing for or was it just a natural progression of where you saw the medium going?

Our game director doubled up as cutscene director, so basically he suggested new interactive ideas regarding the cutscenes from the very beginning of the project. If team members came up with good ideas, we sometimes tried to implement those. Our camera specialist and the game director worked in tandem and made all decisions regarding the camerawork. Of course, the game director had the final say, but we were really putting film direction at the heart of the project.

I see you partially mocapped the GEKKO for MGS4 and were involved in the rigging. Were there any particular challenges you had to overcome in retargeting to these nonhumanoid characters?

I think that as far as challenges go, the biggest one I had to overcome was that I sometimes had to do everything by myself. The GEKKO's concept was that it was a "living" weapon. That's why I suggested we use mocap. We weren't sure whether mocap would be a good fit for the GEKKO's movement, so had to run some tests. It was our first time using our in-house mocap studio and I had some colleagues help me at first and then I tried mocap acting by myself. After that I worked on the postprocessing marker data and retargeted the data, and created the rig and animations on my own.

The point here is that when we wanted to try new expressions, each animator did everything on their own. This way, when they found some problems, we were able to proceed while fixing issues without interrupting anyone else's work. Additionally, it was easy to iterate—I think it's one of the advantages being a generalist. Since the GEKKO movements are myself, they are the most memorable characters! From that experience, I started to build our mocap pipeline seriously. Thanks to that, we were able to significantly cut production costs on MGS5.

You've worked on quite a few mocap-heavy action games, and have even ventured into the suit yourself. Do you find the mocap experience has helped or hindered your development as a keyframe animator?

Of course, the more I handled mocap data, the better my understanding of physics and of what realistic movement looks like became. Actually, I did quite a lot of mocap acting! As an animator I have first-hand experience regarding the kind of amplitude each gesture requires in order to be able to capture and then reproduce natural movement with mocap. Thanks to that, I believe I became much better at directing actors for producing mocap, and conversely, the number of mistakes and retakes was significantly reduced. I would like every animator to fully embrace all aspects of mocap, including acting!

CHAPTER 13

Our Project: Polish & Debug

In the closing laps of the race, the project is all but done and it's all about putting it in a box or on a digital storefront. But the game has likely never been more broken, as everything is crammed in at the end. Now is the time to polish what's there and fix what's broken. But no team (irrespective of size) can polish and fix everything. Applying an equal level of sheen across the entire game is not nearly as valuable as making it more polished where it counts and less so where it doesn't.

Closing Stages of a Project

Before tackling bug-fixing, it's worth knowing the closing stages of a game project and what will be expected of the game animator at each stage as the project wraps. Standard closing stages in the delivery of software, the Alpha, Beta, and final Gold Master, are often confused even by game developers, especially as some teams choose to ignore the real purpose of each stage and the checks and balances they are designed to provide.

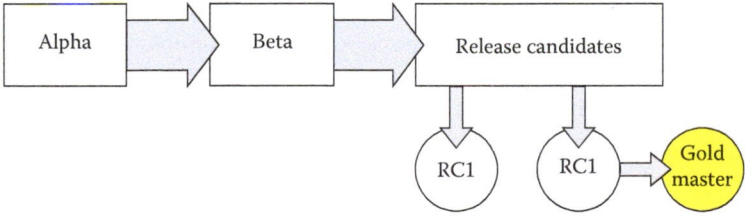

Important deadlines toward the end of a project.

Alpha

While every studio's definition differs slightly, the aim of Alpha is to achieve a content-complete stage for the project with the express purpose of allowing the entire game to be visible and playable by the team in its unfinished state, regardless of quality. For the animation team, this means implementation of all gameplay animations and cinematics in one form or another such that they can be playable and/or understood by a playtester as to what is happening in the cutscene or gameplay sequence. Sliding T-posed characters simply won't cut it.

The purpose of this stage is such that edits and cuts can be made that were previously impossible to appraise before the entire game was visible, revealing its strengths and weaknesses, overall pacing, and, crucially, what is and is not important for the core experience. Making edits or cuts to elements already added to the game even in rough form can be tough, but warning signs at this stage can and will have a massive adverse effect on the final game's quality if they go unnoticed or ignored. Importantly, the content-complete nature of Alpha is a misnomer because oftentimes new content will have to be added to fix or make edits, but as long as these additions are planned for, then it shouldn't blow out the schedule.

Beta

Beta must come long enough after Alpha in order to allow time to implement the edits and other changes resulting from Alpha. By the Beta phase, ideally all animations should be "shippable" and the team should only be fixing bugs from that point onward. When fixing an issue, the animator is expected to also catch visual problems if they can be solved at the same time.

Realistically, however, dedicated creatives will attempt to polish until the very last second. If you've spent several years working toward this point, then it's only natural to give it your all before your work goes out into the world.

Release Candidates & Gold Master

Unlike disciplines like programming, design, and other technical disciplines required to fix and optimize (plus audio and VFX that are always last over the finish line), the animation team along with other art-related fields will likely be hands off at this stage. The final days are spent building potential "release candidates" of the game to submit for publishing, first-party console approval, or disc printing (and in the case of digital self-publishing, actual release). QA will be joined by freed up team members in playing the game in order to find last-minute bugs.

Even at this late stage, it's best to hold off on vacations because animators may still need to be on hand to help fix any last-minute showstoppers, but at this stage, any aesthetic bugs found will likely be waived. Rest assured that at this point, it will be painful to let go, as you will likely still be discovering visual issues that from the animator's standpoint are easy to fix but can be ruinous if they break something else. As such, it's too risky to be making changes to the game in the very final days for anything other than progression-stopping issues or easily-reproducible glitches that will be encountered by everyone playing through.

Once a release candidate has passed through all quality assurance (developer and publisher) and been approved, then it's considered the Gold Master—the final version of the game that will be delivered or uploaded to the world for players to experience. Now all that's left is a well-earned break before returning and anxiously awaiting press reviews, hopefully followed by a celebratory release party with the team!

Animation Polish Hints & Tips

The last few weeks of a project will be spent working through the (hopefully decreasing) list of bugs assigned to you by either QA or other team members to fix as many issues as possible and ensure the game is not only in a stable state but doesn't feature noticeable visual glitches in the animations.

Below is a selection of the most common animation bugs to look out for, as well as some tips as to where to focus polish and bug-fixing efforts in the project's closing stages.

Foot-sliding

When the feet don't lock to the ground, they look floaty and greatly reduce a character's connect to the world. Fixing in a single animation is simply a visual task, but this most commonly occurs either when the speed of a character's translation and animation don't match during something like a run cycle, or during bad blends, causing the FK legs to swing the feet out.

For the former, the issue is avoided with animators completely controlling the speed of translation in the game. If, however, design can modify speed, then the animator must bring that new value back into the DCC to match the animation (remembering to remove the designer's modification once done).

The latter case is much more complicated. Each case will be unique, but they generally occur when blending between two animations, where the blend itself causes an awkward movement that noticeably distracts from the source animations. For example, if an idle has the left foot forward but the run cycle starts with the left foot raised rather than the right, it will cause the left foot to move backward when blending to the running motion, which is undesirable.

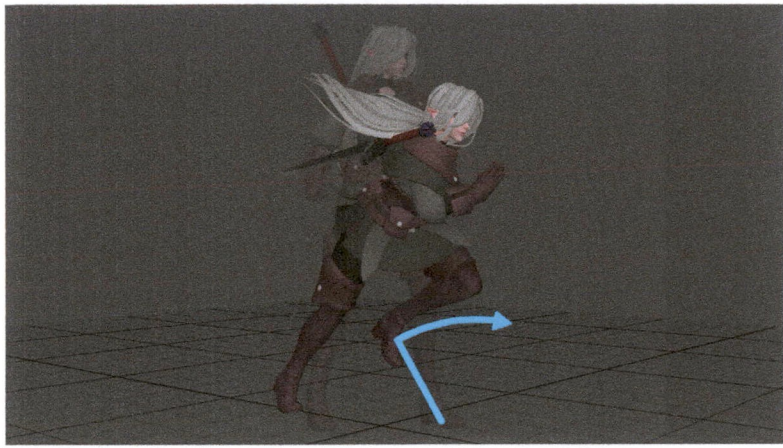

Idle to run displaying foot-sliding during blend.

The solution would be to instead start the run cycle with the right foot up, so the blend accounts for the right (back) foot moving forward across the blend frames as the character moves forward from the idle to the run. Whenever blending, the motion of limbs and so on must be considered for the duration of the blend. We are essentially still animating between two "poses" when blending.

Popping

Again, easily fixed within a single animation but more often occurring between them, popping is when the character noticeably jumps over a single or small number of frames, destroying the fluidity.

Between animations, it's usually not blending long enough between two poses that differ enough to be noticeable. When overly short blends are used, it is most likely for a gameplay purpose, so instead try to utilize longer blends or transitions with the ability to regain character control early via interrupt flags or body-part blends, as covered earlier. If none of these is the culprit, follow up with programming or the technical animators, as there may be a process running in the background causing issues. It's always good to ask around first if you can't immediately identify the cause of a bug, rather than simply sending the bug off to someone else, as it may still be your responsibility.

Contact Points

During cutscenes and other times when the camera is close, the level of fidelity must increase to match. While during the fast action of combat it was acceptable for your character's hands to slightly float above the enemies' shoulders during a throw, in an intimate cutscene close-up when the fingers must rest on a table, they need to match perfectly or stand out as being wrong.

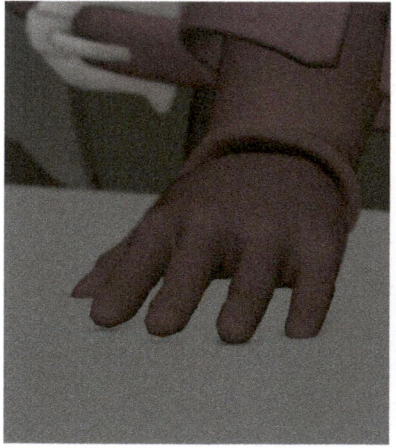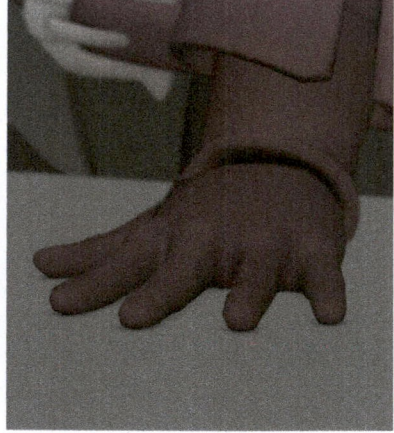

Finger touch points before and after polish.

Naturally, IK performs this job best, and depending on rig complexity and desired visual fidelity, you can utilize IK setups for individual fingers if required. The most universal solution, however, is the ability to "snap" one object to another over a series of frames. For example, if one character's hand touches another's shoulder for a few frames, attach a locator or similar helper to the second character's shoulders and use that to snap or constrain the hand location for the contact duration.

> If there's a task such as matching hands to weapons or other objects that occurs often in your production, consider having the technical team automate the process or create a tool that allows you to do it faster. This rule goes for any repetitive action that could be automated by a technical animator.

Momentum Inconsistency

In player character animation, it is painfully apparent when the character is, for example, running full-tilt toward an obstacle, then, on performing a vault action over it, has a noticeable drop in momentum as he or she starts the vault. A complete pass over all animations to ensure consistency and preservation of momentum between actions is essential once all gameplay systems are in place. If the action can be performed coming from a variety of speeds, then consider unique versions or transitions in/out of the action for each speed.

A common example is an action like landing from a jump or fall that relies on the game detecting the ground collision to interrupt the falling animation with the land. If there is too long a blend, then the ground impact will naturally feel too soft, but more often than not, the detection may delay a frame or two, causing the character to be visibly stopping on the ground before even starting the land animation. Instances such as this can be discovered by enabling slow motion in the engine if available or, even better, stepping forward a frame at a time while playing the game—both helpful engine tools for that final level of animation polish.

Interpenetration

Coming with a variety of names (crashing, clipping, interpenetration and so on), intersection of 3D elements is a common occurrence in unpolished games, be it characters intersecting the environment or, more commonly, a character's limbs intersecting their body—both of which are immersion-breakers that contribute to a game feeling less solid and polished than it might otherwise.

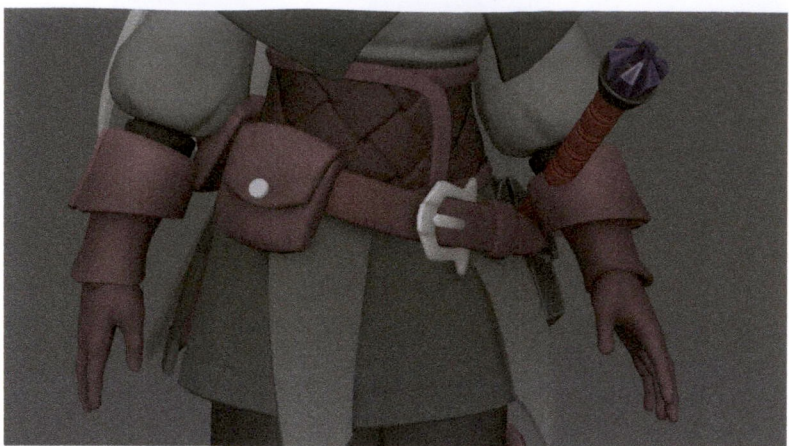

Incorrect weapon placement can cause arms to interpenetrate.

A degree of interpenetration is expected when the character is customizable (can wear different armor or clothes) or when animation is shared across multiple characters—especially those of different sizes. However, this can be minimized by animating to your larger, chunkier characters and considering variable sizes in your idle poses and so on (where interpenetration may be more prolonged and noticeable) by holding the arms away from the body somewhat. Also consider weapon or other item placement on a character as to how it might interpenetrate with the arms—keeping the waist and hip areas clear is recommended, with weapons cleanly stored on the back being optimal.

Custom rigging can be utilized to move intersecting clothing elements, such as high collars intersecting the neck or head, away from the offending body parts, though this will need to be done in real time unless it can be prebaked with every animation.

> Assigning yourself bugs is a great way to create a task list toward the end of a project and allows you to hold onto superficial visual bugs that only you care about and wish to fix (time permitting), as you will likely be unable to submit changes to the game without a corresponding bug task past a certain point.

Targeted Polishing

Why not polish everything equally? Because a thousand animations equally polished to a good level are far less valuable than the hundred or so seen repeatedly throughout the game polished to an excellent degree. Concentrate where the player will see it most and the perception of the game will be raised higher overall. If your game's core gameplay centers around melee combat, then that's where to spend your efforts. If it's story, then perhaps the facial and other acting-related actions and systems should be your main target.

It is a large part of the role of lead or animation director to understand what is key to the game. What are the signature moves or the ones with the most flair that will likely be seen over and over again and become synonymous with the game or individual character? Ensuring these individual actions or the systems that enable them are absolutely flawless and memorable will impart to the player an impression of quality where it matters the most.

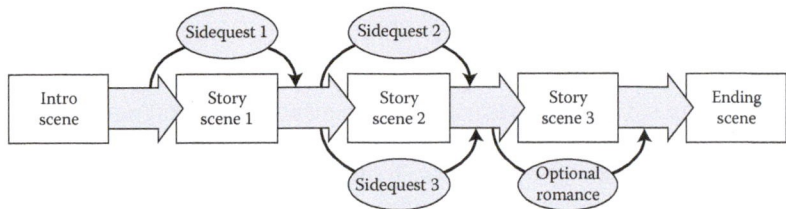

The "critical path" denotes where to focus animation polish efforts.

If the game has a story that the player must complete to "finish" it, this is referred to as the "critical path." While gameplay animations can generally be performed anywhere, independent of location, polishing one-off animations such as cinematics or environmental animations around the critical path should always take precedence over optional side content. Importantly, however, don't selectively polish so much that a gulf of quality is created between polished and unpolished animations where less-critical examples look worse by comparison.

Memory Management & Compression

One major battle toward the end of a project, as every discipline rushes to get all their data such as animations, level art, audio, and so on into the

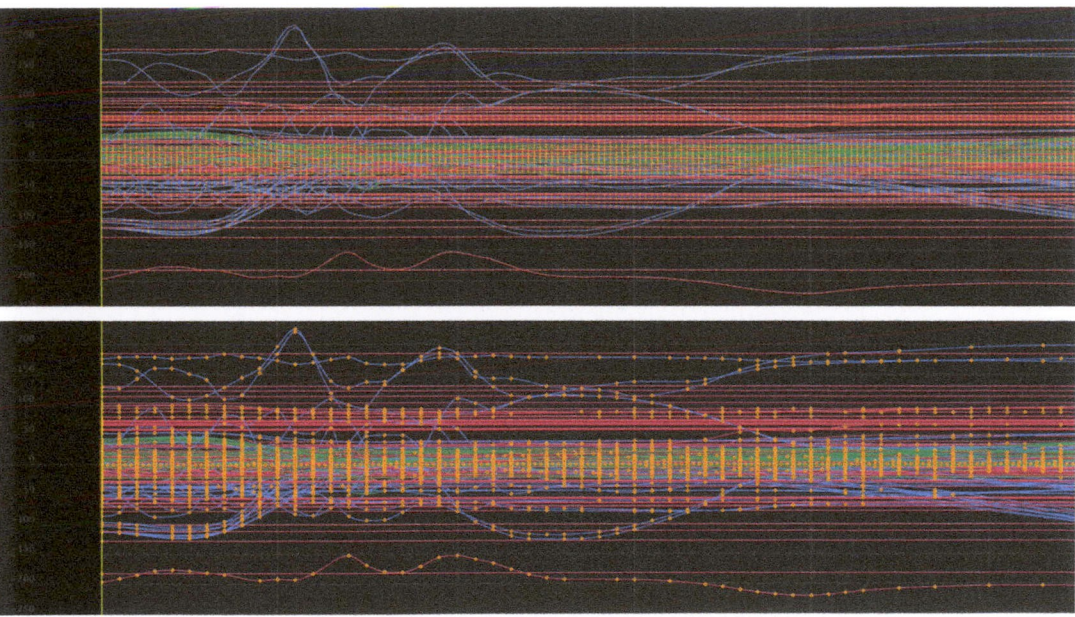

Original uncompressed curves vs the same curve postcompression.

game, is likely hitting animation memory limits. Game projects typically establish memory allocations for each department at the start of the project, depending on each area's needs or importance to achieving the final result. With each console generation, animation teams benefit from greater and greater space allocation, but we always find ways to fill it up, so it's always good to work efficiently regardless.

To aid this, game engines use a variety of compression algorithms and other tricks and techniques to make each animation you export run with a minimum amount of memory footprint while still retaining as much quality as possible. Ultimately, however, it is a tradeoff between memory and quality, so it is highly recommended to manage memory throughout the project as well as to devise a plan early for dealing with memory compression during the closing stages.

Too many games hastily apply a blanket compression value across the entire game's animation rather than carefully selecting areas for more or less compression or using custom settings, resulting in games with high animation quantities sometimes displaying jerky movement across the board, even on important high-visibility assets.

Depending on your engine, the ideal setup allows the technical animators to preset types of compression (not just percentage values) for individual or groups of animations depending on the type of action. For example, simple static/standing actions might favor avoiding foot-sliding by retaining a higher fidelity in the legs, whereas actions that have both character's hands holding a two-handed weapon will benefit from higher quality in the arms so the object doesn't "swim" (float around) in the hands.

That way, the settings of these presets can be adjusted to squeeze more space across the board while retaining different levels of quality where you want it and further increasing the overall perception of fluidity and quality. Failing this level of control, at least ensure you are on top of compression before it comes to the last days to avoid necessitating a panicked drop in quality game-wide right before ship.

Debugging Best Practices

Test/Modify Elements One by One

When the cause of a bug can be one of several potential issues, it is imperative that you work through each possibility one at a time rather than changing several variables in one go before testing. If you fix it after changing several variables, then you can't be sure which variable was the correct one. Searching for solutions should be a process of elimination, changing one element at a time so you can be sure which change fixed the issue—which only helps you recognize similar problems in the future to aid in narrowing down the solution faster.

Late in the project, while attempting to fix two bugs on the same asset in one go is recommended (i.e., a single animation that has two separate animation pops), fixing animation pops in two or more different cinematics then submitting in one version-control change list is inadvisable. This is because one of these changes may break something and you'll have to then go back to figure out which one, and if you submitted all the changes at once, you will have to revert all of them despite only needing to fix one. For maximum efficiency, work through your bug list in a methodical manner.

> There are few things scarier than a bug that fixes itself when you don't really learn what happened, because it will probably come back, likely at an inopportune time. If pressed for time, then it may be okay to let it go, but otherwise, it's always recommended to determine what happened for future reference. Be equally suspicious of errors you can clearly see that "should" break something but mysteriously don't, such as a clearly mislabeled naming convention. It's likely it's just not happened yet, and you're better off keeping everything in good working order, so fix it in advance.

Version Control Comments

Correctly commenting in version control about each change you make, not just for bug fixing but when iterating on an animation at every stage, allows you to go back to prior versions should you wish to make changes for bug-fixing reasons or, more likely, when you may want to use the older animation to solve a task elsewhere.

Moreover, there's always the common scenario where you fall sick or are otherwise off work at a crucial time and your colleagues need to refer to changes in your work. As such, go beyond simple "updated" or "work-in-progress" and similarly useless comments to instead detail what changed in the latest commit to help yourself and others get to the version they need in a bind.

Revision	Date	Action	Description
8	19-03-05	edit	Polish pass
7	19-03-04	edit	Retimed to match updated VO
6	19-03-03	edit	Deleted temp reference meshes
5	19-03-03	edit	Baked down all layers
4	19-03-02	edit	Added mocap
3	19-03-02	edit	Moved to correct scene location
2	19-03-01	edit	First pass blocking
1	19-03-01	add	Added

Useful version control comments enable backtracking.

Avoid Incrementally Fine-Tuning

Take the example of modifying the length of a blend that if too short will cause popping, but too long and it will feel sluggish. If the blend is currently 2 frames, you could simply keep incrementing it 1 frame longer until it just works, but you may get to 7 frames and find you've gone too far, but should you go back to 6 or 5? Even worse, what if you reach 7 and feel it should still be higher and you wasted all that iteration time?

In instances like this, it is recommended to modify in large increments, then take a hot/cold approach to which direction to try next. For instance, in the above example, it would be faster to jump immediately to 10 frames. We're fairly confident it wouldn't be higher, but we just need to eliminate everything above 10 just in case. Next, we drop back down to 6 (halfway between 2 and 10), and it feels even better, but it's now a little too fast again. So next, we move it to 8 frames (halfway between 6 and 10), and now we've gone too far back to it being too slow. Now we know the best value is 7.

Using this faster/slower, hotter/colder approach to "feel" out a blend time (or really any time you need to input a variable) is far better than simple guesswork and will ensure you arrive at exactly the correct number in as few iterations as possible. The more experienced you become, the fewer iterations you will take to arrive at the best look and feel.

Troubleshooting

Every engine differs in its vulnerabilities and fragilities, so only through experience will you learn the particular common ways animations can break in your workflow. However, there are some fairly standard ways you can break a game animation, regardless of the engine. Here is a quick list of what to look out for and how you might fix these problems once recognized.

- **Naming error/mismatch**: The designer or programmer was expecting one name, and you gave them something else (usually via a typo). This is perhaps the most common way to call a supposedly missing animation and will usually result in a T-pose. Best check back through your exported filenames.
- **Wrong file address**: Some engines expect game files to point to or be built from a DCC scene file. Here, the animation exists but is pointing to the wrong file, and will result in the wrong animation being created. Ensure your exported animation points to the correct scene and has no typos in the address.
- **Missing scene file**: The same as above, but the file either never existed or was somehow deleted. Either way, if you find the animation asset is pointing to a file that simply does not exist, the first stop should be the version control of the scene, hopefully just requiring it to be restored.
- **Broken scene file**: The scene file is either broken/corrupted or contains something it shouldn't that is preventing export. It is most likely (especially if not referencing the rig/character) that the rig itself has been modified inadvertently, but may also be attributed to additional hidden elements existing in the scene.
- **Jerky movement**: Within a single animation, the character pops and moves robotically, different from the original animation. This is most likely caused by the animation being overly compressed on export.

- **Frames out of sync**: If, via game debug info, frame 15 of your animation in game looks like frame 25 of the animation in the scene file, for example, then you likely entered the wrong frame count for export, starting 10 frames too late. Either that or a naughty designer scripted the animation to skip the first 10 frames.
- **Animation plays at wrong speed**: Same as above, but that same evil designer sped up your animation without telling you. Get the value from them and modify your animation to work with the same timing, then kindly ask them to remove their time scaling.
- **Character doesn't end in correct location**: The game only knows where the character is located based on the collision, so if an animation ends and jumps the character back to the starting position, for example, it is likely that the collision wasn't following or was animated incorrectly. Best check it in the DCC scene file after viewing the collision debug display.

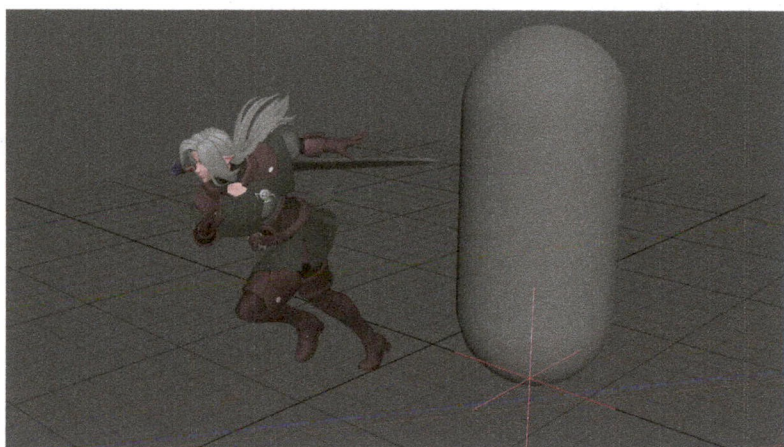

Collision erroneously animated away from character.

- **Entire character broken**: The animations are likely fine, but the character model/rig asset itself was updated incorrectly. This is the most likely cause when every single animation for that character doesn't work. Follow up with the rigging/character team.
- **Animation explodes character**: Usually an issue with the rig, animation scene file, or exporter mismatching the bones. When there's a mismatch in bone count between the character and your exported animation, you'll likely witness the correct animation playing on the wrong bones, which can look horrific. This is because engines often match bones not by names but via an index or list. If the count is off, even by one, it will affect all others in the list following the offending bone. This is not usually something that an animator alone can solve, so get technical animators or programmers involved.

If the animation appears to double the character over, scaling up all joints to double their length in a freakish sight, this is usually an additive animation issue. It means the full source additive animation is combining with the underlying animations rather than just the offset between the additive animation and a selected pose. This is usually a technical issue in script or code, or the additive animation was set up incorrectly.

- **Character position is offset**: Animations play offset from where they should be. Most commonly caused by incorrect scaling of the character in the engine or DCC, but can also involve the process the game engine uses to modify the origin of location-specific scenes like cutscenes. Ensure everything is set up correctly in the DCC if the issue only occurs with that one scene. Collision in-game can also push characters out from the environment or other characters, so it may need to be worked around or turned off.
- **Character stretches back to origin**: Select vertices of the character or other animated object stretch back to the origin, likely because these vertices are incorrectly skinned on the current in-game character asset, even if they are fine in your DCC. Follow up with the technical animators or character team.

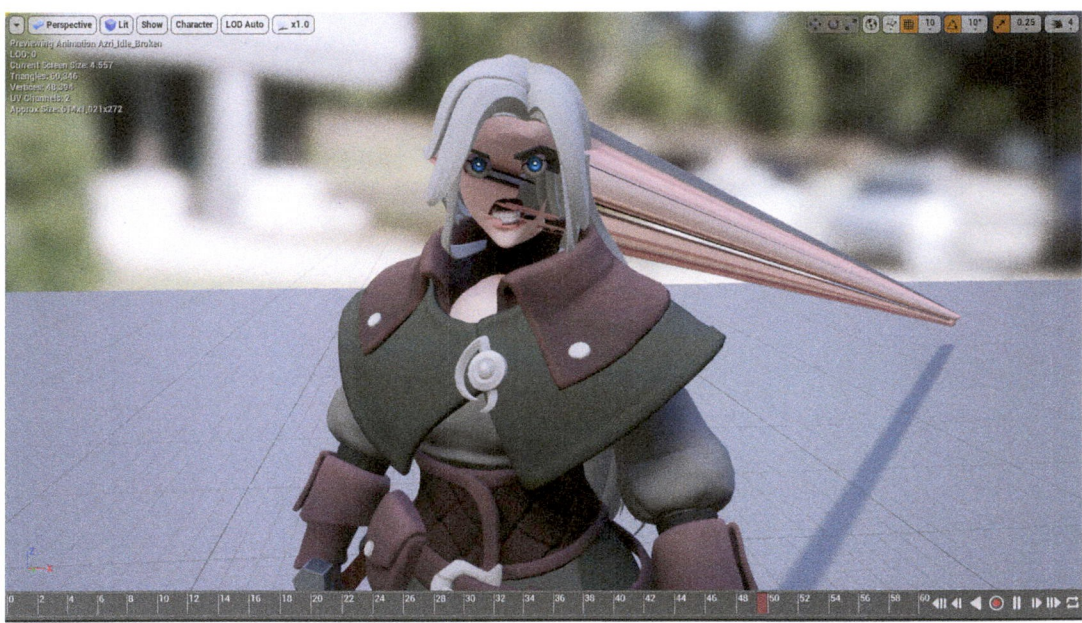

Missing/unskinned vertices cause skin to stretch back to the origin.

Understand that throughout development, you'll be breaking things. It really is impossible to make an omelet without breaking a few eggs, and games are an incredibly complex omelet. As such, it's important not to worry too much about these bugs appearing, but the more you fix them, the faster you'll get at recognizing issues and ideally preventing them before they occur—making you a better game animator all around.

If you still can't figure out the issue despite the above list, here are some "Hail-Mary" tips to test if you're just blindly stabbing in the dark, usually involving a process of elimination.

- Point the game asset to another animation or scene file and see if that works. If so, then you know it's your animation asset or scene and not the code/tech playing it in game.
- View your animation in an available in-game viewer if you have one; that way, you can be sure the animation itself has exported fine, and this time it's more likely the code/tech playing it in the game.
- Duplicate an in-game animation asset you know is working and modify from there, rather than starting from scratch. This ensures you have all the correct settings in place as a sanity check.
- More complicated, but open the exported animation file in a text editor and compare with a similar one that works, looking for inconsistencies. This eliminates the exporter as a potential issue.
- If all else fails and you can't see what's wrong in your scene but you know it's the culprit, blow away your old scene and rebuild from scratch (copying across your animation, of course). This nuclear option is sometimes faster than the time it takes to guess the issue with a seemingly innocuous scene that simply isn't working.

Interview: Alex Drouin
Animation Director—Assassin's Creed & Prince of Persia: The Sands of Time

(Copyright 2007–2017 Ubisoft Entertainment. All Rights Reserved. Assassin's Creed, Ubisoft, and the Ubisoft logo are trademarks of Ubisoft Entertainment in the US and/or other countries.)

The original Prince of Persia was an animation pioneer and Sands of Time more than lived up to that legacy. What attracted you to take up the challenge of that series, and was that always a pressure?

The legacy was more an inspiration than a challenge. It ended up affording me more influence on the project because everybody wanted the animation to deliver the quality of the original title. I never really felt pressure because I sincerely never really thought about it and my only motivation and focus was on the end result—delivering a great game. We were just trying to make our character more real than the average game. Creating a new experience for the player, something magical; something that would fit in the tales of the Arabian Nights.

What led you to the approach of using many more small transition animations for fluidity and control than was the norm at the time?

First, I think it is important that I was working full time in a duo with a gameplay programmer and that our dynamic made the creation of that character possible. Often, I would start by making a small 3D previsualization of how it could look and then break things down into a flowchart. We were really aiming for fluidity more than anything else. There was a quality that we wanted to reach and we would add animation transitions here and there to achieve it. As soon as it started to give us great result, we began to apply that methodology everywhere and it became the way to approach and envision all gameplay recipes.

Similarly, Assassin's Creed was a pioneer in motion-capture for gameplay. What made you unafraid to adopt this new unproven technology?

As mentioned earlier, delivering a great game should always be the main focus. As I moved from Sands of Time to AC, we passed from a linear experience to an open world. The content of the game was a lot bigger and realism was a huge focus. As an animation director, I had to come up with game mechanic recipes, make flowcharts, supervise other animators, and I still wanted to animate at least 50% of my time. So how could I achieve that by keyframing the whole thing and also keep the animation team small?

Since I already had tried a little mocap for Sands of Time, it appeared to me to be a great solution to quickly produce a lot of realistic data and level up the animation style and quality through all the different animators. Still, mocap could only be used for the main actions. All the various transitions and variations, which would end up being most of the data, would still be keyframed.

The weight of the character was a key component in Assassin's look and feel. Do you have any advice for animators looking to retain weight without sacrificing gameplay feel?

That's a tough one. First, I would say that I never try to achieve a style that I would describe as "realistic." I'd rather aim at something that would qualify as "believable." By keeping that in mind, you won't approach animation the same way. Instead of trying to replicate life, you will try emulate the feel of it. Human beings obviously do not react as fast as a videogame character.

For a good feel on the joypad, actions have to be interruptible at any time. As soon as the player gives a new input, it needs to manifest on the screen. The first step is to stop the actual motion and start going toward the next one. In term of animation, the next one to play does not have to be the actual desired motion, it need only be a transition going towards it. That's how we ended up having a massive amount of transition animations. It has to cover all changes of the character state, and if you want to get a reactive character, you will always have to sacrifice a minimum of believability. Then it just becomes a question of choice and taste to know where and when to manifest it.

As for the illusion of weight, I would almost never use a straight mocap data file but instead make a lot of variations on it like taking frames out here and there to add snap or weight, add more up and down on the hip movement, et cetera. It is important to put it inside the engine to validate all your choices because the feeling could change from what you have animated inside your 3D software.

Is there anything else you might like to add about your general philosophies on game animation?

As a game is played, the game designers are constantly trying to communicate with the player, and the first channel is often via the character itself. The main role of an animation is to communicate the game design intention, so be knowledgeable of the design and what it is trying to say. In the conception phase, pre-render fake gameplay situations. It will give you a general idea of the different animations needed and how they are going to flow. You can then use this footage to start identifying the main branching poses. It is also helpful to communicate your intention with the rest of the team.

Remember, an animation is only a little piece of a big puzzle and you need to focus on the puzzle and not the individual pieces. Make animations flow with those before and after and keep everything simple. Nothing should stand out too much to attract the eye, as the player is going to see them many, many times. The impression it gives is more important than the actual look of an animation. Of course, when animations are more important and intended to communicate more, focus on them. As you start pushing and assembling stuff in the game engine, you should focus on the pleasure on the joypad. Is it fun to play? Does it read well? Cutting or adding one or two frames here and there can change the flow and the experience of a mechanic. Work closely with the programmers; it is really important if you want to obtain a great result!

CHAPTER 14

The Future

Getting a Job

Whether currently gainfully employed or attempting to break into the industry, it's always good to have your "ducks in a row" with regards to future employment options, all of which should be online. Nowadays it's seen as unusual for an artist to have no web presence, so not just your reel but your CV should all be online to be discoverable and point anyone to in an instant.

Animators should always have a relatively up-to-date (no more than a few years old) demo reel of your best work because you never know when you might need to search for work in a bind. Even the most promising game projects, through no fault of your own, can get cancelled on the whim of decisions made beyond your control. It's rare to meet a developer who hasn't had a least one cancelled game under his or her belt, and game studio closures and layoffs are sadly all-too-common events in the industry.

It is highly advisable to squirrel away a greatest-hits collection of videos or scenes throughout a project to a single location for easy access. Most studios will be fine with you making a reel once the work is in the public eye, so it can't hurt for you to prep so as to have as little overlap as possible after ship. If you're especially lucky and the game is a hit, you may even ride on any marketing or media buzz the game generates for even more exposure!

The Game Animation Demo Reel

So what makes a good game animation demo reel, and how do you stand out from the crowd when it's likely that tens or hundreds of animators are flooding recruiters' inboxes with applications? It makes sense to present the work you are most happy with creating so far, edited in a digestible form (only the best sequences from cinematics rather than the entire cutscene, for example). Below are tips on what shots to include to maximize your hiring potential into a game studio, and what to add to your reel to round it out if they're not immediately biting.

While a degree of similarity is expected, students should limit presenting only their coursework with the same characters as the rest of their class. There are a growing number of resources online for animators looking to experiment with different rigs so as to avoid having the exact same reel as scores of others. Including personal animations shows a level of creative fertility and enthusiasm that can help you stand out above your peers.

What to Include

Every animator's experience will be different, and the game projects they work on will likely not cover all the items below, so it's worth creating a few shots specifically for the reel should you wish to cover all your bases. Here are a few suggestions that exemplify a lot of the varying tasks one might be expected to perform as a general game animator.

Navigating an assault course is an excellent way to include a sequence of moves typical of gameplay.

- *Dialogue scene*: Showing acting, lip-sync to audio, and potentially camera-work. Should ideally include a change in emotion, and is best with two characters conversing.
- *Two-person interaction*: Usually a combat encounter, potentially including extended contact like a throw.
- *Environmental navigation*: Parkour, jumping over obstacles, climbing, and so on. The more interesting/complex an assault-course, the better.
- *Multihit weapon combo*: Illustrates an understanding of weight and fluidity.
- *Walk/run cycle(s)*: The video game equivalent of a still-life bowl of fruit. Everyone tries, but very hard to master.
- *Realistic mocap cleanup*: If you are lucky enough to have access to raw unedited mocap, show a before and after to share your understanding of plusing and exaggerating mocap.

- *Extreme exaggeration*: Keyframe an action from scratch that's either hyperexaggerated or cartoony to show your understanding of keyframe fundamentals.

While it's not possible to create one for every occasion (some suggest having multiple reels for different kinds of jobs), tailoring your reel for the type of job you desire is recommended. If you enjoy hyperrealism, aim for mocap or realistic keyframe. If you just love exaggerated colorful characters, then be sure to lean toward that. The most important thing is to have fun while making your reel. You should enjoy animating it, after all, and it will only show through!

> The best way to be inspired is to reference other examples of game animation demo reels. Check out www.gameanim.com/book for an ever-increasing gallery of professional game animation reels.

Editing Your Reel

There are a few general rules when editing the work that goes into your reel for maximizing impact and holding the viewer's attention. Ultimately, the quality of the animation is the single biggest factor, but when competing against animators of equal talent, the way your reel is put together will only help your chances of a callback.

Cutting your reel to music in a video sequencer.

- *Start with your best work*: You want to instantly stand out from the crowd. Beginning with something eye-catching and unique will set the expectations for what is to follow. Interviewers will likely ask you which work you rate the highest and why, so showing what they might consider the best work later in a reel raises concerns.
- *Only show good work*: A shorter reel of high quality beats a longer one with filler that gradually descends to unimpressive work, leaving a bad final impression at the end.

- *No more than 2–3 min*: Those involved with hiring will be viewing many reels in an attempt to whittle down the best, and so going over a certain length will be detrimental to their attention span. Potential employers will expect a student reel to be shorter still due to no work history, so don't stress if that comes in around the 1-min mark.

Beyond those decisions, editing to your preferred music helps inspire and give energy and pacing to a reel—just avoid anything potentially irritating. Importantly, take time to render shots cleanly—the visual polish of your reel goes a long way in conveying how perfectionist you'll be on the job.

The Reel Breakdown

An important element to include with your reel is the shot breakdown, carefully detailing which element of each shot you worked on to avoid confusion as to your responsibilities on collaborative team efforts.

This is best included with the video description or wherever you're pointing prospective employers to, such as a page on your site. Both YouTube and Vimeo include a handy formatting trick to allow direct linking to timestamps in the video. Entering numerical timestamps as below will cause the time to form a link directly to the shot in question:

▷ 1,097   ♡ 16   ⊜ 0   ♀ 1   ⬇ **Download**   ◁ **Share**

0:02 Character Reveal Cutscene: Body mocap cleanup and facial keyframe/mocap.
0:18 Level Action Sequence: Previz, prototyping, cameras, mocap direction/cleanup, keyframe, facial and simulation animation.
0:26 Chase Action Sequence: Previz, prototyping, cameras, gameplay aiming animations, all truck and destructible keyframe and non-realtime simulations. (Additional animation & final camera by Joe Smith).
0:49 Death Action Sequence: Previz, prototyping, camera, mocap direction.cleanup, object animation and simulation.
0:53 Dramatic Prop-Break Sequence: Prototyping, camera, keyframe and simulation animation.
0:57 Environment Collapse Sequence: Previz, prototyping, keyframe and simulation animation, mocap direction.
1:04 Finale Action Sequence: Previz, keyframe and simulation animations (minus simulation).
1:20 Action Chase Previz: All previz level layout, character keyframe and test object creation and animation. (Final animation in boxout by awesome animation team colleagues).
2:02 Multiplayer Actions: Mocap direction/cleanup and prop keyframe animation, (directed the majority of multiplayer actions).
2:18 Cartoon Game Previz: Rigged and animated Character.

Adding the time-stamped breakdown to Vimeo or YouTube provides direct links to shots.

> Being caught claiming work you did not do as your own is the worst blight an aspiring animator can have on his or her career, and the industry is small enough that it will carry on to future jobs. Yet it's surprising how often it happens, and if not caught in the initial application process, it will become apparent as soon as the work produced on the job fails to match the reel's quality.

The last thing to remember about the game animation reel is that it needn't be static. Keep updating it every time you improve or add a new sequence.

Vimeo in particular allows you to overwrite previous versions, while YouTube will require a new video upload so previous links sent out will become obsolete (so it is recommended to only link potential employers to a page that contains the YouTube version embedded, such as on your LinkedIn profile or personal website) rather than the video directly.

Your Résumé

Game animation and game development as a whole has become an ever more desirable career as years have progressed. While new job opportunities have certainly sprouted with the democratization of game development tools and digital distribution, the competition for those positions has increased in lockstep. The quality of students leaving schools gets better every year, so in order to stand out from the crowd, you need a stronger portfolio than ever.

Concessions will be made by employers when comparing junior and senior portfolios and résumés (juniors cost less, after all), so don't worry about your lack of AAA titles or the 5+ years of experience a job posting might be asking for—just get your résumé out there and get applying.

Make sure your résumé is up to date on LinkedIn and prominently features a link to your reel. Your opening statement should be a condensed version of your cover letter, discussing high-level goals such as reasons for wanting to become a game animator, with your actual cover letter uniquely tailored to each application and why you want to work at that particular studio.

One of the most impressive pieces a prospective student can include in an application is evidence of working on a team and showing work in a game engine. This allows an applicant to leapfrog over another of similar skill who has only touched the artistic side of game animation. Including game footage of real-time projects already illustrates a level of comfort and competence in a game engine that will allow you to more quickly grasp your role at a studio.

Be sure to include awards that you or your teams might have won, even if not animation-related, as the animator's involvement in gameplay is always relevant. Steer clear of statements on your proficiency in different tools—all DCCs are similar enough that you can learn on the job, so there's no need to hobble yourself at this stage if the studio uses a different DCC for example.

Just like your demo reel, focus on experience relevant to games. While animators starting out will likely wish to detail their school-era experience, once employed in the field, it's better to focus on the game projects you've shipped rather than detailing the work experience you used to help pay your way through college. That said, a varied life experience is a huge bonus to help you stand out from others, so be sure to include your pursuits beyond videogames or that year of traveling abroad. The least-imaginative video games are made by those who list only games as their hobby after all.

LinkedIn, like Twitter, is a great way to connect with others in the field—just be wary of hounding recruiters or game developers in your keenness to learn. If someone does take the time to answer questions you might have or provide feedback on your reel, don't immediately follow up with another round of questions. If you don't wish to take advantage of LinkedIn, it's still a good model to start from should you write your résumé elsewhere—(including an offline version with your cover letter is acceptable, just make sure to link to your online spaces too).

Your Web Presence

It used to be the case that the only way to get your work out there was to build a website from scratch, with sections for your portfolio and résumé easily linked to in an emailed application. Not much has changed with that except that social media has essentially standardized the locations for content to be placed, foregoing the need for a personal site. It helps immmeasurably to have a presence in these online venues.

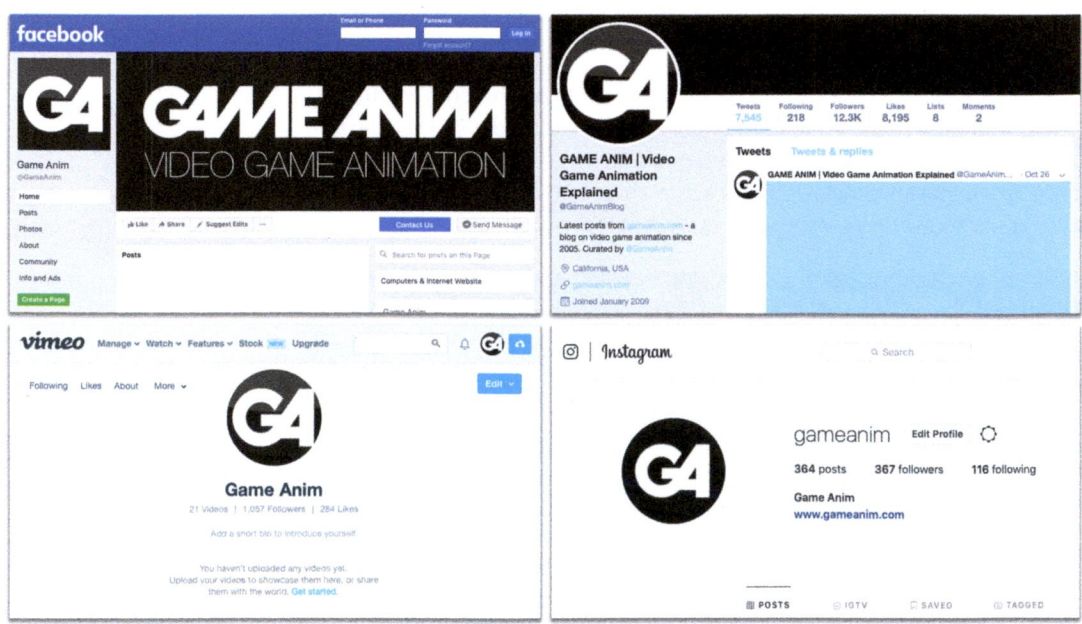

Maintain a consistent web presence for easier portfolio discovery.

- *LinkedIn*: The de facto location for résumés, allowing direct linking to your demo reel and clearly marked sections for all relevant materials, not to mention the ability to directly connect with professionals and recruiters.
- *YouTube*: Gets your reel out to the widest audience possible while also allowing some nice markup of videos to make reel breakdowns interactive.
- *Vimeo*: Better compression quality than YouTube; this should be the version you send out for applications. Allows password protection for sensitive material, as well as better grouping of videos for portfolio creation.

- *ArtStation*: The definitive location for video game art and animation portfolios, allowing you to combine all your work in one place.
- *Twitter*: Take part in a growing game animation community with connections made and knowledge shared primarily on Twitter. Link back to your résumé and demo reel from here, as this is the most front-facing and accessible point of discovery.

That's not to say a portfolio site is useless, it's just now best used as a landing page to point to all these other locations. Game animation applications these days still consist of a digitally enclosed cover letter and résumé, but once picked up by an interested studio, it's more often than not the links to your online résumé and reel that will be shared among those involved in hiring. As is likely the case for every field now, how you conduct and present yourself online will certainly play into a studio's first impression—so play nice.

> For best visibility for hiring, avoid using multiple aliases across your various social media sites. Consistent image and name "branding" makes it easier for other artists and potential employers to find and follow you across the internet.

The Animation Test

Once a reel has caught the attention of a studio, before they offer an interview, there is likely one last hurdle to overcome. Every studio worth its salt may request an animation test to illustrate your skill under a fixed time—allowing them to compare like vs like with other potential candidates, as well as to highlight strengths and weaknesses to give some context and points of discussion in the following interview if successful.

Every test will be tailored for the studio/position, but they'll generally involve some of the elements already listed in the ideal reel contents earlier. A gameplay position will request some specific navigation or combat scenario, whereas a cinematic one will likely require acting and camerawork. Here are some tips for completing the test if required:

- It can be difficult to make time if you're already working a job or have other commitments, but some animators believe they are "above" testing and that their reel should be enough. Part of the reason for testing is to weed out attitudes like that, so make the time.
- Set aside a weekend for the test, free of obligations. Studios will generally let you choose your start time, so make sure you are distraction free, and they will send you the relevant files and brief when ready.
- Read the brief carefully. Failing to understand and follow it raises a red flag as to how you'll work on the job, and oversights like this can waste time and money once working.
- Prepare for the test if it's in a DCC you're unfamiliar with via a practice run beforehand with another scene. Once you do have the brief, be sure to

collect reference for the best quality possible—this should not contribute to the time limit.

- As when animating games for real, work in blocking passes rather than straight-ahead animation. This ensures that you won't come up short as time runs out (which would likely be a fail), with your remaining concern being the final quality only.
- Lastly, don't go over the limit. There's a degree of trust involved in a remote test, but the team likely sees many of these so has a good idea of how much work can realistically be achieved in the allotted time.

Incoming Technologies

By its very nature, video game development is a technology-based medium (though don't confuse it with the tech industry—games are first and foremost in the business of entertainment, with technology used only as a tool). Great game experiences are made by people, not tools or technology—they only enable developers to better realize their ideas.

Nevertheless, being aware of new technology coming around the corner can allow forward-thinking game animators to get a leg up on the competition. Knowing where you should be investing your efforts ahead of time makes it easier to see creative opportunities as new techniques arise. Here are some of the current and upcoming technological advancements that will make an impact on the medium in the near-to-medium future.

Virtual Reality

Virtual reality opens up two new areas related to game animation, one being the type of games we can hope to make with new levels of immersion, and the other being new ways of working. VR limits us in some ways such as no longer having camera control or the option to cut, so cutscenes no longer work, as they traditionally remove all interaction. VR does, however, allow us a higher degree of detail and focus on subtlety as intricate movements up close are even more impressive than the big-budget explosions we've traded on in the past. Similarly, character realization becomes much more important, as we feel we're right there with characters, who need to behave more believably than ever before.

Perhaps more exciting, however, is how it might change our daily workflow. Manipulating characters in a virtual 3D space like a stop-motion animator becomes an altogether different and more active experience from sitting at a desk and computer screen, though whether it's better remains to be seen. Eventually, it'll be more likely that we instead employ some form of augmented reality as a screen replacement rather than truly immersing ourselves, with it enabling not only different methods of animating characters but also new opportunities for communication and remote working.

Affordable Motion Capture

The affordability of depth-perceiving cameras such as webcams or those included with games consoles has given birth to middleware software that allows users to string them together to create rudimentary motion capture volumes. Phone cameras can already provide the same tech, but with built-in software to perform rudimentary facial performance capture. Motion capture based solely on video footage, despite its lower quality, can satisfy smaller studios and single-person teams on a budget—broadening the scope of modest projects from a character perspective. The most recent advancements incorporate facial tracking to complement body data.

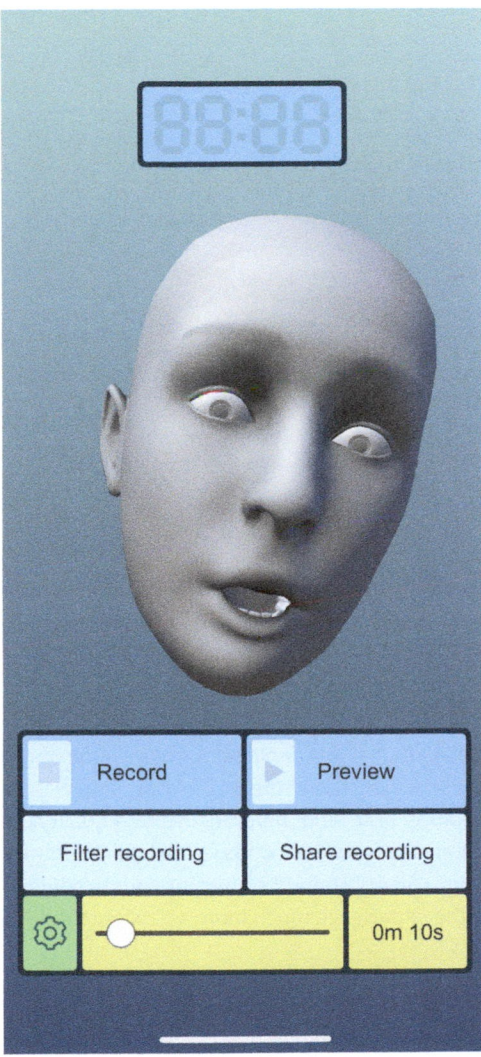

Even phone cameras can record rudimentary facial mocap. (FaceCap, Courtesy of Niels Jansson.)

Runtime Rigs

Standardization of skeletons may soon be a thing of the past, with animation data being transferred cleanly onto a variety of skeletons with different sizes and proportions taken into account at runtime. This will allow future games to have a more diverse cast of characters with a variety of silhouettes, allowing animation creation to tend toward unique characterful work rather than homogenized movements.

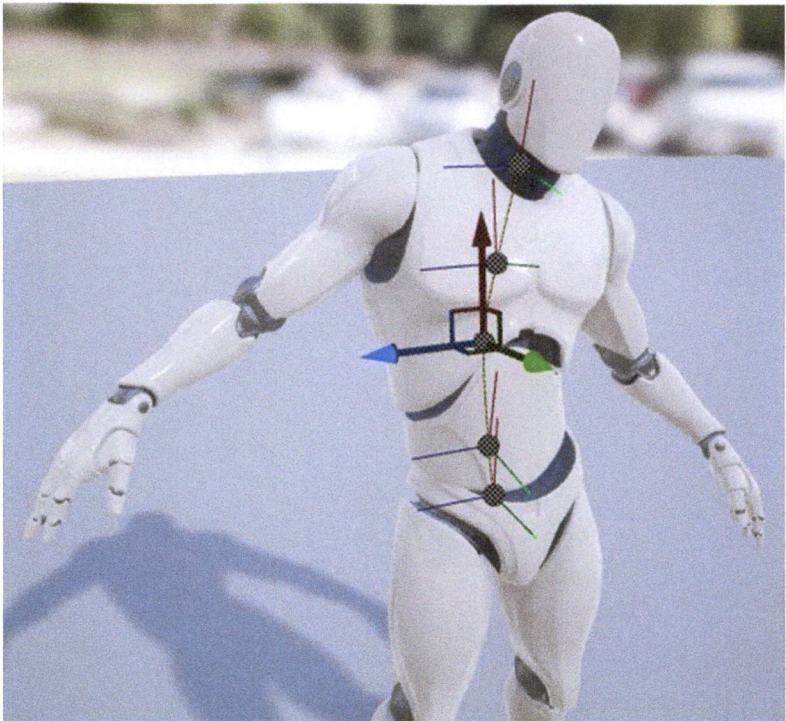

Real-time control rig within Unreal Engine 4. (Copyright 2018 Epic Games, Inc.)

In-Game Workflow

Once rigs are working in real time, animating them in the engine is the next logical step. Eschewing the entire DCC/export step will not only greatly reduce iteration time (and therefore increase quality), but animating characters with final meshes at 30–60 fps in the final environment while tweaking mid-game can only improve an animator's productivity, not to mention making the experience much more accurate to the final result.

Motion Matching

Previously unfeasible in video games due to memory constraints, this is one of the biggest areas of interest on the horizon for motion capture, not just for improved visuals but better player handling and an exciting change of approach to capturing character motion.

Historically, game animations are exported and read merely as position and rotation values on bones, but this approach parses data on momentum, velocity, and matching poses to offer automatic and flawless transitioning between motions. No longer requiring idle poses and move cycles to be curated into small looping cycles throughout the project, now large motion-capture takes more easily implemented in the game will free animators to create a wider variety and volume of unique animations for each character.

Procedural Movement

Already aiding ragdoll and physics motion, advanced procedural physics systems convert an animator's work to physical behaviours that can then be adjusted with a variety of parameters to fill in the blanks, foregoing the need for functional transition animations and allowing the animator to concentrate instead on a smaller set of character-defining animations. Procedural movement should correctly handle shifting of weight and momentum, as well as more convincing movement between animations by replicating motor strengths of a character's joints and muscles.

Machine Learning

Already useful for the two above examples, combining both motion matching and procedural movement with machine learning can utilize the same motion-captured datasets to not just provide a bank of animations to blend between, but to "teach" the character how to walk, run, or whatever actions are fed into the system. Machine learning is a universal approach to using the processing power of computers to precompute solutions (rather than compute in real time), taking the challenge of character movement offline so developers can teach characters movements for them to perform at runtime—even modifying the results to match variable parameters such as navigation of complex terrain. This process shifts the cost of movement from memory to computation and will likely be the biggest pursuit after we once again begin hitting animation memory limits.

Machine learning is perhaps the broadest term for advances in AI and computation right now, as it's more a technique than a technology, so the applications for it are only limited by the imaginations of those using it in game development.

Ultimately, what matters most when using any new technology is that it allows animators to focus on the foremost challenge of bringing game characters to life with results that players will enjoy. Like previous technological leaps such as the advent of 3D, and later, motion-capture, it simply frees animators up so that they can instead focus efforts on the animations that really count without having to fear the ever-increasing number of actions required for fluid movement.

No technology on its own will ever make appealing characters that become player favorites; instead, this relies on the combined efforts of animators and their colleagues to create life where there was none so that players can explore and enjoy the future of this growing medium, inhabiting and interacting with characters in ever deeper and more rewarding ways.

Index